MRS GASKELL
NOVELIST AND BIOGRAPHER

for
JOHN *and* ANDREW

Mrs Gaskell in her twenty-first year,
from a miniature by Joseph Thomson
of Edinburgh

MRS GASKELL

Novelist and Biographer

by

ARTHUR POLLARD

HARVARD UNIVERSITY PRESS
CAMBRIDGE, MASSACHUSETTS
1966

Printed in Great Britain

CONTENTS

	page
PREFACE	vii
NOTE ON REFERENCES	viii
BRIEF CHRONOLOGY	ix
I INTRODUCTION	I
Then and Now	
II MRS GASKELL HERSELF	12
III 'MARY BARTON'	32
IV 'CRANFORD'	62
V 'RUTH'	86
VI 'NORTH AND SOUTH'	108
VII 'THE LIFE OF CHARLOTTE BRONTË'	139
VIII SHORT STORIES AND SHORT NOVELS	172
IX 'SYLVIA'S LOVERS'	194
X 'WIVES AND DAUGHTERS'	224
XI ESTIMATE	248
INDEX	263

ILLUSTRATIONS

The Frontispiece and Plate III are from *Mrs Gaskell, a brief biography*, by George A. Payne, published by Sherratt & Hughes, Manchester, in 1929. Plate I is reproduced by courtesy of the National Portrait Gallery. Plate II is from *The Works of Mrs Gaskell*, edited by A. W. Ward, published by John Murray, 1906.

Mrs Gaskell in her twenty-first year   *frontispiece*
    from a miniature by Joseph Thomson of Edinburgh

PLATE

  I   Mrs Gaskell, 1851   *facing page* 21
       from the chalk drawing by George Richmond, R.A.

 II   Mrs Gaskell, 1864–5   196
       from the portrait by Samuel Laurence

III   Water-colour drawing of Mrs Gaskell   213
       by her daughter, Meta, 1865

PREFACE

THIS short study took its birth from a prolonged and increasingly appreciative acquaintance with Mrs Gaskell's work. It is, however, no mere eulogy. I have sought to give praise where it is due, but I have tried also to be properly critical.

I would like to record my debt to my fellow-editor of Mrs Gaskell's letters, Mr John Chapple, for stimulating discussion of her writings and to Professors Kathleen Tillotson and John Jump who read the manuscript and made extremely valuable criticisms. But for them this book would have had far more blemishes than it has.

Chapter VII has already appeared in *The Bulletin of John Rylands Library* and part of Chapter VIII in *The Cambridge Review*, and I am indebted to the editors of these Journals for permission to reproduce them here. I would also like to thank Mrs Lynne Woolfenden and Mrs Nanette Chappell, who typed the manuscript and managed to read my handwriting so successfully, and Mr T. L. Jones of the Manchester University Press for his professional help at all stages. My final expression of gratitude must go to those who have suffered my work on Mrs Gaskell so long and so patiently—my own family.

ARTHUR POLLARD

Timbersbrook,
  Congleton, Cheshire.

NOTE ON REFERENCES

ALL page references are to the Knutsford edition of Mrs Gaskell's works, ed. A. W. Ward, 8 volumes, Smith, Elder, 1906, with the exception of *The Life of Charlotte Brontë* which was not included in Ward's edition. References to this work are to the third edition (1857), except in places where it is indicated that the reference is to the first edition (1857).

A single number in brackets, e.g. (520), refers to the numbering of letters as they appear in *The Letters of Mrs Gaskell*, ed. A. Pollard and J. A. V. Chapple, Manchester University Press, 1966.

'Hopkins' indicates reference to A. B. Hopkins: *Mrs Gaskell, Her Life and Work*, John Lehmann, 1952.

BRIEF CHRONOLOGY

1810	29 Sept.	Elizabeth Cleghorn Stevenson born at Chelsea.
1811	Nov.	Passes into the care of Aunt Lumb at Knutsford.
1825–7		At Avonbank School, Stratford-upon-Avon.
1827–9		Mainly in London. Her father died on 22 March 1829.
1829–31		Visits to Newcastle-upon-Tyne, Edinburgh, Manchester.
1832	30 Aug.	Married William Gaskell (1805–84) at Knutsford Parish Church.
	29 Sept.	Settled at 14 Dover Street, Manchester—after honeymoon in North Wales.
1833		First daughter: still-born.
1834	12 Sept.	Marianne born.
1837	Jan.	'Sketches Among the Poor', No. 1, *Blackwood's Magazine*.
	5 Feb.	Margaret Emily (Meta) born.
	1 May	Aunt Lumb died.
1841		Tour of the Rhineland.
1842	7 Oct.	Florence Elizabeth born.
		Move to 121 Upper Rumford Street, Manchester.
1844	23 Oct.	William born.
1845	10 Oct.	William died.
1846	3 Sept.	Julia Bradford born.
1847–8		'Libbie Marsh's Three Eras', 'The Sexton's Hero' and 'Christmas Storms and Sunshine' published in *Howitt's Journal*.

1848		*Mary Barton*—2 vols., Chapman and Hall.
1849		Move to Plymouth Grove, Manchester.
1850	30 Mar.	'Lizzie Leigh', *Household Words*.
	19 Aug.	Meeting with Charlotte Brontë.
	Dec.	*The Moorland Cottage*, Chapman and Hall (Christmas book).
	28 Dec.	'The Heart of John Middleton', *Household Words*.
1851	Feb.–April	'Mr. Harrison's Confessions', *The Ladies' Companion*.
1851	Dec.–May 1853	*Cranford, Household Words*.
1852	Dec.	'The Old Nurse's Story', *Household Words*, Extra Christmas Number.
1853	Jan.	*Ruth*—3 vols., Chapman and Hall.
	June	*Cranford*, Chapman and Hall.
		Holiday in Normandy.
	Sept.	Visit to Charlotte Brontë at Haworth.
	Dec.	'The Squire's Story', *Household Words*, Extra Christmas Number.
1854		William Gaskell became senior minister of Cross Street Chapel, Manchester.
		Mrs Gaskell and Marianne visited France.
	Sept.–Jan. 1855	*North and South, Household Words*.
1855		Mrs Gaskell and Meta stayed with Madame Mohl in Paris.
	June	Requested to write *Life of Charlotte Brontë*.
		North and South—2 vols., Chapman and Hall.
	6–20 Oct.	'Half a Life-time Ago', *Household Words*.
		Lizzie Leigh and Other Stories, Chapman and Hall.

1856 Dec.		'The Poor Clare', *Household Words*.
1857 Feb.		*The Life of Charlotte Brontë*, Smith, Elder.
		Visit to Rome with Marianne and Meta.
1858 Jan.		'The Doom of the Griffiths', *Harper's Magazine*.
	June–Sept.	*My Lady Ludlow*, *Household Words*.
	Autumn	Visit to Heidelberg with Meta and Florence, and to Madame Mohl.
	27 Nov.	'Right at Last', *Household Words* (as 'The Sin of a Father').
	7 Dec.	'The Manchester Marriage', *Household Words* (as 'A House to Let').
1859		'The Crooked Branch', *All the Year Round* (as 'The Ghost in the Garden Room').
		Round the Sofa and Other Tales, Sampson, Low.
	8–22 Oct.	'Lois the Witch', *All the Year Round*.
	Nov.	Visit to Whitby.
1860		*Right at Last and Other Tales*, Sampson, Low.
1861 5–19 Jan.		'The Grey Woman', *All the Year Round*.
1861 Feb.		Visit to Normandy and Brittany with Meta.
	May	'Six Weeks at Heppenheim', *Cornhill Magazine*.
1863 Jan.–March		'A Dark Night's Work', *All the Year Round*.
	Feb.	Visit to Madame Mohl, and then to Rome.
	8 Sept.	Florence married to Charles Crompton.

Nov.–Feb. 1864   *Cousin Phillis, Cornhill Magazine.*
                         Sylvia's Lovers—3 vols., Smith, Elder.
1864   Visit to Pontresina.
Aug.–Jan. 1866   *Wives and Daughters, Cornhill Magazine.*
1865   *The Grey Woman and Other Tales,* Smith, Elder.
                         Purchase of The Lawn, Holybourne, Alton.
12 Nov.   Death at Holybourne.
16 Nov.   Buried at Brook Street Chapel, Knutsford.

CHAPTER I

INTRODUCTION

Then and Now

'LET Mrs Gaskell's novels be read after the lapse of a hundred years, and one feels that the verdict delivered then would be that they were penned by a true observer —one who not only studied human nature with a desire, but a capacity, to comprehend it.' Thus wrote G. B. S[mith] in a *Cornhill Magazine* article in 1874.[1] Smith listed her qualities as individuality, force, truthfulness and purity. The time has come to test this judgment.

Some twenty years ago in an article in *Penguin New Writing* Rosamond Lehmann described *Wives and Daughters* as a 'neglected Victorian classic'. One wonders whether this phrase may not be aptly used to describe the work of Mrs Gaskell as a whole. In two decades which have witnessed a widespread and sustained revival of interest in a number of her contemporaries she herself does not seem to have shared in this resuscitation of the Victorian novel. Dickens has been the subject of many books and there have been at least two major works on Thackeray. Trollope has continued to be popular, and George Eliot has been placed in 'the great tradition'. Mrs Gaskell has been the subject of Annette Hopkins' sympathetic and perceptive critique,[2] but this book stands virtually alone. There is a disparity in stature amongst

[1] 'Mrs Gaskell and Her Novels', *Cornhill Magazine*, vol. XXIX, p. 212.
[2] *Elizabeth Gaskell, Her Life and Work*, 1952.

these Victorian writers, but the treatment they have received has been disproportionate and disadvantageous to Mrs Gaskell. Perhaps in this centenary year the balance may be in some degree redressed.

When she died in November 1865, she received an array of tributes that was in itself testimony to her contemporary reputation. In the judgment of the obituary-writers[1] the reputation of *Cranford* was secure. *The Unitarian Herald* and *Macmillan's Magazine* also placed the *Life of Charlotte Brontë* in the forefront of her achievement. *The Nation* and *The Athenaeum* both dismissed *Ruth*, the one ascribing its failure to Mrs Gaskell's purity of mind which made her ill-equipped to deal with the subject, the other allowing it to be a powerful tale but 'based on a mistake, and . . . essentially untrue to truth.' About the other novels the verdicts varied. Masson in *Macmillan's* praised *Wives and Daughters*, but felt that, with *Cranford*, *North and South* would remain the most popular of her novels, not least for its 'vivid delineations of lives of common men and common women'. *The Athenaeum*, however, condemned it as the product of 'the author's intense but prejudiced desire to right what is wrong'. Even more at odds were the judgments of *The Nation* and *The Saturday Review* about *Sylvia's Lovers*. The former discovered in it an 'inability to comprehend, or at any rate to depict, passion of the highest order', whereas the latter, conceding that it might affect various tastes in different ways, found it 'full of vivid and changeful passion, of swift and forcible incident, of carefully woven

[1] *Athenaeum*, 18 Nov. 1865, pp. 689–90; *Nation*, 7 Dec. 1865, i, pp. 716–17; *Macmillan's Magazine*, Dec. 1865, pp. 153–6; *Saturday Review*, 18 Nov. 1865, pp. 638–9; *Unitarian Herald*, 17 Nov. 1865, No. 238, p. 366.

plot, of human character in the full strength of youth and manhood acted upon by the absorbing motives of human life'. This view was as rare as it was perceptive at the time. The same commentator felt that *Mary Barton* would be 'comparatively forgotten for all its power and its pathos' when *Sylvia's Lovers* and *Cranford*, 'the opposite poles of Mrs Gaskell's powers in writing . . . are still eagerly read and widely admired'. His statement implies the popularity of a book which none of these writers singled out for lasting fame, but which, *Macmillan's* also admitted, commanded the most permanent circulation.

This view is supported by an article in *The British Quarterly Review* in 1867. This essay with two others[1] will serve to estimate Mrs Gaskell's immediately post-humous reputation. Of *Mary Barton*, *The British Quarterly* felt that, whilst it had aroused sympathy for the poor, it 'may also have wrought real mischief in the hot heads of angry unionists by granting impunity to murder'.[2] The political dislike of the book still remained. The reviewer liked *Ruth* least, but he also criticized the *Life of Charlotte Brontë*. Although he thought it 'tender, just and true', he thought also that Mrs Gaskell had not been intimate or sympathetic enough with her subject to get 'at the core of the recluse, all whose joys were spiritual, all her miseries physical and external'.[3] The chief merit of this article is its recognition of the worth of *Wives and Daughters*, 'the finest of Mrs Gaskell's productions. . . .

---

[1] 'The Works of Mrs Gaskell', *British Quarterly Review*, April 1867, vol. XLV, pp. 399–429; G. B. S[mith], op cit., pp. 191–212; W. Minto, 'Mrs Gaskell's Novels', *Fortnightly Review*, Sept. 1878, vol. XXX (N.S. XXIV), pp. 353–69.

[2] *British Quarterly Review*, vol. XLV, p. 405.

[3] Ibid., p. 417.

The moral atmosphere is sweet, bracing, invigorating; the human feeling good and kind throughout'.[1] Smith in his *Cornhill* article also attributed a peculiar perfection to this novel, but his praise was not unmixed with criticism. Dividing Mrs Gaskell's achievement into three stages represented by *Mary Barton*, *Sylvia's Lovers* and *Wives and Daughters* he thought this last was 'told rather with quietness than with demonstration of power'[2] and that it lacked Dickens' vivacity and Thackeray's penetration. He found *North and South* unequal in its performance and for *Ruth* his praise was moral rather than literary. He commended the pathos of *Cranford* and the very different pathos of *Sylvia's Lovers*. Most notable of his comments, however, is the praise which he bestows upon *Mary Barton*, which he distinguishes for force, truthfulness and concentrativeness or 'the absolute imprisonment of emotion in a few pages'.[3] Smith found Mrs Gaskell's characters less individualized than those of Charlotte Brontë and George Eliot, whilst Minto in *The Fortnightly Review* felt that there were few set descriptions in her novels. This is surely a misjudgment, and so also is his suggestion that *Sybil* probably suggested the writing of *Mary Barton*. With Minto we seem to be moving into the phase of regarding Mrs Gaskell as a second-class novelist. He noted her rich experience and active imagination, but he found her style homely and to her last novels the most he was prepared to concede was a greater art in the management of her story. He concluded that she would have 'a high place among those who are comparatively unambitious in their efforts'.[4]

[1] *British Quarterly Review*, vol. XLV, p. 424.
[2] Smith, op. cit., p. 209.   [3] Ibid., p. 200.
[4] Minto, op. cit., p. 368.

The next period of interest was that which was marked
by the publication of two major collections of her work,
A. W. Ward's Knutsford edition (8 volumes, 1906) and
Clement Shorter's World's Classics edition (10 volumes,
1906–19). The latter's introductions are very brief, and
the former's, though much fuller, deal mainly with matters of background and literary influence. Amongst
Ward's few critical comments we may note his high
estimate of *North and South* ('one of the finest of modern
English fictions' with 'almost faultless' construction) and
his praise of *Wives and Daughters* with 'its wealth of
closely observed, delicately drawn and impressively contrasted characters'. There is a sensitive review of Ward's
edition in Paul Elmer More's *Shelburne Essays*[1] which
originally appeared in *The Nation*.[2] He allowed that there
is 'nothing recondite in either the beauties or the limitations of Mrs Gaskell's genius', but he singled out *Cranford*, *Sylvia's Lovers*, *Cousin Phillis* and *Mary Barton* for
especial praise. The resurgence in the popularity of the
sociological novels probably begins with Louis Cazamian's chapter in *Le Roman Social en Angleterre* (1904),
where he pointed to the appreciation in *North and South*
of the splendour and beauty of industrial civilization[3] and
argued that '*Marie Barton* prêche un interventionisme
sentimental, fondé sur une notion religieuse de la soli-
darité humaine'.[4] Among the articles written on the
centenary of Mrs Gaskell's birth in 1910 mention need
only be made of one, that of Lewis Melville in *The
Nineteenth Century*[5] which is unmatched for the virulence

[1] 5th Series, 1908, pp. 66–85.   [2] 11 April 1907.
[3] *Le Roman Social en Angleterre*, 1904, p. 410.
[4] Ibid., p. 388.
[5] Sept. 1910, pp. 467–82.

of its criticism. *Cranford* he allowed to be her master-piece, but elsewhere Melville found 'straining after sensational effect', 'stereotyped situations', 'sickly sentiment', 'characterization . . . elbowed aside, . . . the most wooden of puppets', and 'if anything is worse . . . than the character-drawing, it is the dialogue'.[1] *Wives and Daughters* is considered competent but dull, with Molly alone worthy of much esteem. The best of the long novels is *Sylvia's Lovers*, which 'has a well-constructed story, and the characters talk as people really do talk, which is not usual with Mrs Gaskell's creations'.[2]

Between the wars the best study of Mrs Gaskell was A. Stanton Whitfield's.[3] His emphasis was, as I believe rightly, upon character, and his estimates of *Ruth* and *Wives and Daughters*, the latter as a precursor of the modern psychological novel, are particularly sensitive. He decided that *Cranford*, *Sylvia's Lovers* and *Wives and Daughters* must be reckoned as her best books. G. de Witt Sanders, whose work (1929) is more sketchy and too dependent upon quotation, substituted *Cousin Phillis* for *Sylvia's Lovers* in this trio. C. S. Northup's excellent bibliography is incorporated with Sanders' study. Elizabeth Haldane's work on *Mrs Gaskell and Her Friends* (1931) makes good use of letters, but the criticism of the writer is always subsidiary to the biography of the woman. In her essay in *Women Writers of the Nineteenth Century*[4] Marjorie A. Bald considered each of the novels within chapters devoted respectively to atmosphere, humour,

[1] Sept. 1910, pp. 476–7.   [2] Ibid., p. 482.
[3] *Mrs Gaskell, Her Life and Work*, 1929. As most of the works in the modern period are easily accessible, they are not dealt with at the same length as the earlier articles.
[4] 1923, pp. 100–61.

pathos, the woman's point of view, social problems and moral theory. She concluded that 'Mrs Gaskell's peculiar achievement was the power of combining the life of genius with a round of common interests'.[1] Lord David Cecil stressed the femininity of Mrs Gaskell in his *Early Victorian Novelists* (1934), noticing her taste, command of detail, freshness of outlook and sense of social values. He felt that hers was a narrow world, and in particular he complained about the inadequacy of her men characters and of her sociological novels. He therefore selected *Cranford*, *Sylvia's Lovers*, *Wives and Daughters* together with *Cousin Phillis* as her significant achievement.

Since the War, apart from Aina Rubenius's specialized study of *The Woman Question in Mrs Gaskell's Life and Works*,[2] there have been two books, the extensive biography-cum-criticism of Miss Hopkins and a shorter work by Yvonne Ffrench.[3] This latter is decisive in its views but rather superficial at times in its treatment of separate works. Miss Ffrench praised the construction of *North and South*, the characterization of Hepburn in *Sylvia's Lovers* and Mrs Gaskell's management of sensational action such as strikes, fires and riots. Whilst criticizing the early work for 'the artificial dialogue, the mawkishness of sentiment, the abundant coincidence, the innumerable death beds',[4] she singled out *Ruth* for commendation. In his essay in *From Dickens to Hardy*[5] Arnold Kettle agreed with Miss Ffrench in finding the emigration at the end of *Mary Barton* a somewhat defeatist solution. This novel, however, has risen in general regard, and besides Kettle, who was on the whole appreciative, it has

[1] Ibid., p. 161.
[2] Uppsala, 1950.
[3] *Mrs Gaskell*, 1949.
[4] Ibid., p. 25.
[5] Ed. Boris Ford, 1958.

received favourable notice from Kathleen Tillotson[1] and Raymond Williams.[2] Mrs Tillotson insisted that its unity is more complex than that merely of social purpose, that it has 'a unity rather of theme and tone', and Mr Williams agreed with her in emphasizing the central and fundamental importance of John Barton. It is not possible within brief compass to summarize Miss Hopkins' achievement. As biography her work will not easily be surpassed. Her criticism was embodied within the biography. Whilst always displaying a sympathetic understanding of her subject's work, she was at times hardly critical enough. By contrast, H. P. Collins's review-article, 'The Naked Sensibility: Elizabeth Gaskell',[3] is a little too severe. He considered that Mrs Gaskell 'did not *think* hard enough; and collaterally she took experience too hard'[4] and that 'she had no force of inner conviction',[5] but that 'she exhibits the one consistent merit of being Elizabeth Gaskell'.[6] Her virtues he listed as 'sensitiveness, sympathy with human nature, humour, playfullness and insight into not-too-complex character, above all acute feeling for the beauty of the English scene at its best'.[7]

Where does Mrs Gaskell stand in 1965? 'The mood of the twentieth century is far from favourable to Elizabeth Gaskell, her *tone* in fiction is unsophisticated and démodé; the style is neither intellectually modulated nor terse and colloquial and it is unlikely that a culture already impatient of convention will ever be attuned to it.' So wrote Collins.[8] Much of what he says is true, but I am by no means so pessimistic about her. In 1960 I described

[1] *Novels of the Eighteen-Forties*, 1954.

[2] *Culture and Society, 1780–1950*, 1958.

[3] In *Essays in Criticism*, vol. III, no. 1, Jan. 1953.   [4] Ibid., p. 65.

[5] Ibid., p. 67.   [6] Ibid., p. 67.   [7] Ibid., p. 69.   [8] Ibid., p. 71.

her as 'a major minor novelist'.[1] Further acquaintance has generated deeper appreciation. In this study which is presented as a straightforward introduction to Mrs Gaskell's work I have been more critical than Miss Hopkins, but my overall estimate is higher than that which I held in 1960. I have sought by an examination of each of the major works in turn to pass a judgment on all of them and then in my final chapter to summarize and consolidate the conclusions I have reached about Mrs Gaskell's achievement as a whole.

Basically, Mrs Gaskell is a simple writer, 'unsophisticated' in Collins' phrase, 'nothing recondite' in that of Paul Elmer More. The most appropriate method of interpretation I suggest therefore should itself be a simple one. This may seem as old-fashioned as Collins thinks this century finds Mrs Gaskell herself. It seems to me, however, that the search for pseudo-complexity has had too long a run anyway, and that we are altogether, in Swift's phrase, 'too far gone In all the modern critics' jargon'; but of all the authors one may choose to name Mrs Gaskell must surely be among those least likely to respond to such treatment. Certainly one recent Freudian analysis of *Cranford* looked more ingenious than sensible.

Lionel Stevenson has laid down three specifications for the novel, 'structural unity, individualized characters, and the pre-eminent illusion of reality'.[2] Mrs Gaskell would not have disagreed with this judgment. In a comment on a work, *The Three Paths* by 'Herbert Gray', submitted for her consideration in 1859 she advised him thus:

Every day your life brings you into contact with live men

---

[1] Pollard, 'The Novels of Mrs Gaskell', *Bulletin of the John Rylands Library*, vol. 43, no. 2, p. 423.   [2] *The English Novel*, 1960, p. 8.

and women. . . . Think if you can not imagine a complication of events in their life which would form a good plot. . . . The plot must grow, and culminate in a crisis; not a character must be introduced who does not conduce to this growth & progress of events. The plot is like the anatomical drawing of an artist; he must have an idea of his skeleton, before he can clothe it with muscle and flesh, much more before he can drape it. Study hard at your plot. . . . Set to & imagine yourself a spectator of every scene & event. . . . If you but think eagerly of your story, till *you see it in action*, good simple strong words will come,—just as if you saw an accident in the street that impressed you strongly you would describe it forcibly (420).

In the following pages I have tried to concentrate more deliberately than previous critics have generally done on matters of plot, character, setting, information and moral purposes as separate entities within each of Mrs Gaskell's works. I have sought to show her practice in such matters as the pattern and function of plot, the types and relationship of characters, the place of atmosphere and environment, the use of sheer information in her work, and her application of moral judgment. Occasionally it has been necessary to give some outline of plot and sketches of character, but I have tried to relate these strictly to my critical intention.

I hope that I have succeeded in showing that Mrs Gaskell is far more than merely the author of *Cranford*. I have, in any case, tried to show that that work is a more complex achievement than it is often thought to be, but in addition to this, I have also been anxious to confirm the standing of *Wives and Daughters*, to raise that of the unjustly neglected *Sylvia's Lovers*, to mark the importance of *North and South* in Mrs Gaskell's development as a novelist and to indicate the ways in which we may profitably read the early novels without feeling it necessary to ignore or apologize for their faults. In so doing, I would like to think that, whilst not ridiculously promoting excessive claims for her as the equal of her greater contemporaries, I may yet have done something to restore her to that degree of favour which she enjoyed in her lifetime and for some years afterwards.

CHAPTER II

MRS GASKELL HERSELF

ELIZABETH Cleghorn Stevenson was born on 29 September 1810 at 93 Cheyne Walk, Chelsea, the eighth and last child of William Stevenson and his wife Elizabeth (*née* Holland). Her father, a Scot, had been Unitarian minister at Failsworth, near Manchester, but resigned his orders on conscientious grounds. He then took up scientific farming, but his efforts did not meet with success. His subsequent career included literary work as editor of *The Scots Magazine* and as contributor to *The Edinburgh Review*. In 1806 he became private secretary to the Earl of Lauderdale who was to have become Governor-General of India. This appointment, however, did not materialize, and Stevenson, being no longer needed, appears as compensation to have been nominated Keeper of the Treasury Records. He kept this post until his death in 1829. It was thus that the Stevensons came to London, and it was there that Elizabeth was born and that her mother died in 1811, when the young child was but thirteen months old.

Elizabeth Stevenson, the mother, came of the Cheshire branch of the old family of Holland, Unitarians bound by ties of kinship to such families as the Wedgwoods, the Darwins and the Turners. It was to Cheshire that the baby Elizabeth went on her mother's death, to Aunt Lumb at Knutsford. She grew up in her aunt's house at Heathside, coming to love her as a mother and by daily acquaintance acquiring that deep affection for the little Cheshire town which she repeatedly displays in her stories and novels. Place after place—the Royal George Hotel, Brook Street Chapel, the entrance gates to Tatton Park and a host of others—is familiar to readers of Mrs Gaskell who have never been to Knutsford. In one of her letters (197) she tells of the town's old customs known to her in her youth and either dead or fast dying at the time of writing in the eighteen-fifties. Knutsford remained her home until her marriage, but she spent nearly three years at the Miss Byerleys' school at Avonbank, Stratford-on-Avon, and from 1827 to 1831 was away from home for long periods. She helped to nurse her father in his last illness and then stayed in London for a time at the home of her uncle, Swinton Holland, in Park Lane. She may there have seen something of that fashionable life which she portrays in *North and South*, though her description of this may also derive from her increasing knowledge of London life after her first literary success with *Mary Barton* in 1848. After London, she stayed with the Turners at Newcastle upon Tyne, and then during the cholera epidemic of 1831 she went with Anne Turner to Edinburgh, where the Dunbar bust and the miniature by Thompson were executed. Together these give the impression of a strikingly beautiful and vivacious young woman. Elizabeth Stevenson next stayed in Manchester with Anne Turner's sister, Mrs Robberds, and her husband, who was the minister of Cross Street Unitarian Chapel. It was there that she met Robberds' colleague, William Gaskell.

Gaskell, born at Warrington in 1805, was educated at the local dissenting Academy and at Glasgow University. After further training at the Unitarian Manchester College in York he came to Cross Street in 1828. He was to spend the rest of his life there, becoming senior minister on the death of Robberds in 1855 and holding that position till his own death in 1884. His marriage to Elizabeth Stevenson took place at Knutsford on 30 August 1832. The honeymoon was spent in North Wales. Mrs Gaskell's love and happy memories of that area are expressed in a letter to her sister-in-law Eliza who was staying there in 1838 (9). The Gaskells returned to Manchester on Elizabeth's birthday, to their new home in Dover Street. Their first child, a daughter, was stillborn in the summer of 1833.[1] Thereafter they had four other daughters, Marianne, born on 12 September 1834, Margaret Emily (or Meta) on 5 February 1837, Florence Elizabeth on 7 October 1842 and Julia Bradford on 3 September 1846 —and a son, William, born on 23 October 1844, to die from scarlet fever some ten months later on 10 August 1845. Of that event his mother wrote: 'That wound will never heal on earth, although hardly anyone knows how it has changed me' (25a). It is said that her husband encouraged her to take up writing during the period of severe depression following their son's death, and that *Mary Barton* was the result.

The relationship of husband and wife is one that has caused some speculation.[2] William Gaskell seems to have been a peculiarly self-sufficient person with a variety of interests into which he threw himself whole-heartedly. In addition to his work at Cross Street and the demands made upon him by other churches as a visiting preacher,

---

[1] Did she die on or around 4 July? Cf. Mrs Gaskell's poem 'On visiting the grave of my still-born little girl, Sunday, July 4th, 1836' (printed in A. W. Ward's Knutsford edition of *The Works of Mrs Gaskell*, vol. i, pp. xxvi–vii).

[2] Cf. Aina Rubenius, *The Woman Question in Mrs Gaskell's Life and Works*, 1950.

he gave lectures to Mechanics' Institutes and other such organizations. He was Professor of English History and Literature at Manchester New College from 1846 to 1853; he gave classes in Logic and English Literature at Owens College (later to be the University of Manchester); and he acted as private tutor to a number of pupils. His Unitarian activities included the principalship of the Home Mission Board; and from 1861 to 1875 he was editor of *The Unitarian Herald*. He was a member of the Manchester Literary and Philosophical Society, for over forty years chairman of the Portico Library, and a regular visitor to the annual gatherings of the British Association. He was also active in social philanthropy, being a member, for instance, of committees concerned with better sanitation and with the control of beerhouses and places of public amusement. Charlotte Winkworth wrote of the impression he had made on Anglican colleagues and continued: 'He clearly feels that he has found his right place, and Lily is proud that he is appreciated by people whose appreciation she cares for'.[1] It is expressions such as this that we need to regard when claims are made for some kind of marital disagreement. There were differences. Mrs Gaskell at times regretted his isolating himself so much in his study and his going on holiday alone, free from responsibility for his family (489, 490). She seems also not to have received the support which at times she might have expected. Such an occasion was the stormy aftermath of the publication of the *Life of Charlotte Brontë* in 1857, when she 'never needed kind words so much,— and no one gives me them' (352).[2] Though William Gaskell seems to have controlled his wife's earnings, as he had every right to do before the passing of the Married

[1] Hopkins, p. 306.   [2] Cf. Hopkins, p. 304.

15

Women's Property Act in 1872, in most respects the relationship seems to have been a most enlightened one. There appears to have been no attempt on his part to prevent his wife from travelling and generally following the independent way of life which became hers after her literary success. She wrote to her friend Eliza ('Tottie') Fox: 'I don't believe William would ever have *commanded* me' (69). Whatever may have been the difficulties or shortcomings of the marriage, there is evidence that it remained firmly affectionate to the end. Mrs Gaskell was indefatigable in trying to free her husband from his various commitments to enable him to visit Italy in 1864 (531), and perhaps most convincing of all is the public testimony she gave in 1863 by dedicating *Sylvia's Lovers* to 'my dear husband by her who best knows his value'.

Mrs Gaskell took great delight in her children. Marianne, the eldest, was always very close to her mother's heart. Her earliest years were recorded in *My Diary* which her mother kept and 'which, if I should not live to give it her myself, will I trust be reserved for her as a token of her mother's love and extreme anxiety in the formation of her little daughter's character'. The sense of possible premature death gave rise to a tender, anxious and perceptive letter to her sister-in-law Nancy Robson on 23 December 1841, in which Mrs Gaskell asked Nancy to watch over Marianne if she herself should die. 'William I dare say kindly won't allow me ever to talk to him about anxieties', and Marianne, as well as being delicate in health is also 'a peculiar character—*very* dependent on those around her . . . love and sympathy are very *very* much required by MA' (16). To the same sister-in-law she wrote ten years later of Florence being 'nervous and anxious; she will require so much strength

16

to hold her up through life' (101). By this time, however, Mrs Gaskell was speaking of Marianne's 'sense of duty'. Meta was independent from the start and seems to have had her father's self-sufficiency. She was also intellectually the best endowed of the sisters with well-developed talents in music, painting and reading. The youngest, Julia, was witty and vivacious. The dependent pair, Marianne and Florence, found the support they presumably needed in marriage; Meta and Julia remained unmarried, the former after a broken engagement to an Engineer officer in the army. Mrs Gaskell seems to have contemplated such a future in a letter of 1860 to Charles Eliot Norton, in which she wondered why 'no one ever gives them a chance' (453). She concluded that the Unitarian young men of Manchester did not appreciate their qualities, and that 'the new school of enlightened and liberal young men' from elsewhere was probably prevented by their fathers' bigotry from intimacy with Unitarians. This seems to be an inference, for which she had some basis in the behaviour of young Charles Bosanquet. A year or two later Florence was to marry Charles Crompton, and shortly after her mother's death Marianne married her second cousin, Thurstan Holland, in 1866. This latter alliance was a source of some objection from his family (553), but Mrs Gaskell seems to have had a ready and considerable confidence in him (510). Though Thurstan was a little younger than Marianne, the marriage was to be a comparatively short one, for he died at the age of forty-eight in 1884, the same year as Mr Gaskell. Marianne outlived all her sisters to die in 1920. The letters tell a detailed story of the mother's care for and intimacy with this eldest daughter. The anxieties over childhood delicacy, the problems of school and education, guidance against a too ready tendency to espouse political and religious opinions and a host of other matters are covered.

This care of her children represents just one aspect of Mrs Gaskell's active domestic life. In addition, she was the mistress of a busy household. Her letters tell, often amusingly but sometimes in irritated vein, of her problems as a housewife. In those of 1849 and 1850 we can sense the excitement as she and her husband contemplated the building of a new house (e.g. 60). In fact, they moved into one already built, 42 Plymouth Grove, where Mrs Gaskell was to spend the rest of her life. Here she was able to indulge in some gardening (there was also a greenhouse) and to keep hens and a cow. Hence the problems of butter-making and getting eggs for sitting, buying roses and planting out at the right time that we read about in the letters. Indoors there was the problem of staffing, interviewing new cooks who admitted to outbursts of temper and dismissing girls who proved 'shapeless', to use one of William Gaskell's Lancashire dialectal terms. The house seems almost always to have been full of visitors, both great and not so great. Parties were often held for Manchester friends; and visitors, frequent like the Greens from Knutsford (e.g. 20) or the Winkworths from Alderley, often stayed for a few days. More celebrated figures such as the Carlyles, Charlotte Brontë, Harriet Beecher Stowe and the Dickens also came. 1857, the year of the great Art Exhibition in Manchester, was a particularly busy time. Besides being hostess to friends at large, Mrs Gaskell was also active as minister's wife in the work at Cross Street Chapel. Early letters tell of bazaars (7, 13), and of instruction to the Sunday School girls (32). In addition to this, there was her own participation in social welfare work which showed itself, for example, in interest in day nurseries (83), workers' emigration (61) and homes for factory girls (630).

Such in brief outline was the life and background of the woman who came to the notice of the literary world at the age of thirty-eight when she published *Mary Barton*. On 25 September 1862 she wrote to an unidentified prospective authoress, no doubt recalling her own experience, though not with fullest accuracy, for Julia was but a baby and Florence not much more when *Mary Barton* appeared:

When I had *little* children I do not think I could have written stories, because I should have become too much absorbed in my *fictitious* people to attend to my *real* ones. . . . Besides viewing the subject from a solely artistic point of view a good writer of fiction must have *lived* an active and sympathetic life if she wishes her books to have strength and vitality in them. When you are forty, and if you have a gift for being an authoress you will write ten times as good a novel as you could do now, just because you will have gone through much more of the interests of a wife and a mother (515).

The tension between the demands of her fictitious people and her real ones remained with Mrs Gaskell to the end of her life, but there is no doubt, as she herself so fully recognized, that the demands of the real ones which had necessitated her living an active and sympathetic life enriched her books immeasurably.

Mrs Gaskell's first published work was a piece written in collaboration with her husband in imitation of Crabbe and published as 'Sketches Among the Poor No. 1' in *Blackwood's Magazine* for January 1837. It would appear from the numeral that others were intended, but none appeared. It may have been to these imitations that she was referring in a letter to Eliza Gaskell on 13 May 1836 when she wrote: 'I have brought Coleridge with me, and am *doing* him and Wordsworth. . . . I have done all my *composition* of Ld B——, and done Crabbe outright since you left and got up Dryden and Pope' (4). Nothing more appeared from her pen until 1847 when she published the first of three short stories in *Howitt's Journal*. She had met William and Mary Howitt at Heidelberg in 1841 and had corresponded with them before that. The three stories of 1847 and 1848 were 'Libbie Marsh's Three Eras', 'The Sexton's Hero' and 'Christmas Storms and Sunshine'.

The work which occupied her principal attention in the years 1845 to 1848 was her first novel, *Mary Barton*. It was submitted through the Howitts to the publishers Chapman and Hall, whose reader John Forster quickly recognized its worth. The book took its origin from Mrs Gaskell's awareness of the apparent injustice of the economy of boom and slump, and especially the latter, as it affected the workers. The years 1838–42 had been particularly difficult and strife-ridden for the cotton industry, and the distress and trouble had stirred writers to base novels upon them. John Barton, the worker-hero, is at the centre of the book, but, as originally conceived, he was even more obviously so (42). He gave his name to the title of the book, but this was changed at the request of the publishers (39). This first novel brought Mrs Gaskell frustration and annoyance with Chapman and Hall. There are letters showing the anxiety and impatience of the new author as she asks for a date of publication (22, 23, 24) and her ill-concealed exasperation at the delay in payment of £100 agreed upon for the novel (33). In this last-mentioned letter she also refers to the consequence of her anonymity, the 'extreme annoy-

PLATE I

Mrs Gaskell, 1851, from the chalk drawing by
George Richmond, R.A.

ance to me, from the impertinent and unjustifiable curiosity of people, who have tried to force me either into an absolute denial, or an acknowledgement of what they must have seen the writer wished to keep concealed'. The embarrassment was mingled with 'self-reproaches for the deceit I have practised, and into which I have almost been forced by impertinent enquiry' (34). Not for the last time was she to say: 'I am not thinking of writing anything else: le jeu ne vaut pas la chandelle' (41). This reaction, however, arose not only from the troubles with her publisher and some of her acquaintances; it derived mainly from the criticism which poured down upon her from the cotton masters and some of the reviewers. Some, such as the enlightened Potter, were said to have bought it for their men (36); and many distinguished figures in literature, learning and politics commended it. The periodicals, however, were divided, and some attacked it fiercely. The most telling criticism was William Rathbone Greg's article in the *Edinburgh Review*. Greg was a member of a Manchester manufacturing family, whose attitude to their workers was amongst the most progressive in the industry. When the estimates of *Mary Barton* are considered as a whole, it is clear that Mrs Gaskell had little need for depression. The condemnation was severe but it was also ephemeral. The book continued to be praised, and her fame was established.

It made her known in London and led to her association with Dickens. Beginning with 'Lizzie Leigh' in March 1850, Mrs Gaskell contributed to Dickens' periodical *Household Words* in every year up to 1858, with the exception of 1857, an omission explained by work on the *Life of Charlotte Brontë*, her distress at the reception of that work and the domestic preoccupations of that year. She also contributed five pieces to Dickens' later periodical, *All the Year Round*, in 1859, 1861 and 1863. Her best work, however, she reserved in these latter years for her new publisher (George Smith)'s magazine, *The Cornhill*, in which both *Cousin Phillis* and *Wives and Daughters* were serialized. This was a monthly, capable of taking longer sections of work than Dickens' weeklies, and not therefore so dependent on the need for quickly succeeding crises in the action. The pace could be much more leisurely. Mrs Gaskell had many trials with Dickens as an editor. These did not appear with *Cranford* which came out as nine pieces over a period of eighteen months from December 1851 to May 1853, each one self-contained and independent. They arose, however, with *North and South* which was more closely organized and was published in regular weekly contributions from September 1854 to January 1855. She told her fellow-writer, Anna Jameson, something of her troubles:

Though I had the plot and characters in my head long ago, I have often been in despair about the working of them out; because of course, in this way of publishing it, I had to write pretty hard without waiting for the happy leisure hours. And then 20 numbers was, I found my allowance; instead of the too scant 22, which I had fancied were included in 'five months'; and at last the story is huddled and hurried up (225).

There was a note of weariness and apathy in her words as she sent the penultimate portion: 'I have tried to shorten and compress it, both because it were [*sic*] a dull piece, and to get it into reasonable length. . . . I never wish to see its face again; but, *if you will keep the MS for me, and shorten it as you think best for HW*, I shall be very glad' (220). She received £600 for the work from its serialization and from its publication in book form by Chapman and Hall. This was the last of her works which they issued. Thereafter her publishers were Smith, Elder. Chapman and Hall seem never to have been very satisfactory in their dealings, and she had still further trouble in later years over the question of re-issues and the transfer of copyrights to Smith, Elder.

North and South, like *Cranford*, was generally welcomed on its appearance, but the book which Mrs Gaskell wrote between these two met a reception even stormier than that accorded in some quarters to *Mary Barton*. *Ruth* was published in January 1853. It is the story of an unmarried mother, a young girl seduced, rescued and yet ultimately disgraced, who nevertheless is noble and leads a noble life and meets a noble death. Mrs Gaskell's courage in treating such a subject was not matched by sufficient generosity in the reception of the work, even among some of her friends. She told Nancy Robson: 'I had a terrible fit of crying all Saty. night at the unkind things people were saying' (148), and to Tottie Fox she wrote: 'I think I must be an improper woman without knowing it' (150). But by April 1853 she was telling Lady Kay-Shuttleworth:

From the very warmth with which people have discussed the tale I take heart of grace; it has made them talk and think a little on a subject which is so painful that it requires all one's bravery not to hide one's head like an ostrich and try by doing so to forget that the evil exists (154).

This mention of Lady Kay-Shuttleworth reminds us of the directions in which Mrs Gaskell's friendships were widening in these years. She stayed with the Kay-Shuttleworths at Briery Close, Windermere, and there met

Charlotte Brontë. Also in the Lake District she met the Arnolds and Mrs Wordsworth. She came to know Ruskin, whose wife had been at the same school as Mrs Gaskell. Two letters discuss at some length the Ruskins' estrangement (195, 211). In the second of these Mrs Gaskell is reporting what she had heard from the Nightingales, reminder of yet another important friendship which she established in the eighteen-fifties. She writes feelingly and at length in admiration of Florence Nightingale's work at the Middlesex Hospital (211) and sends an extract of one of Florence's letters to Catherine Winkworth describing her work in the Crimea (213). Part of *North and South* was written at the Nightingales' Derbyshire home, Lea Hurst near Matlock. This recalls the fact that Mrs Gaskell travelled extensively in the years of her fame. Besides family holidays, often spent at Silverdale on the coast of Morecambe Bay but also including visits to Normandy in 1853, Rome in 1857 and 1863 and Germany in 1858 and 1860, there were frequent and extended stays with friends who had country seats, Edward Holland (Thurstan's father) at Dumbleton, the Whitmore Isaacs at Boughton, the Ewarts at Broad Leas in Wiltshire, Frederick Holland at Ashbourne Hall, and Mrs Davenport at Capesthorne and after her marriage to Lord Hatherton at Teddesley. There were numerous visits to London and also to friends in Winchester and Canterbury and, very memorably, Oxford. Perhaps dearest of all the friends with whom Mrs Gaskell loved to stay was that remarkable Englishwoman in Paris, Madame Mohl. One obviously enjoyable visit with Meta in 1854 is described in two letters to Marianne (229, 230). The breadth of Madame Mohl's interests brought Mrs Gaskell and her daughter into contact with people famous in literary, artistic, scientific and political activities. It is sad that the correspondence between these two intelligent and vital women seems to have completely disappeared.

Mrs Gaskell's acquaintance with the literary life of London must have been particularly pleasant for her. Her active interest in literature is evident from the earliest of her letters. She told her sister-in-law Nancy Robson in 1841 of her reactions to Harriet Martineau's latest book, *The Hour and the Man*, in which she found characterization and conversation interesting, but of the story she commented, 'one knows all along how it must end' (16). She expressed her praise of *David Copperfield* (44a), *Framley Parsonage* (456) and *The Bigelow Papers* (584), whilst of George Eliot's *Scenes from Clerical Life* and *Adam Bede* she wrote: 'I have never read anything so complete, and beautiful in fiction, in my whole life before' (445; cf. 431). This appreciation is the more notable in that she found it difficult to reconcile the beauty of the books with the author's way of life. Mrs Gaskell was always impressed by the moral tone of a book. She criticized Aïdé's *Rita* for introducing the reader 'into the kind of disreputable society one keeps clear of with such scrupulous care in real life. . . . I don't think it is "corrupting", but it is disagreeable,—a sort of dragging one's petticoats through mud' (413). This explains her anxiety to indicate the reasons (as she thought, Branwell's responsibility) for the presence of 'coarse expressions' in *Wuthering Heights* and *The Tenant of Wildfell Hall*. Her criticism of Charlotte Brontë's *Villette* shows a sensitive understanding of the relationship of the author's life to her work:

I believe it to be a very correct account of one part of her life; which is very vivid and distinct in her remembrance, with all the feelings that were called out at that period, forcibly present in her mind whenever she recurs to the recollection of it (154).

Mrs Gaskell admitted that some part of her judgment of *Villette* was 'founded entirely on imagination; but some of it rests on the fact that many times over I recognised incidents of which she had told me as connected with that visit to Brussels'. To discover such intimate experiences from one so reserved as Charlotte Brontë is itself testimony to Mrs Gaskell's rare genius for friendship. Charlotte stayed in Manchester in April 1853 and May 1854, and Mrs Gaskell paid a visit to Haworth in September 1853. When Charlotte died, Mrs Gaskell determined to write a memoir of her friend. Patrick Brontë, however, asked her to write an authorized biography of his daughter. This brought her in touch with her new publisher, George Smith of Smith, Elder; thus commenced a business relationship which quickly blossomed into a friendship. Mrs Gaskell embarked on her new task with vigour. She visited Haworth and there spoke with Charlotte's father and with the curate, Nicholls, her husband. She wrote to the local stationer John Greenwood for details and drew upon his memories of the sisters. She sought out Charlotte's close school friend, Ellen Nussey. She travelled even as far as Brussels in the course of her research, there interviewing Monsieur Héger, the schoolmaster in whose house Charlotte had lived for a while. At times she seems hardly to have allowed a week to pass without asking Smith for details of publication of Charlotte's books and other such information. Once she had gathered her material Mrs Gaskell wrote quickly; too quickly it seems, for after a burst of activity on holiday she had to take a rest. 'I wrote 120 *new* pages', she told Emily Shaen, '. . . but I found my head and health suffering' (308). Nevertheless, just over three weeks after this letter was written she was reporting to Smith that she had 'written upwards of 300 of *my* (foolscap) pages, and I am just ending the year 1845. The next nine or ten years will be very interesting I have got such good materials. . . . I *think* it will be nearly 600 pages in all' (314).

In this same letter she expressed a fear about one of the troubles which she foresaw her work might encounter. 'I am very sore about reviews; I know it is a weakness, but unfavourable ones depress me very much.' She hastened to qualify 'unfavourable' as meaning not 'severe' but 'supercilious or personal ones, or impertinently flattering ones'. She went on to say that an unfavourable review would seem to her 'as if I had done her [Charlotte] an injury'. Mrs Gaskell regarded the writing of the *Life* as an act of piety; all must be done appropriately to commemorate Charlotte Brontë and to make her appear before the world as the noble woman she was. This led Mrs Gaskell into other troubles, into attacking people who in their turn were to protest and even threaten legal action. The Lady Scott and Carus Wilson affairs were the most notable of these, but so integral are the sections concerned to a proper judgment of the biography as a whole that the reader must be referred for a fuller treatment of these matters to the chapter on the *Life*. Suffice it here to say that Mrs Gaskell finished her task, went off with Meta to Rome to escape the reviews and returned in June 1857 to find the veritable 'hornet's nest' that she had to some extent anticipated buzzing madly and woundingly about her head. Her bitterness took on a tinge of cynicism. She wrote to Mr (later Sir) William Fairbairn quoting approvingly a suggested preface for the third edition which had been sent to her:

If anybody is displeased with any statement in this book, they are requested to believe it withdrawn, and my deep regret expressed for its insertion, as truth is too expensive an article to be laid before the British public (358).

The difficulties she had with Nicholls in the writing of the book led her to assert that she would never write another biography; its reception no doubt confirmed her in this resolve.

Whatever else had happened, however, there was to be placed on the credit side of this endeavour the newly formed friendship with Smith. In contrast with the unbusinesslike methods which characterized Chapman's dealings with her, Smith seems readily to have accepted any reasonable suggestion of Mrs Gaskell's in their commercial transactions. He quickly raised the offer for the *Life* from £600 to £800 when she pointed out that she had received the former sum from *North and South* which had entailed only half the labour and nothing of the research expenses of the *Life* (326, 328). At the same time as we take note of this, we should also recognize the generosity which she herself showed. When Sampson Low offered her £1,000 for a novel in April 1859, she wrote to Smith telling him that she 'would much rather have 800£ from [him] than 1,000£ from them' (430). She did, in fact, receive £1,000 from Smith for what turned out to be *Sylvia's Lovers*, but she was sincere in her offer. For her last work, *Wives and Daughters*, Mrs Gaskell received £2,000, but it was a source of discontent that at the same time as she was writing this book Wilkie Collins was being promised £5,000 by Smith for his next novel (582).

With her name firmly established among the writers of her time, with increasing financial sufficiency, with the opportunities, as her family grew up, of satisfying her love of travel, Mrs Gaskell does not seem to have laboured under the same pressure to produce after 1859. *Sylvia's Lovers*, which took its origin from the visit to Whitby in November 1859, did not appear until 1863, and there is a marked decline in the number of her contributions to periodicals. Chief among these latter, and worthy of mention as so fine an example of short fiction, is *Cousin Phillis* which appeared in *The Cornhill* from November 1863 to February 1864. The pressure returned, however, with her agreement to write *Wives and Daughters* for serial publication in the same magazine. With this pressure there came bad headaches, an illness of three weeks, and perpetual tiredness ('oh *how* dead I feel!' (582)). She hoped with the money she received to buy and furnish a home for her husband in his retirement. The last letters are full of detailed preparations, particulars of the purchase, the finding of a suitable tenant in the first place, the shopping for carpets and furniture (cf. 580, 582). After much searching and some disappointment she bought The Lawn at Holybourne near Alton (Hampshire). She took possession at the end of September 1865 but spent most of October in Dieppe and Boulogne. She returned to stay at The Lawn on 28 October. A letter to Marianne describes the house, still not properly ready for occupation, furniture not delivered, upholstery to be done, carpets to be cut, and yet 'Every day we like it better & better even in the midst of all the *half* furnished

29

state, painters, & charwomen' (588). Her joy was to be very short-lived, to last but a fortnight. With her family around her—all but her beloved Marianne and the husband for whom the new house was to be a surprise— she was taking tea on Sunday, 12 November 1865 'when *quite* suddenly', in Meta's words to Ellen Nussey,[1] 'without a moment's warning, in the midst of a sentence, she fell forwards—dead'.

Those who know Mrs Gaskell only by *Cranford* are sometimes inclined to think of her as a quiet, perhaps somewhat prim Victorian lady. Hardly anything could be farther from the truth. She was extremely active as a mother, a minister's wife and a hostess. When she had time to spare from these duties, there were the calls of visiting, of apparently indefatigable letter-writing and the passion for travel. Wherever she went, she made friends. Possessed of a serene beauty, considerable gifts of conversation, a lively personality and a ready sense of humour, she was endowed to succeed socially. To these gifts she added the psychological capacity of a keen observer and student of human nature, the intellectual and cultural ability of a well-stocked mind and a well-formed taste, and the moral courage and seriousness which expressed itself in her firm yet liberal religious convictions, her delicate personal sympathies and her sustained social purpose. Her friend Susanna Winkworth left an account of her qualities. In it she spoke of 'all her great intellectual gifts—her quick keen observation, her marvellous memory, her wealth of imaginative power, her rare felicity of instinct, her graceful and racy humour ... so warmed and brightened by sympathy and feeling'.[2]

[1] Letter of 22 Jan. 1866. [2] Quoted Hopkins, p. 312.

She spoke also of 'the atmosphere of ease, leisure, and playful geniality' that surrounded Mrs Gaskell, and of her expression being 'like the gleaming ripple and rush of a clear deep stream in sunshine'. Her qualities as a person are reflected abundantly in her books. Charles Eliot Norton testified to this when he wrote:

She is like the best things in her books; full of generous and tender sympathies, of thoughtful kindness, of pleasant humour, of quick appreciation, of utmost simplicity and truthfulness, and uniting with perfect delicacy and retirement a strength of principle and purpose and straightforwardness of action, such as few women possess.[1]

That is why her books are so much worth reading.

[1] To J. R. Lowell, *Letters of Charles Eliot Norton*, ed. S. Norton and M. A. de Wolfe Howe, Boston, 1913, p. 172.

CHAPTER III

'MARY BARTON'

To Mrs Gaskell was given the triumph that must be every novelist's ambition. Her fame was established almost from the day on which her first novel appeared. *Mary Barton* was an immediate, if controversial, success. Perhaps its success arose in part because it was controversial. The novel appeared at exactly the right moment. 1848 was the year of revolutions. Italy, Hungary and France surged up in popular revolt. In England also the unrest that had for years expressed itself in Chartism found new strength for what turned out to be the last expiring demonstration of that movement. A great meeting had been called for 10 April on Kennington Common and a mighty procession was to march to the Houses of Parliament with a petition for the Chartist demands. Prompt official action reduced the whole affair to a fiasco. Chartism was dead, but who was to know that? The European uprisings took place after the Chartist demonstration. The kind of people who read *Mary Barton* were living with uneasy minds when that book appeared in October 1848.

Thirty years before, in August 1819, in Mrs Gaskell's own city of Manchester, the troopers had dispersed with sabres a meeting in St Peter's Fields. 'Peterloo' showed that the class-war was real. The next three decades did nothing to mitigate its ferocity. In these years the transition of large parts of England from a predominantly agricultural to a manufacturing economy was accelerated and completed at a terrible cost in human suffering. The new working-classes sought some improvement in their lot through political agitation. Many of them had supported the movement for electoral reform, out of which issued the Reform Act of 1832. That act, however, was a cruel disappointment for them, in that it failed to extend the franchise far enough. Out of this disappointment came Chartism with its precise proposals for reform, the most important of which was the demand for universal suffrage. The 1839 petition for the Charter was rejected by Parliament. In the years of increasing economic distress that followed, political hopes seemed to have been doomed. It appeared to many more appropriate, as well as more likely, to seek some form of economic relief. Powerful support for this was forthcoming, for here was a cause to which manufacturer as well as workman might give his support. That cause expressed itself in the movement for the repeal of the protectionist Corn Laws. Two Manchester men, Cobden and Bright, were found at the head of the Anti-Corn Law League, established in 1838. They campaigned for repeal with increasing vigour in the first half of the eighteen-forties, and by the middle of that decade they found themselves with a grim ally at their side. Whatever might be the suffering in England, it was nothing compared with what happened in Ireland when the potato crop failed in successive years. After various delays the Corn Laws were repealed in 1846. Whether this relief seemed as illusory as that after the Reform Act of 1832 we do not know, but certainly there was room for still further action by the workers as the 1848 agitation abundantly shows. The middle and upper-classes must have felt as though they were sitting on a volcano.

There were those who had already given much thought

and concern to the question. Thomas Carlyle, the great seminal thinker of the period, had written on Chartism in 1839. In this essay and in *Past and Present* (1843) he spelled out in vivid terms and violent, disturbing style the nature of the crisis and the urgent need for action. Laissez-faire, every man for himself, the reckless and unqualified pursuit of private profit, was wrong, said Carlyle; it was not only wrong, it was stupid. Men could not escape their obligations to one another. 'Never, on this Earth, was the relation of man to man long carried on by cash-payment alone.'[1] Many of the manufacturers, hard self-made men, thought they knew better.

The conscience of the nation was disturbed, and it found expression in literature. Among the first novels on the subject of life in industrial areas are Mrs Trollope's *Michael Armstrong, the Factory Boy* (1840) and Charlotte Elizabeth (Tonna)'s *Helen Fleetwood* (1840). Both these novels provide quite moving pictures of the sufferings of young people in the mills, but neither author was able to realize the individuality of her characters sufficiently to make these works into considerable literary statements of the social problem. Disraeli did better in *Sybil* (1845). He saw England divided into the 'two nations' of rich and poor, and amongst the latter one does not easily forget his presentation of Warner, the starving hand-loom weaver, or the brutalized inhabitants of Wodgate. *Sybil* is the work of an intelligent and supremely aware observer, but it is not the work of a participant, of one who knew from daily experience the plight of those about whom he wrote. The book also tends to mingle the undiluted realism of Blue Book evidence with the somewhat fanciful symbolism by which Sybil is made to lead to-

[1] *Past and Present*, Bk. III, c. x.

wards Disraeli's political solution. Of the books which followed *Mary Barton*, bred partly out of that novel's success and partly from the prevailing concern, mention must be made of Dickens' *Hard Times* and of Kingsley's *Alton Locke* and *Yeast*. The first of these is less realistic than *Sybil*; it reads more like an allegory. This is not to deny its force, though it possesses the passion neither of Kingsley nor of Mrs Gaskell. The former's two novels deal with conditions in London tailoring sweat-shops and with agricultural distress. Kingsley knew what he was writing about.

So did Mrs Gaskell. She knew because, like Kingsley, she had lived amongst the conditions about which she wrote. *Mary Barton* is set, not in Coketown of *Hard Times*, but in Manchester, actual as ever anything was, 'the shock city' of the 1840s.[1] We must be careful to note what it is about. Perhaps the necessary distinction may be best expressed by saying that it is not about industrial conditions, but about people living in those conditions. *Mary Barton* is about humanity, about the indissoluble bond that binds man to man beneath the all-seeing eye of God. Mrs Gaskell is with Carlyle. He saw 'Sooty Manchester . . . built on the infinite Abysses . . . and there is birth in it, and death in it'.[2]

Mrs Gaskell saw much of that birth and death. Premature death in children seems, in fact, to have had some part in compelling her to write *Mary Barton*. She told a fellow social worker, Travers Madge, of a speech which gave her the idea for the novel:

She was trying hard to speak comfort, and to allay those bitter

---

[1] Asa Briggs, *Victorian Cities*, 1963, p. 92.
[2] *Past and Present*, Bk. III, c. xv.

feelings against the rich which were so common with the poor, when the head of the family took hold of her arm, and grasping it tightly said, with tears in his eyes, 'Ay, ma'am, but have ye ever seen a child clemmed to death.'[1]

Mrs Gaskell sets out to reveal such suffering in *Mary Barton*. In the preface she speaks of 'her deep sympathy with the careworn men, who looked as if doomed to struggle through their lives in strange alternations between work and want' and of 'the bitter complaints made by them, of the neglect which they experienced from the prosperous—especially from the masters whose fortunes they had helped to build up'. Thus arose her determination to give 'some utterance to the agony which, from time to time, convulses this dumb people'.[2]

Because what Manchester was is so important for a proper understanding of the compulsion which made Mrs Gaskell choose the subject she did for her first novel, it will be useful to describe the situation she knew so well and felt about so strongly. Who were these 'dumb people' to whom she refers?[3] The combined population of the Manchester, Salford, and Chorlton Unions in 1801 was just over 118,000. In 1831 it was 275,000, and in 1841 354,000; that is, it trebled over forty years and in the last ten years of the period increased by over a quarter. Many of the newcomers were Irish, accustomed to lower standards of life even than the English labourers. A whole

---

[1] M. Hompes, 'Mrs E. C. Gaskell', *The Gentleman's Magazine*, vol. LV (N.S.), 1895, pp. 124 f.

[2] *Mary Barton*, pp. xxxiii–iv.

[3] Information in this section is based on J. Adshead, *Distress in Manchester*, 1842; J. P. Kay, *The Moral and Physical Conditions of the Working Classes in Manchester*, 1832; L. Faucher, *Manchester in 1844*; B. Love, *The Handbook of Manchester*, 1842.

area on the city side of the loop which the river Medlock makes behind Oxford Road station was called 'Little Ireland'. There some four-hundred back-to-back cottages housed some four thousand people. Many of the poor lived in cellars 'neither drained nor soughed. They [were] consequently damp,—always liable to be flooded, and [were] almost entirely without the means of ventilation.'[1] There were no yards or privies, and refuse and ordure were indiscriminately hurled into the streets. Kay speaks of an area west of Deansgate where there was one privy for 380 people. The streets were either ill-paved or not paved at all. The rooms and cellars were 'destitute of furniture. Bricks and logs of wood were the substitutes for tables and chairs. Heaps of shavings, litters of straw, defiled with all sorts of impurities served them for beds. Frequently several families occupied different corners of the same chamber, and there was no separation of the sexes, save the distance between the beds of straw.'[2]

In times of prosperity wages ran from about nine shillings for tenters and reelers to twenty-five shillings for spinners,[3] but there was considerable fluctuation. The average wage, for instance, at one mill in December 1841 was only 11s. 3d. One class, however, was condemned to suffer continuous and increasing hardship.[4] This was the handloom-weavers, who, after a public petition in July 1841, rioted a year later and brought work in the factories to a standstill. Troops had to be recalled from Ireland to restore the situation. In time of distress the poor had either to starve or else to resort to desperate devices. In illness and bereavement they might, if they had been prudent, obtain help from a benefit-society to

[1] Adshead, p. 14.   [2] Faucher, p. 146.
[3] Love, p. 98.   [4] Faucher, p. 150.

which they had contributed. In times of unemployment, however, they could look only to charity, always inadequate, to the pawn-shop or to crime. Adshead reports a case of a man with three children, who, having pawned his own clothes, then had to pawn those of his children as well. Other cases of distress in 1842 included that of a dyer with a wife lately confined and four children who had been 'whole days without any food'.[1] It is not surprising that industrial relations were so bad, strikes frequent and often violent. The supply of labour, however, was such that the employers could usually defy the strikers.

It is not surprising either (and Kay as a doctor and social investigator was not surprised), that, given these conditions of work and at times of lack of work, crime, prostitution and drunkenness flourished. We hear of the beer-house and the gin-shop, full of customers, as many as four hundred in an hour, men and women alike, drinking on credit or even paying in food or clothes for their liquor.[2] Neale in his pamphlet on juvenile delinquency[3] painted a grim picture of the criminal areas of Manchester with their pawnbrokers' shops, illicit distilleries, beer and spirit shops, prostitutes' haunts and low lodging-houses. The increase in crime may be judged from a comparison of the figures of persons held in custody in 1831 when it was 2,423 with those for 1841, 13,345, an increase of five and a half times.[4] The police report for 1843 showed that there were some 330 brothels in Manchester with an estimated prostitute population of 1,500. Logan, a city missionary who investigated the problem, postulated five chief causes of prostitution, namely, the seduc-

[1] Adshead, p. 27.　　　　　　[2] Cf. e.g. Faucher, pp. 50–1.
[3] Quoted Love, pp. 147–8.　　[4] Love, p. 148.

tion of servants in public houses, the free mixing of the
sexes in factories, the work of procuresses, deception by
young men and encouragement by unscrupulous mothers.
To these the translator of Faucher's book on Manchester
added one other 'powerful cause', the 'seasons of commercial distress, when trade becomes paralysed—the mills
closed—and honest labour denied an honest livelihood'.[1]

Behind all this struggle and suffering lay the separation
of the classes. Here indeed were Disraeli's two nations,
in a situation made none the easier by the fact that many
of the successful manufacturers had themselves risen from
the ranks of the workers and possessed therefore the
ruthlessness needed for such success mingled with contempt for their less fortunate fellows. Of course, there
were enlightened employers like Mrs Gaskell's friends the
Gregs and Ashton of Hyde,[2] but the general picture was
no doubt accurately painted by Canon Parkinson when
he said:

There is no town in the world where the distance between the
rich and the poor is so great, or the barrier between them so
difficult to be crossed. . . . There is far less *personal* communication between the master cotton spinner and his workmen
. . . than there is between the Duke of Wellington and the
humblest labourer on his estate.[3]

Reviewers of *Mary Barton* were not always well disposed towards Mrs Gaskell's portrayal of Manchester and
its people. In a cumbersome circumlocution the *Manchester Guardian*[4] claimed that the book 'sinned generally
against the truth in matters of fact, either above the comprehension of its authoress or beyond her sphere of

[1] Faucher, pp. 42–3.   [2] Faucher, pp. 96–7; Kay, pp. 64–5.
[3] Quoted Briggs, op. cit., pp. 110–11.   [4] 28 Feb. 1849.

39

knowledge'. Was Mrs Gaskell's picture untrue? Did she exaggerate? The outline of conditions has been given above in order to assist in answering questions like these. I have deliberately omitted reference to Engels' *Condition of the Working Classes in England* because of the propagandist intention of that work, and chosen four writers, only one of whom, Benjamin Love, had a distinct bias, and that was against the working-classes. How much of their picture of Manchester does Mrs Gaskell reproduce? The immediately striking phenomenon is not what she reproduces, but what she omits, or omits to emphasize. The worst of the social investigators' revelations are not to be found in *Mary Barton*—nothing about the depraved Irish, nothing beyond a brief reference of Esther's to the extreme debauchery of drunkenness, nothing about the indiscriminate mixing of the sexes in overcrowded living conditions, little more than hints about the worst sanitary conditions, limited reference to prostitution, the pawn-shop and the plight of the handloom-weavers, and nothing about the actual conditions of work. This last Mrs Gaskell did not know enough about, and perhaps she did not know enough either about some of the other phenomena. She may therefore have decided to remain wisely silent. Whether that be so or not, she can scarcely be accused of exaggeration in her descriptions. If she exaggerated the separation of masters and men, she did so because the sympathetic angle of her book originated from her feelings for and with the workers. Even on this question of class-division, however, she had weighty testimony on her side.

There were moral and artistic reasons for Mrs Gaskell's particular treatment of the social situation. The basic ills in her book are the sufferings of decent upright people—

poor wages, uncertain employment, bad housing—not the more spectacular and, as she would probably have thought, the more deserved afflictions of the less worthy arising from profligacy and drunkenness. Moreover, she was not writing a social treatise. The danger in works of that kind is that people become abstract figures in the social catastrophe. For Mrs Gaskell the social catastrophe is what happens to people, to a few characters either already well-known to the reader or else carefully delineated for the particular occasion. Her novel was didactic by intention. The epigraph quotes Carlyle in recording a desire to be 'the means, under Providence, of instilling somewhat'. It was, however, a lesson in sympathy rather than in political economy that Mrs Gaskell wanted to teach.

Mary Barton is set in the years around 1839 to 1842 (p. 94), a period of continuous industrial recession associated with Chartist agitation. The Chartist meeting on Kersal Moor was held on 24 September 1838 and the petition presented to Parliament in the following June. The book follows a twofold but interlocking course in tracing the histories of John Barton and his daughter Mary. Originally Mrs Gaskell intended to entitle the book *John Barton*, but she altered this to suit her publishers. Despite the greater prominence consequently given to Mary, John Barton remains the hero, always well to the forefront of the story. The whole of the first part belongs to him with the incidents of the visit to London, the strike, the meeting with the employers and the murder of young Carson. Mrs Gaskell, however, skilfully balances this with Mary's adventures, the philandering of young Carson and the faithful devotion of Jem Wilson culminating in the quarrel of the two men. The two lines of the story merge with the arrest and trial of Jem on suspicion of murdering Carson, Mary's realization of her love, her efforts on his behalf, Barton's return home broken in mind and body and his death-bed reconciliation with Carson's father. The plot has its faults. It suffers from what appears to have been a re-arrangement of emphasis as a result of the change of title. Moreover, the imaginative energy resides in a succession of parts rather than in the whole, and as a result passages in which the reader is deeply engaged alternate with passages that fall flat. We do not really need a half-chapter about Job Legh and the baby Margaret, nor Will Wilson's traveller's tales. There are incidents of high excitement, but the book is not wholly free from melodrama. There is a cloak-and-dagger air about the trade-union scene when lots are drawn for the task of murdering Carson. Excitement and melodrama co-exist in the chase down the Mersey for Will Wilson and his last-minute appearance as the crucial witness at the trial.

There is a lot of death in *Mary Barton*. It is surprising that the dangers of sentimentality that so often intrude upon death-scenes are, on the whole, successfully avoided. Davenport and the Wilson twins die in justifiable ex-emplification of the book's social theme, young Carson and John Barton die for the needs of the plot and the moral, and Mary's aunt, the prostitute Esther, for the needs of another and subsidiary moral. The murder of Harry Carson is sensational, even melodramatic, but the exaggeration implicit in the incident is effective. Mrs Gaskell demonstrates that disaster of such magnitude proceeds out of a trivial thing when men are as desperate as John Barton and his friends. The murder also vividly, frighteningly crystallizes the emotional situation of the novel, the two sides implacably and destructively arrayed against each other. There is one other death, the most important of all, that of John Barton. This, like the murder, has both a realistic dramatic and a representative didactic significance. It does not seem to embody these two values equally nor to express them with comparable adequacy, but of this more will be said in its place.

Working as a counter against the narrative crudities of the book, its melodrama and extreme emotions, its occasional arid didacticism and even sheer irrelevance is its use of irony and contrast. Esther's good deed, warning Jem Wilson of the dangers in which Mary stands as a result of young Carson's attentions is an example of incidental irony. From this proceeds the quarrel and the arrest. Jem accepts that Mary is in love with Carson. The irony is that she is not; she has realized the stupidity of her infatuation and ended the affair. Even more ironic is Barton's killing of Carson for an offence insignificant by comparison with the cause he might have had, had he but known that Carson was attempting to seduce Mary. On the broad canvas of the novel as a whole what I may call the public and private themes counterpoint each other in a contrary progress. The opposition of masters and men moves blindly, inexorably, to tragedy and death, whereas the personal history of Jem Wilson and Mary Barton proceeds through difficulty and misunderstanding to love and happiness. It is appropriate that this life-value through the most intimate of personal relationships should implicitly read a lesson by contrast, placed as it is in juxtaposition with the defective public relationships of social organization. The contrast in the degree of development in the two kinds of relationship is evident enough when the union of the loving Jem and the contrite Mary is seen side by side with the strong, yet obviously con-trived, reconciliation of John Barton and the elder Carson.

The novel begins with a scene of deceptive and inevit-ably temporary joy. Green fields, black and white farm-houses, the lowing of cattle and the cackle of poultry, all this idyll of a May evening in the country makes an un-likely prelude to a 'tale of Manchester life'. The sardonic note is emphasized as we read more and more about the Manchester that has been outlined above. The simple happiness, purity and naturalness of Greenheys Fields is never forgotten. It acts as an implicit condemnation of the places that are subsequently described. The contrast, however, is not simply one of place. Place matters for what it does to people, and within a page or two John Barton remarks:

You see them Buckinghamshire people as comes to work here has quite a different look with them to us Manchester folk. You'll not see among the Manchester wenches such fresh rosy cheeks . . . as my wife and Esther had (p. 6).

This contrast is also found between the Mancunian John Barton ('a stunted look about him; and his wan, colour-less face') and his friend Wilson who came from Lonsdale ('more handsome and less sensible-looking . . . hearty and hopeful, and although his age was greater, yet there was far more of youth's buoyancy in his appearance') (p. 4). Two minor characters also play their part as a commentary on the destroying city: Esther, showing, as John Barton says, that in such a place beauty is a snare, and old Alice Wilson, for ever nostalgically reminiscing on her youth in Lonsdale and at the end deliriously re-enacting incidents of her childhood. Mrs Gaskell effec-tively points the difference between this last sad scene in a

lonely Manchester dwelling and that earlier happiness
with 'the sister of her youth, who had for nearly as many
years slept in a grassy grave in the little churchyard
beyond Burton' (p. 250). There is a double poignancy in
the recollection of a better place and a better time, but
this is reinforced by the fact that the place and time were
associated with the happiness of innocent childhood with
a playmate long departed. It is not accidental, either, that
the delirious Alice remembers their childish transgression
in failing to tell their mother that they had left church
early to play in the spring day. This detail both emphasizes the 'innocent child-like spirit' of old Alice and
reminds us that the city's temptations were of a far more
sinister and corrupting kind.

Esther's defection represents these latter, but apart from
the mention of this defection the beginning of the book
is serene. This serenity is noticeable in John Barton himself ('At the time of which I write, the good predomin-
ated over the bad in his countenance' (p. 4)); and the
tea-party at the Bartons' house is a scene of high happiness. Mrs Gaskell with her usual skill in detailed description tells of the comfort and cleanliness of the house, its
comparative spaciousness, the abundance of crockery and
of furniture, this latter 'sure sign of good times among
the mills' (p. 13). Prosperity is also implied in Mrs
Barton's instructions to Mary to go for ham, eggs, bread
and milk, and rum. The degree of comfort here is quickly
emphasized by contrast with Alice Wilson's cellar which,
though 'the perfection of cleanliness', is scantily furnished
and irremediably damp. Nor does Alice Wilson fail to
notice the difference in the fire, food and light compared
with what she is accustomed to.

Shortly after the party Mrs Barton dies in child-labour,

brought on by the shock of Esther's disappearance. Two or three years pass, trade worsens, wages drop and unemployment is widespread. Mrs Gaskell tells of the stripping of the Barton household, the steady departure of loved possessions to the pawnshop, and notably the smart japanned tea-tray and caddy to which she had drawn particular attention in her earlier description. The house has become dingy, comfortless, fireless (pp. 130, 132). The trade-cycle that brings economic depression for the masters means destitution for the workers. But it is not the Barton household which demonstrates the lowest depths of poverty and suffering; that is revealed by the sufferings of the Davenports. This family lives in a cellar in Berry Street, a street

unpaved: and down the middle a gutter forced its way, every now and then forming pools in the holes with which the street abounded . . . women from their door tossed household slops of *every* description into the gutter. . . . [The cellar was] very dark inside. The window-panes many of them were broken and stuffed with rags . . . the smell was so foetid as almost to knock the two men down . . . three or four little children rolling on the damp, nay wet brick floor, through which the stagnant filthy moisture of the street oozed up (pp. 65–6).

The Davenport cellar contrasts not only with the Barton house of happier days, but also, as a set piece within the same chapter, with the Carson ménage. With increasing affluence the manufacturers had begun to move out of the city. A former middle-class house in the same street as Carson's mill now presents a sadly bizarre appearance with 'its painted walls, its pillared recesses, its gilded and gorgeous fittings-up, its miserable squalid inmates. It [is] a gin palace' (p. 54). Carson's house is two miles from the city, almost in the country, 'furnished with disregard to expense' (p. 74). Besides simple description, Mrs Gaskell tellingly inserts dialogue to reinforce the contrast with the plight of the Davenports. Mrs Carson, the servant announces, will have cold partridge and 'plenty of cream in her coffee' for breakfast (p. 75). Harry Carson is to buy his sister a small new rose costing half a guinea (p. 76). The ostentation of the women is worse than that of the men (cf. the description of Mrs Hunter, p. 25); nor does Mrs Gaskell fail to remark upon their *ennui*—Mrs Carson, for instance,

indulging in the luxury of a headache . . . without education enough to value the resources of wealth and leisure, she was so circumstanced as to command both. It would have done her more good than all the ether and sal-volatile she was daily in the habit of swallowing, if she might have taken the work of one of her housemaids for a week (pp. 233-4).

That or something like it might easily have been her fate, for Bessy Witter might well have married Wilson 'and Carson warn't so much above her, as they're both above us all now' (p. 136).

It is this kind of touch which gives to Mrs Gaskell's sociological novels a note more authentic than is generally found among the other practitioners in this mode. She is aware of background and history. She can suggest so much of this by a single remark. It is the effect of intimacy. She knows the type of people she is writing about. It is this which enables her to distinguish among the masters as none of her fellow-writers do. She notes the range of attitudes both among the different employers and between the different generations of the employers. Their diverse views are well illustrated in

47

the scraps of conversation before the men arrive for the meeting with the masters. Some appreciate the men's sufferings and are willing to grant a rise in wages; others are adamant and characterize conciliation as surrender (p. 210). It is the younger generation, personified in Harry Carson, that proves totally unyielding. He is the child of wealth and comfort; his father, hard though he is, had in childhood and youth 'been accustomed to poverty' (p. 429). The father possesses an understanding born of experience and denied to the son. The men are rebuffed by Harry Carson's resolution, and his pitiless cartoon is the occasion for tragic violence.

Political and social attitudes are abstract things which find expression through association. Action and suffering, however, are personal. Harry Carson dies, and John Barton commits murder. The deed comes out of association and attitudes. The masters are ruthless, but the Trade Union is no less so in its mode of retaliation. Mrs Gaskell's portrayal of the furtive behaviour characterizing the union's proceedings has an unsatisfactory air about it, but she was able to recognize the appeal which association made, its 'wild and visionary' quality, and 'visionary is something. It shows a soul . . . a creature who looks forward for others, if not for himself' (p. 196). Mainly, however, she sees combination as 'an awful power . . . capable of almost unlimited good or evil'; and in this case she sees it working towards evil. At best, it exercises an inexcusable power over the individual; Job Legh decides to starve in the Union rather than be ostracized and persecuted out of it (pp. 228–9). His is the voice of sanity among Mrs Gaskell's workers. At worst, combination breaks forth in the violence of Carson's death and what is described as 'the real wrong doing of the

Trades' Unions' (p. 199), their persecution of the black-
legs or 'knobsticks' who came in from Burnley, Padiham
and other towns to fill the places of the striking opera-
tives. Mrs Gaskell shows that a defect of imagination can
produce consequences as disastrous to the workers as the
same sort of defect had to the masters. None of them
realizes what they are doing. They are only wise when it
is too late. Herein lies the point of the vitriol-thrower
Jonas Higginbottom's remorse as he asks in prison for
his watch to be sold to relieve his victim's family (p. 218).

  Is this incident incredible? Is it sentimentalized? Is Mrs
Gaskell's sympathy for the workers excessive? Perhaps
it appears so, but her concern was to show man's in-
humanity to man and thereby to inculcate the supreme
need for understanding and kindness. She was avowedly
giving voice to the agony of the poor, expressing things
from their angle. Put simply, that was to say that the poor
suffered and the rich took no heed. As the epigraph to
Chapter VI has it,

> How little can the rich man know
>   Of what the poor man feels . . .
> *He* never heard the maddening cry
>   'Daddy, a bit of bread!'

John Barton alleges that there was even worse than that:
'I've seen a father who had killed his child rather than let
it clem before his eyes; and he were a tender-hearted
man' (p. 217). Desperation comes out of suffering, the
more especially as the masters do not appear to suffer in
bad times (e.g. pp. 23–4). The workman derives comfort
from the parable of Dives and Lazarus. Mrs Gaskell asks:
'Does it haunt the minds of the rich as it does those of
the poor?' (p. 112). The trouble was that there was a

great gulf fixed between the two in this life. 'Class distrusted class, and their want of mutual confidence wrought sorrow to both' (p. 198). Any meeting was bound to fail, because it was sure to end in collision.

Mrs Gaskell carefully qualifies her own position. She does not accept the contrast as the workers see it, but, she goes on, 'What I wish to impress is what the workman feels and thinks' (p. 24). She even accepts the economic theory on which the masters worked. Given the situation of a possible repeat order, she writes: 'It was clearly [the employers'] interest to buy cotton as cheaply, and to beat down wages as low as possible. And in the long run the interests of the workmen would have been thereby benefited' (p. 197). Her economic thinking may seem very naïve. That hardly matters, for her chief concern is not with economics, but with human kindness. This to some extent explains Job Legh's function in the novel. He illustrates the dignity of character in humble life. He eschews the violence of Unions and accepts with noble resignation the ills which life brings. Mrs Tillotson has aptly described him as 'the point of rest in the narrative and in the theme, the embodiment of "the gentle humanities of earth".'[1] He is the good Samaritan, ever ready to relieve distress, helping Jem Wilson in his trial, comforting Mrs Wilson, and finally, and appropriately, bringing Mr Carson to a more enlightened view of the employer's responsibility (p. 451). It is a simple and noble belief that Job Legh holds: 'When God gives a blessing to be enjoyed, He gives it with a duty to be done; and the duty of the happy is to help the suffering to bear their woe' (p. 448). That was Mrs Gaskell's belief as well.

Mary Barton is about the need for human kindness in a

[1] Tillotson, op. cit., 1956 ed., p. 219.

tragic situation. John Barton is the victim. It is important therefore to examine in some detail the process of his characterization and history. In him is embodied the 'agony . . . of this dumb people', pressed to the extremity where it can suffer in silence no more. Mrs Gaskell is careful to make clear, when she introduces him, that he is no mere suffering angel. We are told at the beginning of the story that his expression showed him 'resolute either for good or evil' (p. 4). He is one of those 'who have endured wrongs without complaining, but without either forgetting or forgiving those whom (they believe) have caused all this woe' (p. 24). With the death of his wife the balance of his temperament is altered. 'One of the ties which bound him down to the gentle humanities of earth was loosened. . . . His gloom and sternness became habitual instead of occasional. He was more obstinate' (p. 22). Barton's class-hatred has already shown itself in a bitter, but perhaps too consciously rhetorical speech against the failure of the rich in their charitable responsibilities to the poor. This, however, has to be recognized as a theme-speech of the novel rather than a simple personal statement. The familiar parable-reference is there: 'We pile up their fortunes with the sweat of our brows, and yet we are to live as separate as if we were in two worlds; ay, as separate as Dives and Lazarus, with a great gulf betwixt us: but I know who was best off then' (p. 8). Mrs Gaskell neatly suggests the tragic sadness of the whole relationship in the final words with their cynical mirth. Our Lord's intention in the parable is perverted by this suggestion of delight in prospective revenge.

Barton's cynicism is expressed again in his conjecture about Carsons' contentment with the fire that destroys their obsolescent machinery but allows them to collect a large sum in insurance. Mrs Gaskell, however, specifically shows that there was truth as well as cynicism in Barton's speculation. She does it, moreover, at the beginning of the sixth chapter which goes on to portray the suffering of the workers at its extreme in the plight of the Davenports. In the period of distress she enables us to see John Barton's deepening gloom and hatred, from which his cynicism so often takes its birth; but she also illuminates the portrait periodically with flashes of Barton's kindness, as in this scene in which he readily helps the Davenports with the few victuals that he has, or again later when we are told of his asking that his own Union allowance be paid to Tom Darbyshire, father of seven children, who yet 'was, in his listless, grumbling way, a backbiting enemy of John Barton's' (p. 131). There is a breadth about Barton's response to life that, combined with the customary intensity of his reaction, gives him a fullness of characterization unmatched elsewhere in the book.

He is, however, more than an individual. He represents the workers; in him are personified in heightened form all their attitudes and emotions. They cherish a pathetic optimism (Mrs Gaskell calls it 'fond' and 'forlorn') about the power of Queen and Parliament, and Barton no less than anyone else. The pathos comes out in the naïveté of their instructions to him as to what he must say on his visit to London and in the largeness of their expectations (pp. 97–9). He goes in high hope and returns utterly cast down. The story of Dives and Lazarus is again on his mind, the more so because the luxury of London is more than he had even dreamed about, much less seen, in Manchester. 'Mary, we mun speak to our God to hear us, for man will not hearken; no, not now, when we weep tears o' blood,' he says. Mary hears

Margaret Jennings singing 'Comfort ye, comfort ye, my
people, saith your God'. We may believe Mrs Gaskell
when she says that Mary was comforted; but there is,
nevertheless, an ironic overtone in such a song at such a
time (p. 111). After the London visit increasing harshness
of spirit goes hand in hand with Barton's physical decline. 'Poor John! He never got over his disappointing
journey to London' (p. 194). It proves to be a traumatic
experience. Monomania overtakes him. 'It is hard to live
on when one can no longer hope' (ibid.). A man seeking
so little from life itself is then bidden to commit murder.
It is ironical that the task should fall on him, for he had
been absent from the meeting with the masters at which
the offending caricature had been drawn and had therefore not been satirized in it. It is more ironical still that
Barton should be obliged to kill just after he has seen the
agony of the vitriol-disfigured victim and has declared
that he will have no further part in violence, not even in
attacks on knobsticks. He cannot escape from being the
workers' representative. They are all suffering, and he is
called to avenge that suffering. As their avenger he becomes also their victim, the one who must now suffer
alone, in a sense vicariously for their crime.

After the murder there follows flight, return and final
listlessness. Barton retreats from life in a prolonged
wrestling with his conscience. He must, however, make
his settlement before he goes. Mrs Gaskell gives us a set-
piece with Barton and the elder Carson confronting each
other. It does not altogether succeed. For one thing
Carson's speeches are too theatrical, too full of rhetorical
question and exclamation. For another, the demands of
Mrs Gaskell's thesis are in conflict with her realism.
Barton is dying because of hatred and revenge; Carson

is consumed with the one and seeking the other. Mrs Gaskell believes that masters as well as men must transcend such emotions. By the too obvious device of an incident in which wisdom is made to proceed and convince out of the mouth of babes and sucklings Carson is converted from his lust for revenge to forgiveness. This ending is too contrived. The didactic intention has taken over at the expense of dramatic likelihood. Barton's last speech shows how these two might exist convincingly side by side. It is both didactic and dramatic. 'All along it came natural to love folk . . . I think one time I could e'en have loved the masters if they'd ha' letten me' (p. 431). The pose in which he is found, lying in Carson's arms, seems too obviously didactic. This is not to say that it fails altogether, for its symbolic significance is powerful. The inadequacy lies in Mrs Gaskell's inability to make realism and the symbolic sit easily side by side in the scene as a whole.

She felt that the masters were as capable of attaining salvation as the men, and she felt also that human kindness must be seen to triumph. This is what she tries at the end by assertion to make us accept. What remains convincing, however, is John Barton's simple history of terrible suffering. We see him as the victim of an impossible situation in which oppression suffocates all the willing potentialities for good and stimulates all the tendencies to hate. In John Barton Mrs Gaskell realizes a deeply poignant human condition, namely, that charity is both willing and able to suffer long, but that there is a point beyond which it can be no longer kind. He remains one of her outstanding characters.

She certainly felt more about him and his lot than about his daughter Mary and hers. Mary's part of the story is most unpromisingly conventional. We have a familiar variation of the eternal triangle—a pretty girl, poor and basically good, a young man, honourable suitor, also poor and good, and the rich would-be seducer, be-whiskered villain of Victorian melodrama. The young girl's head is temporarily turned, but she repents in time; not, however, without bringing on much trouble; but after many vicissitudes all ends well. There are appropriate secondary characters—the coarse accomplice of the rich young man, the prostitute who personifies the consequences of listening to blandishments such as his, and the good young girl, for contrast, not half so beautiful as the heroine, seriously studying music instead of flirting, nobly accepting the onset of blindness and at the end, appropriately (and almost predictably) having her sight restored. The wonder is that so much was done so well with such poor material.

Mrs Gaskell ensures that we know in the first chapters that Mary is a better girl than her behaviour might suggest. Moreover, Mary derives a certain degree of sympathy from the reader's anxiety lest she should go the way of her aunt Esther who had also been dazzled by expectations of a good marriage, and then been deserted and reduced to prostitution. In the first half of the book Mary's is a secondary role. Afterwards, however, and presumably as a result of prompting from the publisher (cf. 39), Mrs Gaskell brings her to the fore. She develops Mary's character out of the dilemma in which the girl has been placed in having to prove her lover's innocence without incriminating her father who, she knows, has committed the murder. It is a powerful situation fit, as Maria Edgeworth noted, 'for the highest Greek Tragedy yet not unsuited to the humblest life of a poor tender girl—heroism, as well as, love in a cottage'.[1] Out of the strain of opposite responsibilities Mrs Gaskell demonstrates Mary's love, loyalty and endurance. When Jem Wilson has been saved by her efforts, the strain proves too much. When cause for anxiety has passed, Mary collapses. This is a realistic touch which makes her more credible.

Mary, however, is a very simple character. Her role, too, is simple. She is successfully realized within the limits in which Mrs Gaskell conceived her. The criticism must surely lie against the narrowness of the limits. The possibilities of development both of character and situation are simply neglected. This may seem to be asking for something like *Sylvia's Lovers* some fifteen years before Mrs Gaskell reached that book. It is not. It is rather to say that Mary's creator does not seem to have realized that her character had a heart and a mind. Mrs Gaskell never seems to have got 'inside' Mary. Her heroine's history is one of action rather than of feeling, of responding to events by doing rather than of generating them by being. This may explain why she is so much more convincing in the latter half of the novel. What she does is more interesting than what she is. She is an actor rather than a character. Mrs Gaskell never envisaged her with anything like the same fervour and interest as she did her father. As a result, the love-story, as a whole, seems lacking by comparison in that inspiration which so obviously determined and defined the story of the workers' suffering.

The love-story has its links with this other story. The clash of John Barton with Carson shows how money destroys men. The encounter of Jem Wilson with Car-

[1] R. D. Waller, 'Letters Addressed to Mrs Gaskell by Celebrated Contemporaries', *Bulletin of John Rylands Library*, vol. 19, no. 1, p. 8.

son's son reminds us that money is also destroying love. 'The gentleman; why did he with his range of choice among the ladies of the land, why did he stoop down to carry off the poor man's darling?' (p. 191). The meeting of the two young men is violent, but at the same time it enables Mrs Gaskell to show Jem's awareness of the equality which underlies the difference in economic status. He recognizes the common humanity between them—'a man's a man for a' that' (p. 203), thus demonstrating that he possesses feelings so markedly absent from Carson's character. The whole scene between these two displays extremely well the contrast between the flippancy and superciliousness of Carson and the sturdy dignity and tender concern of Jem. In some ways this may appear too facile and biassed a comparison, and certainly in other places Jem seems too good to be true. The phrases which are used to describe Barton's thoughts of him do not augur well for Jem's later participation in the events of the novel. 'A steady workman at a good trade, a good son to his parents, and a fine manly spirited chap' (p. 47) makes him sound unexceptionable but also uninteresting. Jem is too good, and Harry Carson is too bad. Both are over-simplified.

Esther is better, even though she, too, often seems to be fulfilling a representative function rather than living out a personal history. Her prostitution symbolizes the blighting moral effect of the society in which she is found. Her suffering is irremediable. She may have found her way back to the place she had left, but she can never regain her innocence and happiness. It is thus appropriate that at the threshold of her former home with the Bartons she should come 'as a wounded deer drags its heavy limbs once more to the green coolness of the lair in which it was born, there to die' (p. 455). This simile is emotionally charged, but its evocativeness seems rather too rhetorical. Esther's story is not without sentimental and melodramatic touches, especially in the account of her dreams with the loved figures of childhood passing round her bed, 'all looking at [her] with their sad, stony eyes' (p. 189), but even here we gain a vivid impression of the hunted, outcast quality of her life. These frightful fantasies also give meaning to her insistence on the need to escape through drink.

Of the really minor characters one deserves especial mention. Sally Leadbitter, Carson's intermediary in his affair with Mary, is a superb miniature. All her conversation and action is at one with the description of her vulgar-mindedness which we are given on her introduction to the tale. Even when Mary is beset with anxiety and plunged in grief at the time of the trial, all that Sally can talk of is the pretty appearance that Mary will make at the trial (p. 319). At the end with what would be cruelty, could she feel at all, Sally announces Jem's dismissal to Mary:

Decent men were not going to work with a —— no! I suppose I mustn't say it, seeing you went to such trouble to get up an *alibi*; not that I should think much the worse of a spirited young fellow for falling foul of a rival—they always do at the theatre (p. 417).

The last-moment hesitation, too late to conceal the word she was going to use, looks like belated consideration, but the substituted sentence is more cruel still, and the whole blundering, unfeeling performance is completed by her inability to separate the sufferings of life from the titilating situations of cheap theatre.

By contrast with the opening chapters the last section of the novel moves at a very fast rate. Mrs Gaskell's control and variation of pace is not the least of the book's successes. There is the anxiety of the trial itself, the suspense of the chase after Will Wilson's ship, Mary's collapse and illness, her father's return and decline and death. Jem and Mary are left. The whole tangled history has moved to its close. The past is finished, but the future is theirs. They marry and emigrate to Canada. It may be said that this does not represent a solution, only an escape. This is true enough. There can be no happiness in Manchester. This is surely what Mrs Gaskell really believed, and not what she claimed she believed in the reconciliation of Carson and Barton. That was only what she would have liked to believe and what she wanted others to believe.

Progressive thinkers applauded her for what she had shown. The book brought her congratulatory letters from Carlyle and Dickens, F. D. Maurice (a founder of the Christian Socialist movement) and Kingsley, and the veteran Radical weaver-writer Samuel Bamford among others. It received favourable reviews in *The Athenaeum*, *The Eclectic Review*, *Fraser's Magazine* and *The Westminster Review*. They welcomed it, in general, for its merit as a documentary. For those who thought it faithful, however, there were others who found it biassed. Chief among these latter was a Manchester man, brother of cotton-spinners and friends of Mrs Gaskell, William Rathbone Greg, who objected to the book's excessive sympathy for the workers in an article he wrote for *The Edinburgh Review*. The misery of the poor, he felt, was their own fault. The rich were under no obligation to supply their improvidence. For such as Greg Mrs

Gaskell's statement in the preface that she was concerned only to show how things *seemed* to the poor and her reiterated qualifications, dissociating herself from Barton's statements and attitudes, were of no avail.

In a sense Greg was right, for whatever may be said about Mrs Gaskell's views, *Mary Barton* issued from her compassion for the poor. For her 'the bewildered life of an ignorant thoughtful man of strong power of sympathy, dwelling in a town so full of striking contrasts as this is, was a tragic poem' (39). In another letter she wrote:

Round the character of John Barton all the others formed themselves; he was my hero, *the* person with whom all my sympathies went, with whom I tried to identify myself at the time, because I believed from personal observation that such men were not uncommon, and would well reward such sympathy and love as should throw light upon their groping search after the causes of suffering, and the reason why suffering is sent, and what they can do to lighten it (42).

This quotation makes it clear that Mrs Gaskell saw the whole matter not as a question of economics but of morality and even religion. It is thus that *Mary Barton* differs so obviously from a work such as Harriet Martineau's *A Manchester Strike* which does see the whole problem as a question of economics. The contrast brings out the nobility of Mrs Gaskell's view of the matter all the more strikingly.

A little before in the same letter she spoke of the tale's 'silently forming itself and impressing me with the force of a reality'. We need not be surprised to read this. There is nothing in the least contrived about the underlying inspiration of *Mary Barton*. Like many a first novel, what it has to say was irrepressibly demanding to be said. She felt so keenly both about what was and what she considered ought to be. The book's imaginative energy is nourished on close experience, deep sincerity and immense compassion. In some ways her very triumph in the portrayal of John Barton may make the other parts of the tale seem less convincing than they might otherwise be. The book is unequal in its achievement, but in its principal interest character and event move inexorably to calamity that none would wish and none can foresee. In this sense it is truly a tragic poem.

CHAPTER IV

'CRANFORD'

WITH *Mary Barton* the mid-Victorian sociological novel reached its maturity. Dickens praised the talent that had produced it and it may even have had some part in his decision to try his hand at a similar work in *Hard Times*. As editor of *Household Words* he was quick to enlist the services of a writer of whom he thought so highly. 'Lizzie Leigh' appeared in that periodical in 1850 and was but the first of many short stories that were to follow. It was in the pages of this same weekly that *Cranford* itself saw the light. This work will probably always remain the best known of its author's productions.

Cranford is Knutsford. It is not surprising that, after the success of *Mary Barton*, Mrs Gaskell's thoughts should have turned to a story centred on Knutsford, for this quiet Cheshire town, the scene of her childhood and youth, remained to the end of her life the home of her spirit. That she did turn to Knutsford and her early years, immediately after writing *Mary Barton*, is shown by her tale 'The Last Generation in England' which appeared in *Sartain's Union Magazine* in July 1849. In this tale we have the genesis of *Cranford*, the first draft, as it were, of that book's first chapter. This chapter together with the second appeared as a story in *Household Words* on 13 December 1851. That was all Mrs Gaskell had in mind. 'The beginning of Cranford was one paper in "Household Words"; and I never meant to write more . . .', she told Ruskin

(562). Dickens, however, persuaded her to write more, and the rest of the story appeared as seven episodes at irregular intervals between 1851 and May 1853.[1] The whole tale was published in June 1853.

The Knutsford of Mrs Gaskell's early years was for her the last generation in England. It was the home of Aunt Lumb and all her Holland relatives. It was a world which to the young girl must have seemed to be dominated by what to her were old ladies. Fussy old ladies they were, preoccupied with the niceties of their little lives, controlled by the requirements of genteel trivialities. At one level, but, be it said immediately, a superficial one, the tale that is told about them re-creates nostalgically those pleasant, little, leisured lives. Hugh Thomson caught this aspect perfectly in the well-known illustrations to the 1891 edition. This is the *Cranford* world of lavender and lace, of quarter-hour calls and the right way to address the widows of Scottish peers. It is a world that in its setting and superficial appearance is not far distant from that of Jane Austen. But beneath the surface of Jane Austen's work there is the firm moral and social texture of a world where an Emma answers 'Just what she ought, of course. A lady always does' and where a Mrs Elton is always to be recognized at once as a vulgar interloper. Many readers, however, have failed to penetrate below the surface of *Emma*; and the same is true of *Cranford*. There is obviously more than lavender and lace in a book that Charlotte Brontë could find 'graphic, pithy,

[1] These appeared as follows: 3 Jan. 1852—Chapters III and IV; 13 March 1852—Chapters V and VI; 3 April 1852—Chapters VII and VIII; 15 Jan. 1853—Chapters IX, X and XI; 2 April 1853—Chapters XII and XIII; 7 May 1853—Chapter XIV; 21 May 1853—Chapters XV and XVI.

penetrating, shrewd'.[1] *Cranford* may seem to be a novel about unimportant lives, but, in fact, it is a consideration of fundamental human problems, of money, class, sex, social groupings, and taste. The world of *Cranford*, however, is much less certain of its own values than is that of Jane Austen. This explains some of the reversals of opinion; from this derives much of the book's irony. The social code is not adequate for the human responses. The fear of vulgarity time and again inhibits the display of kindness, but it is never able to suppress it. That is why Charlotte Brontë could also describe *Cranford* as a 'kind and indulgent' book.[2]

It is not one of the main concerns of this short study to examine the literary analogues of *Cranford*, but a brief reference to some of the works with which it has been compared may help to indicate with a degree of precision some of the lines that this examination of the book may profitably pursue. Likenesses have been drawn with the work of Goldsmith, Crabbe, Galt and Miss Mitford. Some of the attempts at comparison proceed from the fact that the writings in question possess a background similar to that of *Cranford*. The setting in each instance is that of a village or very small town. But even in the description of the setting considerable differences may be discerned. Likewise, the relationship of setting to character, the influence of one upon the other, varies from case to case. In *The Vicar of Wakefield*, for instance, there seems to be little such influence, whereas in many of Crabbe's tales not the least of their effect derives from the

[1] Letter to Mrs Gaskell, 9 July 1853: *The Brontës: their Lives, Friendships and Correspondence* (Shakespeare Head Brontë), ed. Wise and Symington, vol. IV, p. 76 (hereafter referred to as S.H.B.).
[2] Ibid.

fact that the characters are what they are because they are where they are. In Galt's *Annals of the Parish* this is also true, but in a different way. Here the characters are the product of their environment, not in terms of their psychological intensity but rather of their social and perhaps even racial attitudes. Galt's work is also difficult to compare with *Cranford*, because of the specialized angle of vision and narration (that of Pastor Balwhidder) and the diverse and unconnected reference resulting from the method of chronicle account which is adopted. In *Our Village* one feels that the characters are often appropriately, but not inevitably, located where they are.

The sense of apt location is stronger in *Cranford*. This proceeds mainly from two causes, the one Mrs Gaskell's greater understanding of, and hence penetration into, character, and the other the reader's greater familiarity with characters who appear throughout the book. When one considers the first of these, one cannot help but reflect that Elizabeth Barrett Browning might more suitably have called Mrs Gaskell rather than Miss Mitford 'a prose Crabbe in the sun'. And yet, though Mrs Gaskell exhibits strong powers of delineating character in terms of her own sunnier disposition, the inappropriateness of this phrase is at once apparent. Crabbe's method of characterization is usually so different, a matter of generally broad strokes with occasional surprising subtle nuances. His procedure is that of the surgeon with the scalpel, laying bare, revealing the character. Mrs Gaskell is at once less intense and more delicate. Admittedly, the nature of her characters and the conventions of their society are different (Crabbe's world is altogether less refined); but then she chose that they should be. Moreover her method of characterization is different. Whereas

65

Crabbe sets the whole unsparingly before us, whereas he reveals, she presents. New facets appear as and when she sees it needful to show them. In addition, her comment is less outspoken. She is content to leave the ladies of *Cranford* speaking of their 'elegant economy'. Crabbe, however, must point the difference between appearance and reality in the plainest terms:

> Our good appearance through the town was known,
> Hunger and thirst were matters of our own.[1]

I mentioned as the second cause of our sense of apt location in *Cranford* the fact that the characters appear throughout the book. It is this fact which to some extent make the comparisons with both Crabbe and Miss Mitford inappropriate. The comparison perhaps arises because of *Cranford's* appearance as a series of episodes, but Mrs Gaskell links her episodes in a manner which distinguishes her from the other two writers. It is not just a matter of the presence of the same people in different situations, either. This is why I must insist on her manner of proceeding in characterization in what is a progressive revelation, in the course of which she tells us not only more about the individual characters but also more richly informs and demonstrates the ethos of the world in which they are set. In this I am arguing for the essential unity of what is only apparently a series of episodes.

We must therefore at this point examine the structure of the work. We have Mrs Gaskell's own word that she never intended to go beyond the end of the present second chapter, and that cannot be gainsaid. In that first part two strongly imagined characters appear and are dismissed by death. Of these two, Captain Brown and

[1] *Tales of the Hall*, VI, 242–3.

Miss (Deborah) Jenkyns, I shall say more later. The characters who assume prominence in the third chapter are those who matter throughout the remainder of the tale. Above all, from this point onwards the book belongs to Miss Matty, who is both so lovable and so inadequate. It has been clear enough in the first two chapters that she has had to live under the autocratic protection of her elder sister. She has done so in that contented passivity, that mood of cheerful and even eager acquiescence, that makes her isolation by her sister's death so pathetic. Mrs Gaskell then skilfully re-directs the reader's sympathy by showing that the pathos of Miss Matty's life had other sources, though—and this increases the pathos—she herself might not have been willing to confess as much. Miss Deborah's autocracy had been blighting as well as protective. The second instalment of *Cranford* in *Household Words* told Miss Matty's love story of far away and long ago. The tragic sense of the past is then prolonged into what are now the fifth and sixth chapters. 'Memory at Cranford', as *Household Words* entitled these chapters, takes the blighting influence back to the father's generation, so that to a sister lost in age have now been added a suitor rejected and a brother lost in youth. At this point we move into the present, and the theme of estrangement is now concentrated upon the person of the Honourable Mrs Jamieson, the new autocrat, determining who is in and who is out in Cranford society. Miss Matty, needless to say, accepts all rulings without demur. The next episode, the conjuring show and the subsequent panic about robbery in Cranford, emphasizes her helplessness and lack of self-confidence. Then, as life seems to be proceeding with its trivial inconsequence, the bank collapses with dramatic suddenness and Miss Matty is impoverished. Her helplessness is now tragic. What can she do? The next chapter is entitled 'Friends in Need'. One of these friends, the most important, we have heard of somewhat unobtrusively, usually at the ends of chapters. It is her servant Martha, whose love affair with the reliable Jem Hearn Miss Matty has reluctantly recognized. It is the marriage of these two which does much to save her. Finally, the long-lost brother Peter, now Aga Jenkyns, returns and all is well. The most sympathetic, because the kindliest, of heroines is saved.

Once we have noted that the book's structural unity depends so much upon the central character, we may seek next for its unity of mood and spirit, the tonal unity, which leaves such a firm impression. An important contribution to this is made by the book's atmosphere, created by the evocation of place and time, and by the attitude of the narrator. Cranford is Knutsford. Mrs Gaskell told Ruskin: 'It is true, too, for I have seen the cow that wore the grey-flannel jacket—and I know the cat that swallowed the lace.' In this literally incidental sense *Cranford* is a history. Many of the places and people have been linked with those that Mrs Gaskell knew. Holbrook may be based on the eccentric Peter Leigh and Mrs Jamieson on Lady Jane Stanley, and possibly the Jenkyns sisters on Mrs Gaskell's cousins Miss Mary and Miss Lucy Holland. The places are identifiable—the George Inn, the Shire Lane and the rest; but the people are not. Of them one can only say 'linked with' and 'based on'. Even, indeed, with the places one must make due allowance for the fact that we know them in *Cranford* not as geographical locations but as imaginative reconstructions. Cranford is —and is not—Knutsford. We do not need to know

Knutsford to know the George Inn, Mr Johnson's shop
or Darkness Lane. In any case, time has brought its
changes to all these. To stand in the Assembly Room at
the Royal George today is to experience a fine pleasure,
but it is not a literary one; it is extra-literary, historical
rather, to feel that Mrs Gaskell was there, and loved it so
much and described it so well. She described it so well,
that is, for her own purposes.

Cranford is a quiet backwater, its separation from the
main stream of life emphasized by the occasional re-
minders of the noise of that great world which is represented by Drumble. This very word is discordant, and
from the place itself will come the death blow to Miss
Matty's perilously maintained independence. Cranford
is not only quiet; it has also seen better days. This is part
of the significance of the pages describing 'my father
the Rector''s time. The county families are no longer
present as Sir Peter Ashley was; they are only talked about.
Cranford is now left to a group of old ladies living empty
lives on limited means. All this is concentrated in the
description of the Assembly Room at the George:

Miss Matty gave a sigh or two to her departed youth, and the
remembrance of the last time she had been there. . . . The
Assembly Room had been added to the inn, about a hundred
years before, by the different county families, who met
together there once a month during the winter to dance and
play at cards. . . . Now, no beauty blushed and dimpled along
the sides of the Cranford Assembly Room; no handsome artist
won hearts by his bow, *chapeau bras* in hand; the old room
was dingy, the salmon-coloured paint had faded into a drab;
great pieces of plaster had chipped off from the white wreaths
and festoons on its walls; but still a mouldy odour of
aristocracy lingered about the place, and a dusty recollection of

the days that were gone made Miss Matty and Mrs Forrester bridle up as they entered, and walk mincingly up the room, as if there were a number of genteel observers, instead of two little boys with a stick of toffy between them with which to beguile the time (pp. 102-3).

What a contrast—elegant economy and two lads with a stick of toffee!

Cranford has not moved with the times. It belongs to the past. Its chief characters are either old or growing old. The book begins in the present—'Cranford *is* in the possession of the Amazons'—but by the fourth paragraph Mrs Gaskell, perhaps unconsciously, has moved into the past tense, and then, as the narrator speaks in her own person, the sense of reminiscence becomes stronger. The narrator is in the present, the events are in the past: 'I imagine that a few of the gentlefolks of Cranford were poor' (p. 3). The survivor is recalling people and occasions past and gone. The sense of the present only returns —and then not completely—with the beginnings of dialogue. The first two chapters are a story of death, the event that puts irrevocable finality upon the past. Captain Brown dies, Miss Brown dies, Miss Jenkyns dies. The first two deaths, related to the main events of the incident, took place a long time before the last. 'The last time I ever saw poor Miss Jenkyns was many years after this' (p. 26), but she, too, is dead. It is all so long ago. And yet there was a past that still affects the present, a past long before this we have been hearing about, a past that has made the present for Miss Matty what it is and that might have made it so different. The next episode describes the meeting with, and visit to, Holbrook, her lover of long ago, and to the place 'round which it is probable that many of her innocent girlish imaginations had clustered'

(p. 37). Then death takes him. The visit takes place in the present; memory goes surging back into the past. The consideration of unfulfilled desire and hope is pathetic enough, but the present returns with death that ends all, setting its sardonic seal on life, confirming that what might have been is a mockery and that even what is is but a frail enough possession, soon to be taken away. This is the fact that not only strikes fantasy down, but also plunges it cruelly into the waters of sorrow and hope-lessness.

After the love-affair we are introduced to a past still further off, to Miss Matty's childhood at the vicarage and further back still, to the letters of her father and mother during their courtship. A whole life passes before us. An additional range of pathos is introduced. A past so long ago is made to convey 'a vivid and intense sense of the present time' (p. 51). Mrs Gaskell sensitively evokes the relationship of the young rector and his girl-bride and follows the history of their marriage, the scholar-husband and his wife busy in domestic and parochial concerns. Though Mrs Gaskell suggests that the degree of satis-faction which husband and wife respectively derived from their letters may have varied in extent (p. 55), she shows also how the letters symbolize the enduring affection between them. The rector is said to have 'treasured' his wife's letters 'as fondly . . . as if they had been M. T. Ciceronis Epistolae' (p. 55). The two are bound together in an ultimate sorrow, so strong in its power that it also works their final separation. Their anguish when Peter runs away from home after being chastised by his father (p. 65) represents one of the grand examples of Mrs Gaskell's delineation of pathos—the mother's restless, anxious searching, the father paralysed by remorse, his simple confession 'I did not think all this would happen', their fear lest Peter had committed suicide.

My father saw no conscious look in his wife's hot dreary eyes, and he missed the sympathy that she had always been ready to give him—strong man as he was, and at the dumb despair in her face his tears began to flow. But when she saw this, a gentle sorrow came over her countenance, and she said, 'Dearest John! don't cry' (p. 66).

Mrs Gaskell goes on to describe the aftermath of Peter's disappearance, stressing the effect on the father, his great tenderness—and 'you see, he saw what we did not—that it was killing my mother' (p. 69). And so to another death, the end of a life that has been spanned in a few pages from joyous girlhood to its sorrowful close.

At this point the narrative moves from recollection into the present, though it is still told in the narrator's past tense. The remainder of the book manipulates time not by length and distance away but by pace and intensity. Cranford time, steady, slow, uneventful, is now affected by outside persons and events. First, in the chapter 'Visiting' we see the norm. Then comes Lady Glenmire and excitement, Signor Brunoni and more excitement. Neither is what Cranford expects. They almost think that Lady Glenmire will arrive wearing her coronet, but the fact is always very different from the fantasy. Signor Brunoni is the conjurer, the personification of fantasy; but the reality is Samuel Brown, a worthy, struggling, very ordinary ex-soldier. Fantasy in his case not only stirs up the excitement of the actual conjuring show, but also provokes the subsequent panic about robberies. Fact supersedes fantasy when Brunoni is discovered to be Brown, lying ill at the Rising Sun. Then more fact still, and more excitement, but this time with more justification—the engagement of Lady Glenmire and the doctor Hoggins and financial disaster for Miss Matty. Imagined crisis has been succeeded by real crisis, in its turn to subside into resolution in terms of the book's pervasive kindliness. The last three chapters are entitled 'Friends in Need', 'A Happy Return' and 'Peace to Cranford'. The fairy-tale ending of Peter's return may appear too good to be true, but it is a neat translation of fantasy into fact. Happiness, however, comes only at the end and can last only for a comparatively short time. Cranford is an elegy, an account of time past and of a fleeting, unimportant present. It is a book of old people, with no significant future.

This sense of age is accentuated by the presence of the narrator. Mary Smith is the daughter of a Drumble businessman, and a frequent visitor to Cranford, staying usually with the Misses Jenkyns. She is the young observer of the main group of elderly people, but she is not just a *spectator ab extra*. She is also a participant, but yet a detached participant. Mary's position of being neither fully of, nor fully out of, the action of the book gives Mrs Gaskell certain advantages. It allows her through Mary Smith to convey the attitude both of sympathetic understanding and of light and tender irony. The use of the first-person narrative helps to moderate some of the strangenesses of the novel and to objectify some of the reader's views about it. The whimsical, for example, is very much itself, highly eccentric, but, because Mary mediates it to us, we are never in danger of doubting its reality. This comes out particularly clearly in her questions in the first chapter, and especially in 'Do you ever see cows dressed in grey flannel in London?' (p. 6).

Time and again the position and behaviour of Miss Matty is emphasized by a dramatic contrast with that of Mary. There is, for instance, the visit to Miss Matty's suitor of long years ago, with all her daintiness and flutter brought out in a scene of tremendous comedy (p. 40)—Holbrook's peas 'going wholesale into his capacious mouth, shovelled up by his large, round-ended knife', Mary following suit, and Miss Matty, 'pick[ing] up her peas, one by one, on the point' of her two-pronged fork! Much more sombre is the scene of the two ladies sitting at breakfast with their letters, Mary's from her father retailing the stories of the Town and County Bank's imminent failure and Miss Matty's a notice of a meeting of the bank's shareholders, about which she brightly and with characteristic good-heartedness remarks: 'I am sure, it is very attentive of them to remember me' (p. 144). She goes on chatting cheerfully about a meeting to which Miss Deborah had been invited years before, whilst Mary—and the reader—beset by grim foreboding, bestow the pity upon Miss Matty that she does not know she needs.

The detachment of Mary Smith allows for the play of Mrs Gaskell's tender irony upon the foibles of her characters, whilst the inclusion of her observer as an actor ensures that the irony is also partially gentle self-derision. Thus the characters of the book are not alienated from the reader's sympathy. At the end of the visit to Lady Glenmire, for instance—'In our pattens we picked our way home with extra care that night, so refined and delicate were our perceptions after drinking tea with "my lady"' (p. 96). Another example, but this time at a greater distance from the characters—a sort of semi-identification merely or at best a retrospective identification is provided by the first appearance of the famous phrase 'Elegant economy!' 'How naturally one falls back into the phraseology of Cranford! There, economy was always "elegant", and money-spending always "vulgar and ostentatious"; a sort of sour-grapeism which made us very peaceful and satisfied' (p. 4).

It is in the opening pages of the book that its characteristic spirit is established. The very first sentence is an ironic exaggeration: 'Cranford is in the possession of the Amazons'; but these Amazons are occupied in keeping trim gardens, frightening away little boys, inquiring curiously into everybody else's business and tending the poor. The idea of eccentric triviality is thus quickly stamped upon the book. With it there comes also the importance of etiquette and a proper concealment of poverty beneath the cloak of gentility. With the atmosphere thus established, we move into the story, Captain Brown's experience in Cranford. It is centred upon three incidents—the affair of Betsy Barker's Alderney cow, the clash with Miss Jenkyns on the relative merits of Dr Johnson and Dickens (Mr Boz), and the deaths of Captain Brown and his elder daughter. There is, it will be noted, a skilful variation in emotional appeal in these events. The first is farcical, the second rather sharp comedy, with Miss Jenkyns the very personification of this old-fashioned world, reactionary incarnate, not content merely to prefer Johnson but attacking Dickens. But what an ineffectual Amazon! Her self-confidence, disgust and scorn have no effect on Captain Brown:

I consider it vulgar, and below the dignity of literature, to publish in numbers.

75

To this he shrewdly—and quietly—replies:

How was the *Rambler* published, ma'am? (p. 11).

Then there is death. We have already heard about that: 'Death was as true and as common as poverty'. It is; these deaths are but the first of that number, of whose importance something has already been said. With death comes a generous display of kindness to the bereaved Jessie Brown, led by the formidable Miss Jenkyns. In a wonderfully comic episode this lady shows us how, rigid though she may be in observance of the correct conventions, these latter must nevertheless give way to human values. Miss Matty, 'large with terror', arrives to report that

'there's a gentleman sitting in the drawing-room with his arm round Miss Jessie's waist'. Miss Jenkyns snubbed her down in an instant. 'The most proper place in the world for his arm to be in. Go away, Matilda, and mind your own business.' This from her sister, who had hitherto been a model of feminine decorum (p. 26).

'Dear Miss Jenkyns, how I honoured her!' (p. 15). Mrs Gaskell chose her words carefully; not 'loved' or just 'respected', but 'honoured'.

The reader's reaction to the death of this strong-minded woman is an ambivalent one. From the moment that we are able to make a comparison, our sympathy rests with Miss Matty, lovable but ineffectual. Miss Jenkyns' death represents an emancipation for Miss Matty, but it is also a setting adrift. It is this which gives an added dimension of sadness to the recollections which follow, to her refusal of Holbrook's offer of marriage largely under Miss Jenkyns' direction and to the loss of Peter, the one

member of her own generation who might have sur-
vived to sustain her. To protect herself Miss Matty now
embraces a rigid code of self-discipline. Ironically, Miss
Jenkyns' power is not reduced by her death, but increased. Miss Matty, gentle dissentient of the earlier day,
becomes the stern self-disciplinarian.

Many a domestic rule and regulation had been a subject of
plaintive whispered murmur to me during Miss Jenkyns's
life; . . . Miss Jenkyns's rules were made more stringent than
ever, because the framer was gone where there could be no
appeal (pp. 30, 32).

Mrs Gaskell continues: 'In all things else Miss Matilda
was meek and undecided to a fault.' This facet of her
character is humorously exploited in the visit to Holbrook
with Miss Matty's remark: 'I only hope it is not improper;
so many pleasant things are!' (p. 41).

From this mixed elegiac and yet mildly comic note Mrs
Gaskell skilfully moves to the next stage in the emotional
structure of the book with the immense intensification
of feeling in the story of Peter. I have already said something of the sorrow and remorse generated by Peter's
flight. In the whole incident Mrs Gaskell maintains a
beautiful balance between the reactions of the two parents. At first the father is prostrate with grief, the mother
actively searching and writing, expressing her concern
to Peter (in the letter which he never received) about his
father's suffering; then in the days that follow the father,
now more tender, but also more strong, watches his
wife's decline to her death. Then there arrives, just too
late, Peter's present for his mother, the Indian shawl, in
which she is buried. Irony could not better reinforce
pathos than in the father's comment: 'It is just such a

shawl as she wished for when she was married, and her mother did not give it her' (p. 70). This is the pathos of recollection.

There is also more immediate pathos arising directly out of the action. This is shown best by the effects on Miss Matty of the bank's collapse. Rumours of the event lead her to her single decisive act in the whole work, the impulsive quixotic generosity as a result of which she gives five sovereigns for the Town and County note which the shopman refused. Once more in this scene irony mingles with pathos. Miss Matty is about to buy her first new dress for years, the first since before her sister's death; in fact, the first she will have ever bought for herself. The decision on the dress causes her endless trouble; the decision to give away money when her whole fortune is threatened receives no consideration. Again, when Miss Matty has settled her accounts and found herself on the verge of homelessness, without any thought of that, she can reflect on the happiness of Lady Glenmire, who, 'instead of being tossed about, and wondering where she is to settle, will be certain of a home among pleasant and kind people' (p. 152). Before that Mrs Gaskell has shown Miss Matty glad that Miss Jenkyns had not come to *her* present condition, the very Miss Jenkyns who was to blame for Miss Matty's plight. And after this reference we read of Miss Matty's 'soft reverie about Mr Holbrook', reminding us of the marriage and security that Miss Jenkyns also had had her part in denying to Miss Matty. The latter's final thought is for Martha, the servant, who will have to leave. This kindness and concern for others is by now expected; what is surprising, and what makes the disaster all the more pathetic, is the bravery with which Miss Matty faces it.

Miss Matty has the nobility which all the other characters lack. They may have rank, social graces and personal qualities, which overshadow those of Miss Matty
in an assembled company, but they are essentially lesser
characters, serving amongst other purposes to emphasize
the worth of this apparently insignificant spinster. The
Honourable Mrs Jamieson, 'fat and inert', represents
aristocracy, firm in determining the limits of social
recognition. Mrs Fitz-Adam, sister of Hoggins the
surgeon, must not be visited, and so, although the other
ladies call on her, Mrs Jamieson 'used to show how
honourable she was by never seeing Mrs Fitz-Adam
when they met at Cranford parties' (pp. 77–8). This
display of *noblesse non oblige* is extended to exclude the
Cranford ladies from meeting Lady Glenmire, Mrs
Jamieson's sister-in-law. She is to be kept for better
guests, but then, finding that she cannot attract other
visitors, Mrs Jamieson performs a *volte face* and invites the
ladies. Miss Matty is not hurt by the refusal, but Miss Pole
is indignant; Miss Matty is not attracted by the invitation,
but Miss Pole accepts at once. Use of character for
contrast here is obvious. Then Lady Glenmire becomes
engaged to the despised surgeon Hoggins. Human values
again triumph over social conventions. 'We all liked
Lady Glenmire the best. She was bright, and kind, and
sociable, and agreeable; and Mrs Jamieson was dull, and
inert, and pompous, and tiresome' (p. 139). Though,
admittedly, she was in London, Mrs Jamieson is, signifi-
cantly, the only absentee from the meeting called to
consider what help can be mustered for Miss Matty in
her need.

Miss Pole is, as it were, the woman of the world in the
little group of Cranford ladies. She is the one who always

has adventures, she is always first with the news. She stumbles on Signor Brunoni in the George Assembly Rooms, she knows first about Lady Glenmire's engagement. She 'had always a great deal of courage and savoir faire' (p. 92), and so it is she who asks, 'Has your ladyship been to Court lately?' The comedy of the egregious question is heightened by the reply: ' "I never was there in my life", said Lady Glenmire, with a broad Scotch accent' (p. 92). It is Miss Pole who pours worldly-wise scorn on the story of the ghosts in Darkness Lane—and then offers the chair-men an extra shilling to take her home by another route (pp. 119, 121)!

Mrs Forrester, by contrast, is quiet and retiring. It is perhaps of some importance that she lives farthest away, and her housekeeping represents elegant economy on the veriest shoestring in a 'baby-house of a dwelling' and 'one little charity-school maiden' as her domestic staff (p. 3). In her house, however, there is hospitality and friendship; reference is made to 'extra preparation', and the conversation is lively, even if rather gruesome (the visit takes place during the great robbery panic). This contrasts with Lady Jamieson's tea-party (p. 93) which is formal and dependent on the whims of the insolent man-servant Mulliner. Mrs Gaskell goes into detail about the perfections of that occasion, the china, the plate, even the thin bread and butter—but there is cream for the dog and milk for the guests; and not until after tea, and then only under the influence of Lady Glenmire, does the occasion 'thaw down'. I have noted Mrs Jamieson's absence from the meeting to assist Miss Matty. On that same occasion Mrs Forrester waited for Mary Smith,

The poor old lady trembling all the time as if it were a great crime which she was exposing to daylight, in telling me how very, very little she had to live upon; a confession which she was brought to make from a dread lest we should think that the small contribution named in her paper bore any proportion to her love and regard for Miss Matty (p. 166).

Not even the humour of *Cranford* is free from pathos, and even the apparently inconsequential story of the cat that swallowed the lace is touched with it, for it is a story told at the grand Mrs Jamieson's by the poor Mrs Forrester, and it relates to the lace she is wearing, 'the sole relic of better days' (p. 94).

Humour and pathos are subtly intermingled in Mrs Gaskell's treatment of sex in *Cranford*. Both are present, for instance, in Miss Matty's account of her special fear of finding a man under her bed and the ridiculous means —rolling a ball from one side to the other—which she adopted to reassure herself (p. 118). Sex is an important theme in the book. There is much in the lives of the Cranford spinsters which suggests sexual unfulfilment. They display a mixture of curiosity and fear about men. Captain Brown, and perhaps in some of the implications Surgeon Hoggins, make their world look very trivial. Out of this comes humour, perhaps best of all in Miss Pole's weighty remark: 'My father was a man, and I know the sex pretty well' (p. 115). There are places in the book's treatment of this theme where pointed contrast is made between the fact that is and the fantasy that might have been, with resultant pathos. Such, for example, is Miss Matty's revelation of her frustrated motherhood-desire. Sometimes, the humour mixes wryly with the pathos, as when she takes to wearing widows' caps after the death of Holbrook (p. 48). There are contrasts also between Holbrook's and Miss Matty's uncompleted lives and the natural emotional development of the servant Martha and her lover Jem Hearn. It is easy, however, to exaggerate, and even with these latter characters it seems better to indicate their importance in terms of general human kindness rather than in those of a more specialized sexual interpretation. Miss Matty's kindness allows Martha to have her 'follower'; in due time that kindness receives its reward in their provision for her at the time of the catastrophe. To claim more than this is to risk the danger of distortion.

Sex is but one theme; others are class, money, taste, the cramping effects of a small provincial, outdated society. The question of rank and class is centred critically upon Mrs Jamieson. All the behaviour of this self-conscious aristocrat is boorish. Not only does she ignore Mrs Fitz-Adam, but in lesser details also Mrs Gaskell takes care to expose her bad manners—in her late arrival at Betsy Barker's tea-party, her supercilious comments (for example, on seed cake reminding her of scented soap) and her greater concern for her pet-dog Carlo than for her social acquaintances (p. 79). Mrs Jamieson exploits her rank, and it is therefore appropriate that her relative and social equal, Lady Glenmire, should explode her pretensions. By contrast with Mrs Jamieson, Martha and Jem Hearn show that humanity matters more than class. They show, too, that it matters more than money. Money does matter, even though the Cranford ladies try to ignore this fact. This is one important point in the chapter on Miss Matty's financial ruin. By changing the bad note she both shows that money does matter and yet ignores the fact that it does. Humanity matters more than money. Yet we are never allowed to ignore elegant economy. Financially life is a struggle, but a small income may yet be a happy sufficiency. Miss Matty's candle, reluctantly lighted and early extinguished, is a recurring image to remind us. Even her ultimate happiness is secured on a competency rather than a fortune. 'I don't believe Mr Peter came home from India as rich as a nabob; he even considered himself poor, . . . he had enough to live on "very genteelly" at Cranford; he and Miss Matty together' (p. 184).

'Genteel' reminds us of standards at Cranford, of matters of taste and etiquette. Everything must be done in the proper way. Appearances must be kept up. Here also Mrs Jamieson's vulgarity is exposed, and never more tellingly than through the insolence of the servant Mulliner who always calls at the front door instead of at the servants' entrance. Mrs Gaskell, however, is for the most part more gentle in her satire on etiquette, as, for instance, in Miss Matty's visit to see the new fashions:

It is not etiquette to go till after twelve; but then, you see, all Cranford will be there. . . . So I thought we would just slip down this morning, soon after breakfast—for I do want half-a-pound of tea (p. 145).

That such things should be thought so important is one mark of the extreme provincialism of Cranford society. This is surely the reason why little incidents in little lives are magnified so much. This, as well as sexual reactions, helps to explain the excitements of the conjuring show and the robbery panic. This helps to make the tea-parties so important. 'Parties in Cranford were solemn festivities, making the ladies feel gravely elated' (p. 8; cf. p. 82). They knew each other's business intimately. 'It was impossible to live a month at Cranford and not know the daily habits of each resident' (p. 12). Where the actual was intrinsically so unimportant it was necessary to make the most of it, and where it failed completely we need not be surprised if fantasy prolifically supplied the deficiency.

Within such a confined and close-built society it is not strange to find rigid conventions of behaviour, and the stress on vulgarity is notable throughout the book. 'Vulgar' was 'a tremendous word in Cranford' (p. 4). It was vulgar, for instance, to be 'ostentatious' or to laugh in a public place (p. 104). The final comment on vulgarity comes on Mrs Jamieson's approval of Peter Jenkyns's sitting cross-legged on the floor. 'I remembered how we had all followed that lady's lead in condemning Mr Hoggins for vulgarity because he simply crossed his legs as he sat still on his chair' (p. 186). Miss Matty had already made her comment about that:

Mr Hoggins is really a very personable man; and as for his manners, why, if they are not very polished, I have known people with very good hearts, and very clever minds too, who were not what some people reckoned refined, but who were both true and tender (p. 152).

Hoggins is the surgeon, the bringer of healing. He restores Signor Brunoni. His is the true magic, but Brunoni also is shown as a force making for life. His story and that of his wife is a history of courage, struggle, tenderness and affection. They, together with other characters from outside such as Lady Glenmire and Peter Jenkyns, are used to demonstrate some of the insufficiencies of Cranford society, to show, above all, that its fear of vulgarity is monstrously exaggerated.

The ultimate impression, however, is not and cannot be a critical one, for the best characters in Cranford show in times of crisis that kindness, the quality that makes for more abundant life, will always triumph over the fear of vulgarity, the merely social inhibition. 'I have known people with very good hearts . . . who were both true and tender.' And none more so than Miss Matty herself. It is right that in concluding our consideration of *Cranford* we should recognize so precisely where the book's greatness resides. Its appeal derives at one level from its comedy based on the inconsequential, the eccentric and the minimally significant. Basically, however, it is concerned with important human attitudes, with truth and tenderness. Mrs Gaskell's triumph lies in the skill with which she has blended the superficial comedy with the fundamental moral seriousness.

CHAPTER V

'RUTH'

FEW books can have been more eagerly awaited than *Ruth*. When it appeared in January 1853, that is, before *Cranford* was published in book form, it was announced as 'By the Author of *Mary Barton*'. The success of this latter novel and the popularity of the instalments of *Cranford* augured well for the new work. *Ruth* was probably the most extensively reviewed of all Mrs Gaskell's writings. In general, it was received favourably. The verdicts of *The Westminster Review*, 'a beautiful novel, satisfies the highest moral sense'[1] and *The North British*, 'a good, righteous, true book'[2] are typical. Many literary and public figures also welcomed its appearance. The reception, however, was far from unanimous. Some periodicals were forthright in their criticism. *The Literary Gazette*, to mention but one, found the book 'insufferably dull'.[3] The objections of this review were literary, in contrast with most of the reactions, both public and private, both favourable and otherwise, which were moral. Mrs Gaskell knew something of the violent personal reactions which *Ruth* aroused. She told her friend Eliza Fox of men who had either burnt the book or forbidden their wives to read it (150). She knew something also of the attitude which lay behind such interdiction, for she wrote to her sister-in-law Nancy Robson: 'Of course it is a prohibited book in *this*, as in many other households.

[1] April 1853, vol. 59, p. 484.
[2] May, 1853, p. 167.   [3] 22 Jan. 1853, p. 79.

Not a book for young people, unless read with someone older.' She went on, however: 'I have spoken out of my mind in the best way I can, and I have no doubt that what was meant so earnestly *must* do some good' (148). Clearly her own intention was a moral one. *Ruth* was meant to be didactic, a *roman à thèse*.

The novel aroused controversy both because of the subject itself and because of Mrs Gaskell's treatment of one aspect of the tale, namely, Benson's lie. *Ruth* is a fable of seduction and illegitimacy and of society's attitude towards the unmarried mother. Mrs Gaskell had already touched on a similar topic in the story of Esther in *Mary Barton* and more fully in 'Lizzie Leigh'. In both these instances, however, there was no significant rescue and restoration to society. Esther followed the conventional path into prostitution and death. Even in 'Lizzie Leigh' where the seduced girl is found by her mother, her subsequent life is clothed in the obscurity of retirement and mourning for the child of her sin, and all of this is conveyed in the last paragraphs of what is in any case a short tale. In fact, 'Lizzie Leigh' is really about the mother rather than the daughter. *Ruth* is a full-length novel with the heroine kept steadily before us. It is a simple tale of an innocent, friendless girl, seduced by a superficially attractive young squire, Bellingham, and then deserted by him. In her forlorn and pregnant condition she is rescued by a Dissenting minister, Benson, and his sister, and in the town where he serves she is passed off by them as a young widow-relative. Years afterwards her identity and history are discovered, and she is disgraced. In particular, one member of Benson's congregation, the Pharisaic Bradshaw, inveighs against her after having employed her as governess and seen her nobility of character. At the end Ruth redeems herself in the eyes of all by her selfless care of the sick during a typhus epidemic, the final victim of which she herself becomes after nursing her former lover Bellingham (now Donne and the local member of parliament) back to health.

Mrs Gaskell is seeking to show that Ruth's downfall was a misfortune rather than a crime. To this end she insists on the innocence of Ruth and on her self-dedication in redemption of her error. Seeing Ruth's plight as she does, Mrs Gaskell opposes enlightenment against convention in the respective attitudes of the Bensons and Bradshaw. Because the story is so simple, some of the characters, Bellingham in particular, seem notably incomplete, and others clearly exist for the moral's sake. It is the plot, however, which the dominating moral intention affects most of all. There is too much contrivance, coincidence and unnecessary suffering. It might be claimed that illness represents the moral unhealthiness of the society described, but this would be difficult to substantiate. The illness too often is accident that happens to fit the needs of the plot. Bellingham falls ill and is taken away, leaving Ruth helpless. Ruth then falls ill, increasing our sympathy for her plight and our admiration for her saviours, the Bensons. Later in the book there is the illness of Leonard, arousing unnecessary fears; and at the end the illness first of Donne and then of Ruth. The sickness of Donne illustrates also the element of coincidence in the book, but there are more obvious examples than that. Perhaps we can accept the misfortune of Ruth's meeting her employer Mrs Mason and of the latter's seeing her with a man but not recognizing him, which results in Ruth's dismissal from her work. The presence of Mrs Mason's sister in Eccleston years later is less easy to accept, especially as we have never heard of this sister before. Most difficult of all, however, is the reappearance of Bellingham, and moreover with a changed name. Then he has to fall ill at the end. Here one feels the awkwardness of contrivance. His illness is the obvious opportunity for the supreme act of Ruth's redemption, her giving herself, as she thinks under obligation, to the one least deserving of her aid.

The feeling of contrivance is much too strong in both small things and great. Events as important as the election and Richard Bradshaw's forgery seems to fail of their full impact because of this sense of prior disposition. As a result the movement of the novel suffers, the pace is far too sluggish, the coherence far too slight. The general narrative inadequacy is revealed most obviously in the contrast which it makes with the effectiveness of the single incident of the lie. The deceptive ease with which the lie is suggested and accepted as a way of passing off Ruth as a respectable young woman, the good intentions underlying the decision, the sombre possibilities which strike the reader immediately and long before they occur to the characters, all these give a weight and force to this episode which is missing elsewhere in the book. Yet this incident has not lacked its critics, both of its necessity and its moral appropriateness. Contemporaries such as the reviewers in *The Guardian* and *The Athenaeum* were doubtful whether Benson would have told the lie, and in a later day A. W. Ward was obviously uncomfortable with what he found to be a difficult problem.[1] Mrs Gaskell exploits the narrative and moral possibilities of the lie elsewhere. Philip Hepburn in *Sylvia's Lovers* profits by deception and falls when the truth is discovered.

[1] Knutsford edition, pp. xix–xx.

Margaret Hale in *North and South* protects her brother by a lie, but at the immediate and prolonged cost of knowing that Thornton is aware of her deceit. In *Ruth* the narrative usage of the lie is in the simplest of its possible variations. The aim behind the falsehood is completely altruistic, even laudable, and there appear to be no misgivings until the truth is revealed and the disaster occurs. Mrs Gaskell seems almost to have anticipated the criticisms of the kind mentioned above. She makes it clear that 'for himself [Benson] was brave enough to tell the truth; for the little helpless baby, about to enter a cruel, biting world, he was tempted to evade the difficulty' (p. 121). In the sentences preceding these words she had also made it clear that this decision was 'the pivot on which the fate of years moved; and he turned it the wrong way' (p. 121). It is just another instance, albeit perhaps most critical, of Mrs Gaskell's variations on the theme that to do evil, however beneficently designed, is not likely to make good prevail.

Despite the contrivance, narratively speaking, *Ruth* is in some ways an advance upon *Mary Barton*. Interest in the story is not dissipated over so many characters. The tale concentrates upon Ruth herself, and only in the last part when Mrs Gaskell finds it necessary to bring in some measure of retribution against the over-righteous Bradshaw is there much attempt to consider the other characters. Ruth herself, however, possesses nothing like the sustained power of interesting that is found in John Barton. The imaginative energy that was able to realize his character and situation so vividly and so compellingly is absent from the later novel. In *Mary Barton* the sympathy sprang from immediate experience and living roots, in *Ruth* it seems to betray a somewhat artificial and theoretical origin. This may also help to explain the apparent sluggishness of the book's movement. It is memorable more as a novel of a few strong, even violent, episodes than as a coherent history. George Eliot may have had this among other things in mind when she wrote of Mrs Gaskell's being in this novel 'constantly misled by a love of sharp contrasts—of "dramatic" effects'.[1] We remember Ruth's betrayal because from the moment of her meeting with Bellingham her too evident simplicity and his too evident villainy make it inevitable. After this, however, it is events such as her desertion, the Bensons' lie, her meeting Bellingham again and Bradshaw's savage denunciation after her exposure that remain in the mind. These scenes are isolated amongst tracts of the uneventful. Public events do not matter; the election, for example, is always very much in the background. Personal lives pursue the even tenor of their way. Admittedly, neither Ruth nor we are allowed to forget her anxiety and the cause there is for it, but of the rest there is either not enough or hardly anything at all. The triangular relationship of Ruth, Jemima Bradshaw and her father's partner Farquhar is tantalizingly under-developed, at once fully sufficient for its subsidiary role in the tale and yet obviously having a potentiality that is never explored. There seem to be so many possibilities here for interaction, for conflict and resolution, that are so obviously missing from so much of the novel as we have it. This absence of sustained conflict may also contribute to the appearance of sluggishness. What tension there is derives mainly from Ruth's own anxiety, chiefly directed to her contemplation of the effects of her exposure on her son Leonard, and from her and the

[1] *Letters*, ed. G. S. Haight, 1954, vol. II, p. 86.

Bensons' fears of Mr Bradshaw. Mrs Gaskell seems deliberately to have put aside opportunities that the lie afforded her of portraying a prolonged moral conflict in the mind of Benson himself. On another level, that of narrative suspense, she appears to have played down the chances which the re-appearance of Bellingham as Donne gave her for revealing the past and exploiting all that that would mean to Ruth. Neglect of possibilities such as these makes one wonder whether Mrs Gaskell had learned the lesson of narrative economy too well after the extravagance of *Mary Barton*. She seems determined not to broaden the canvas nor to heighten the tension too much. She was anxious at once to concentrate attention on, and to divorce any suggestion of the sensational from, her chosen subject, Ruth herself. She told her sister-in-law, Nancy Robson, 'I could have put out much more power, but that I wanted to keep it quiet in tone, lest by the slightest exaggeration, or over-strained sentiment I might weaken the force of what I had to say' (148).

Scenic description has a quite remarkable place in the novel. Not even in the sociological novels where it can contribute so much to the impression of suffering does it play so prominent a part. The sheer extent of it in this book is another decelerating factor in the story. At times indeed it almost appears as though Mrs Gaskell is enjoying it for its own sake. One recalls the lovingly accurate detail of the little common, where Mrs Mason comes upon Ruth and Bellingham, with its golden bloom of the gorse, its clear bright pond, and the martins, water-wagtails, linnets and warblers. Mrs Gaskell is surely describing a place she knew, just as the Dissenting chapel at Eccleston is no doubt based on that of Brook Street, Knutsford. It is sufficient to place two short passages together. Here is a line or two from G. A. Payne's account of Brook Street:

From the inside, the diamond panes, with their background of ivy, stained as they are by green and brown hues, give a subdued light, which adds to the general solemnity of the building.[1]

and here is Mrs Gaskell:

The casement windows of the chapel were made of heavy-leaded, diamond-shaped panes, almost covered with ivy, producing a green gloom, not without its solemnity, within (p. 151).

For the most part, however, setting is used to reflect or contrast with the feelings of the characters. The beauty of the common, for instance, is appropriately idyllic, suiting Ruth's happiness at the time, but for the reader there is something ironic in such beauty as it contributes to such happiness, for he has already read the preceding paragraph which begins: 'Ruth went on her way, all unconscious of the dark phantoms of the future that were gathering around her' (p. 51). Here the link of scene and character is indirect, made by the author, shared with the reader, and unrecognized by the character. Elsewhere it is more explicit and the character is more aware of it. Such an instance is that in which by their differing response to rain Mrs Gaskell points the contrast in the characters of Ruth and Bellingham, between her happy, innocent spontaneous nature and his bored, irritable, complaining attitude (p. 64). This incident occurs during their stay in North Wales. This area is the scene both of Ruth's desertion and her later meeting with her lover. Its sombre

[1] *Mrs Gaskell and Knutsford*, 2nd ed., 1905, p. 46.

aspect aptly symbolizes nature's eternal indifference to human agony, whatever man (or woman) may think. Sometimes it can seem enchanted, as Mrs Gaskell shows in a passage of fine descriptive power:

The soft wind outside sank with a low, long distant moan among the windings of the hills, and lost itself there, and came no more again. Out beyond, under the calm sky, veiled with a mist rather than with a cloud, rose the high, dark outlines of the mountains, shutting in that village as if it lay in a nest. They stood, like giants, solemnly watching for the end of Earth and Time. Here and there a black round shadow reminded Ruth of some 'Cwm', or hollow, where she and her lover had rambled in sun and in gladness. She then thought the land enchanted into everlasting brightness and happiness; she fancied, then, that into a region so lovely no bale or woe could enter, but would be charmed away and disappear before the sight of the glorious guardian mountains (pp. 82–3),

but the next sentence reads: 'Now she knew the truth, that earth has no barrier which avails against agony.' The critical reunion with Donne (Bellingham) on Abermouth Sands illustrates this truth. Mrs Gaskell so describes the scene as to parallel its sombreness with the deepening suffering of Ruth. References to 'purple hills', 'white cottages' and 'the little grey church' give way to the account of the seashore, the 'great shadow made by the rocks', 'the eternal moan [the waves] have made since the world began', 'the skirl of the grey seabirds', and 'the hard echoing sands' (pp. 292–3). After the ordeal of the meeting and her rejection of Donne Ruth is left exhausted and downcast, incapable of 'contemplating anything beyond the dreary present, when the expanse of gray, wild, bleak moors, stretching wide away below a sunless sky, seemed only an outward sign of the waste world within her heart' (pp. 301–2).

The waste world within Ruth's heart is the real subject of the novel. What she has done or rather what she has suffered she can never escape. This, however, is a subject on which there can be little talk, for most of the characters know nothing about it and those who do have no wish to discuss it. Moreover, the intensity of her suffering can only be fully realized by Ruth herself. The subject must therefore be developed by means which allow Mrs Gaskell to concentrate upon Ruth alone. Her relationship to nature is one such means by which Mrs Gaskell conveys the suffering in her heroine's heart. Another, more powerful device is the reference to dream. Mrs Gaskell used it elsewhere, notably in *Sylvia's Lovers*, but it is employed most extensively in *Ruth*. It is ideally suited for the process of exploring a character's inner being. Instead of a direct account of thoughts and feelings, to be taken on the author's testimony, the description of dream gives a dramatic dimension, a sense of greater immediacy and vividness. Thus Ruth's sadness on leaving home after her mother's death is given an added poignancy by her crying in her sleep as she dreams of her mother (p. 9). This is a fairly commonplace example, of which there are a number. Together they enable us to appreciate that the word 'dream' is more than a cliché on occasions such as that on which Ruth is left deserted in Wales ('Life was a horrible dream'—p. 93) or in her reflection on the year that passed before her comfortable settlement with the Bensons ('like a bad, unholy dream'—p. 190). Dream is also used as an image to describe those situations in which Ruth is so confused as to be unable to arrange and assess her attitude, such as, for instance, at the inn where

Bellingham has asked for hospitality after Ruth's meeting with Mrs Mason:

It was a dream—a strange varying, shifting dream—with the old home of her childhood for one scene, with terror of Mrs Mason's unexpected appearance for another; and the strangest, dizziest, happiest of all, there was the consciousness of his love (p. 58).

The real dreams are more simply terrifying, and Mrs Gaskell makes them lead one after another to a crescendo of terror. First, Ruth dreams of her son Leonard growing up 'a repetition of his father' but dragged down by the girl he seduces into 'some pit of horrors into which she dared not look' (p. 162). Then there follows a dream of 'undefined terror' (p. 255), and this is succeeded by one of Leonard's being taken away by his father, in one version going happily, in another struggling to remain with his mother. Mrs Gaskell catches this fantastic variability of dream extremely well and uses it skilfully to intensify our sense of the uncertainty of Ruth's position. The dreaming reaches its frightening dramatic climax in the following passage:

She dreamed that she was once more on the lonely shore, striving to carry away Leonard from some pursuer—some human pursuer—she knew he was human and she knew who he was, although she dared not say his name even to herself, he seemed so close and present, gaining on her flying footsteps, rushing after her as with the sound of the roaring tide. Her feet seemed heavy weights fixed to the ground; they would not move. All at once just near the shore, a great black whirlwind of waves clutched her back to her pursuers; she threw Leonard on to land, which was safety; but whether he reached it or no, or was swept back like her into a mysterious

something too dreadful to be borne, she did not know, for the
terror awakened her (p. 307).

Here dream is no transposition from the actual circumstances of Ruth's life, but nightmare whose only link with
those circumstances lies perhaps in its location on the seashore. Bellingham is also surely there, but he is not named,
an added touch to the terror of it all. The exact details,
particularly at the end, are uncertain and, where we have
them, apparently illogical. How could Leonard be safe on
land? Was she not pursued thence?

The substance of these dreams reminds us of the importance of the child. Relationship to nature provides one
measure, the external, for Ruth's sufferings; the dreams
provide another, the internal. Leonard provides a third,
for he is the character for whom she feels most tenderly,
just because he will be the one, apart from herself, likely
to be most afflicted by any revelation of her past. The
child is also important as a focus of sympathy in that his
suffering will be undeserved and, as Mrs Gaskell is anxious
to show, the result of society's unenlightened attitude.
Child-characters are notoriously difficult to make convincing, and there is much in the portrayal of Leonard
himself that does not quite ring true if he is regarded
simply in realistic terms. We need to see him somewhat
differently. First, he objectifies all Ruth's joys and fears in
motherhood, and Mrs Gaskell stresses that the mother-
child relationship is here no less, in fact if anything more,
intimate than that of married mothers and their offspring;
thus far short of sufficiency falls the speedily expressed
conventional view of the child as 'this badge of her shame'
(p. 118). Secondly, through Benson Mrs Gaskell seeks to
show the necessity for distinguishing between Ruth's 'sin'

and its consequences, both for mother and child. He suggests that God may turn evil to good by making the child His messenger to lead Ruth back to Himself (p. 118) and that it is hardly likely to be His will that the child should be made miserable (p. 119). Appropriately, Benson ends this scene by seeking the 'Father's' help for Ruth and themselves through his 'Holy Son' (p. 120). The concept of God the Father is repeatedly in Ruth's mind in the later stages of the book.

So much in this novel depends on Ruth herself; and at its dramatic centre lies the relationship of Ruth and Leonard, her sense of guilt towards him, her care that he should be protected from knowledge of her past, her fears for him if that should be discovered, her determination to keep him from his father, her desperation when the truth is known. All these enrich the characterization of Ruth by suggesting a sense of the hunted quality of her life, perpetually fearful and periodically savage. This impression of violence is marked in the central scenes with Bellingham when he suggests a reconciliation, and seeks this for the sake of the child. The fearful dream for Leonard's safety is now turned into firm action. The basis of Bellingham's appeal could not have been more inept; 'that very circumstance . . . changed her from the woman into the mother—the stern guardian of her child' (p. 270). This is so exactly right that one finds it difficult to know how a contemporary reviewer could even suggest that Ruth ought to have married Bellingham to legitimize Leonard, doubting whether the child would really be corrupted and whether Bellingham is as bad as Ruth thinks.[1] There appears to be no ground for the reviewer's doubts, and he seems altogether to have missed Mrs

[1] *North British Review*, May 1853, p. 162.

Gaskell's point that there are things far more important than legitimacy.

Because society was wrong in placing so high a value on legitimacy, both Ruth and Leonard have to suffer. This is why the exposure scene is so important, and this almost forms the *raison d'être* for Bradshaw. This character is the embodiment of conventional standards, held at their most pharisaically unbending; 'every moral error or delinquency came under his unsparing comment' (p. 209). The Bensons' 'Think of Mr Bradshaw!' (p. 124) becomes a kind of ominous refrain in the reader's mind. He is heard of so often before he appears. He is almost a caricature—'stern, powerful and authoritative' (p. 152), a churchgoer devoid of the gracious Christian virtues, an upright man who yet will place expediency against principle when it suits him, as in the election incident. Altogether he represents Mrs Gaskell's nearest approach to a character like Gradgrind in *Hard Times*. He has many principles but no feelings.

Bradshaw as a churchgoer but hardly a Christian reminds us that Mrs Gaskell is seeing Ruth's story in explicitly religious terms as a conflict of man's values against God's. This is why prayer is an important element of Ruth's experience. Mrs Gaskell emphasizes that this is no narrow petition for self-protection, but a recognition of God's righteousness and a penitent plea for His power to enable her to bear punishment with 'a meek and docile heart, "for His mercy endureth for ever"' (p. 283). One paragraph ends with these words; the next tellingly begins: 'Mr Bradshaw had felt himself rather wanting in proper attention to his guest [Bellingham].' Without any comment from Mrs Gaskell, the contrast in values is strikingly borne in upon us—the father irresponsible but socially acceptable, the mother far more admirable but lowly, unprotected and fearful, and Bradshaw now so amiably treating the one, soon so brutally to castigate the other.

His part in Ruth's exposure follows quite close upon this contrast. Because it involves the mother-child relationship, what I have called the dramatic centre of the book, at its most crucial point, the exposure scene forms the climax of the novel. It falls into four sections—Bradshaw's entry, 'purple with suppressed agitation', and denunciation of Ruth; her explanation of the whole matter to Leonard; Bradshaw's tirade against Benson; and finally, the latter's interview with Ruth. Bradshaw's ferocity is both in character and in accord with the requirements of the situation. His series of outraged rhetorical questions (p. 336), which in another might look artificial, is appropriate to his nature, and the torrent of his denunciation is in effective contrast to Ruth's brief, subdued replies of a few monosyllables. What might otherwise have become melodramatic is saved because what Bradshaw does arises from what he is, and what he does comes just at the right moment in the narrative. Some have criticized what follows. For them Leonard's intensity of grief is unacceptable. Like Bradshaw, Leonard is not a fully realistic character, but he is by no means so crudely subservient to extra-narrative purposes as, say, the children in *Jude the Obscure*. Like them he illustrates the dealings of a harsh world upon the helpless, but he does more than this. As he has before objectified Ruth's fears, so now he redoubles her sufferings. She suffers both for herself and, even more, for him. He suffers in himself also, and the subsequent prolonged psychological malaise which afflicts him (p. 362) is accurately perceived and described. There is, however, no trace of sentimentalizing. Mrs Gaskell knew children too well for that. Her knowledge and understanding is again evident in her making him hurl childish defiance at those who have injured his mother (p. 341). Finally, it is there once more as she gives Leonard, weeping at Ruth's grave, the simple words addressed to Bradshaw: 'My mother is dead, sir' (p. 454) —so laconic, so obvious and yet so full of feeling. Mrs Gaskell was careful to limit the extent of Leonard's speeches. This is why, apart from his ready realization of the implications of his mother's unmarried state, I find it hard to understand *The Westminster Review's* complaint that his language is 'sheerly impossible'.[1] There is hardly enough of it for such a judgment. Its linking this complaint to Leonard's intensity of grief seems to miss a powerful element in the scene as a whole. Though he may not be fully realistic, Leonard functions successfully as a character both in isolation and in relationship with others. This is more than can be said for some of the other characters in this novel.

The critical episode with which we are dealing finds its conclusion in Benson's interview with Ruth. I have earlier referred to the hunted quality in Ruth's attitude. During Bradshaw's attack Mrs Gaskell makes this explicit in such references as that in which she compares the appearance of Ruth's eyes with 'such a look of terror on a poor dumb animal's countenance' (p. 336) and that in which she likens her defending Leonard to 'a wild creature at bay, past fear now' (p. 337). When Benson finds her, she, like Esther in *Mary Barton* (and we recall that she is described as a 'wounded deer' seeking its birthplace there to die), is preparing to return to the home of her youth. Benson,

[1] April 1853.

however, leads her in overt Christian terms to recognize the need to stay; 'He, having purified you, even as by fire, will make a straight path for your feet' (p. 353).

What follows in the last stages of the book is the process of that purification as Mrs Gaskell saw it. Ruth is a good character, in fact too good, and the incident of the fever epidemic gives her a more than sufficient opportunity to redeem herself. Yet still she has to die. The description of Ruth's last days is powerfully conveyed. Mrs Gaskell makes excellent use of such emotive detail as the reference to her continual singing, something which Ruth had never been heard to do since her mother's death (p. 444). Benson takes an appropriate text for her funeral-sermon: 'These are they which came out of great tribulation and have washed their robes and made them white in the blood of the Lamb' (p. 453). Yet we must ask whether Ruth's death was really necessary? Charlotte Brontë, and others since, doubted it. Her death places conventional judgment under severest conviction (Bradshaw seeks to make amends too late), and yet it comes also to be a concession to the conventional point of view. The price of sin has to be paid in death, at the cost of narrative credibility. Suffering seems to have been pressed too far. Ruth has more to regret than to repent, but she repents and redeems herself. No more should have been required.

Ruth as a story possesses a beginning, a middle and an end, but its middle seems far more convincing than either its end or its beginning. This latter is the least satisfactory part of the book and it involves most fully the book's least satisfactory character, Bellingham. Ruth is described as 'innocent and snow-pure' (p. 43). She is too innocent, too pure, too simple altogether at the beginning. It does not surprise us, but it does not convince us either in any important literary sense, that she falls so readily before the advances of Bellingham. Mrs Gaskell devotes a few sentences to explaining why he should be what he is, the selfish product of an indulged childhood, and in his treatment of Ruth she conveys some sense of the excessive affected concern of the practised seducer, but that is all. In his later appearances we must accept that the earlier developing vices have become settled parts of his character, and his offer of money for Leonard's education after Ruth's death is at one with what we know of him. His inadequacy as a character derives from his narrowness. He is more than just a personification of Lechery, but not much more. It may not be altogether fair, but it is certainly indicative of how much Mrs Gaskell might have made the relationship of Ruth and Bellingham, to mention beside it that of Hetty Sorrel and Arthur Donnithorne. These two are broader characters because they are deeper; they are more fully realized in the present of the novel because their past has been more fully imagined. They have feelings and motives that Mrs Gaskell never seems to envisage for Bellingham and Ruth.

Apart from Ruth's prolonged intense anxiety and suffering Mrs Gaskell understands feeling best of all in a quite minor character, Jemima Bradshaw. Jemima is rare in this novel for her complexity of response. By contrast with her submissive mother and her worthless brother, she stands up to her domineering father, especially in her noble defence of Ruth when he denounces her. This defence is all the more noble, coming as it does after months of jealousy of Ruth because the latter seems to have grown in the favour of Farquhar, Jemima's erstwhile lover. The estrangement between herself and Farquhar has resulted from what she believes to be his willingness to forward the match only from motives of calculation and at her father's encouragement (p. 222). A further cause for admiration of her defence of Ruth lies in the fact that she has had to work her way through the obstructing harshness of her father's code which she has, despite her opposition to him, nevertheless imbibed. The relationship of two girls side by side is better done by Mrs Gaskell only at the end of her career in *Wives and Daughters*. Here in *Ruth* it is not very much developed, another instance perhaps of Mrs Gaskell's denying herself a narrative opportunity. Even so, we may be grateful for the little portrait of Jemima. It is matched at its own level only by the quite different 'comic' character of Sally, the Bensons' servant, another in the long line of its author's memorable domestics.

There is one other important character still to be considered. As Bradshaw represents the severity of the world's judgment, so Benson shows forth the charity of God's judgment. He rescues Ruth, shields her and suffers with her. He shows Christ-like pity in his simple goodness. In doing so he deceives others. The lie is 'the pivot on which the fate of years moved'. Unfortunately, the lie does not seem to create sufficient disturbance in the heart of Benson to keep us ever in mind of this fact. Of course, there is an irony that often arises from his failure to remember the lie. Only very shortly after the plan has been adopted and whilst they are yet discussing it, Benson's reply to his sister's 'Think of Mr Bradshaw!' is 'We must think of a higher than Mr Bradshaw' (p. 124). A little later in the same scene we read: 'Let us try simply to do right actions without thinking of the feelings they are to call out in others. We know that no holy or self-denying effort can fall to the ground vain and useless' (p. 127). Benson, we are assured, 'strove to leave his life in the hands of God, and to forget himself' (p. 141). Despite this assurance, the reader feels that there must have been some aftermath of the lie in Benson's life, but this is never suggested. Indeed, the very assurance of Benson's putting his life so fully in the hands of God makes us feel how great must have been the effect of deceit on such a character. At the time of the election he bluntly tells the agent Hickson: 'We are not to do evil that good may come' (p. 253). Expediency cannot be justified against principle (Bradshaw knew this when he engaged in electoral manœuvre), but that was exactly what Benson had tried to do with Ruth and it is precisely the defence he is to use for his conduct when he confronts Bradshaw—'For a good end' (p. 345). It is in this scene at the crisis of the action that the force of the complaint I am making is most evident. Benson speaks of the 'degradation I have suffered for years, at being a party to a deceit' (p. 345) and of the upbraiding of his own conscience, but we have not been made to feel this. Nevertheless, it is in this scene that he, like Ruth, expresses his nobility through suffering, taking his stand 'with Christ against the world' (p. 347). He recognizes his error: 'God's omnipotence did not need our sin' (p. 358). He plays a full part in these passages that form the zenith of the book's achievement. In their respective errors and in their realization of those errors Benson and Ruth show themselves better than all the upright and self-righteous Bradshaws of this world. By this we recognize that, though Mrs Gaskell seems to have denied herself yet again in not developing Benson's remorse of conscience, she has nevertheless displayed him unmistakably in his principal function of embodying the moral enlightenment, the nobler ethic, which it was her chief purpose to inculcate by this novel.

Ruth is, inescapably, a deliberately moral book. On this ground it appealed so much to its contemporaries. *Bentley's* review spoke of 'the high moral purpose of the story which we must admire. It is better than any sermon'.[1] It is better than any sermon, precisely because it is not a sermon. It proceeds by demonstration rather than exhortation, by didactic exemplification rather than by preaching. G. H. Lewes was right to describe it as 'a moral problem worked out in fiction' with its lesson 'carried straight to the soul by the simple vehicle of the story'.[2] It is not a sermon, but a fable, and a fable, moreover, involving not only moral attitudes but also human feelings. 'Poor Ruth!' (p. 448)—that is the book's subject. Mrs Gaskell wanted to show (not just to declare) the effects of a hard world's treatment of an innocent, ill-used girl, of the harshness and wrongness of that world's judgment and the extent of that wrongness when measured against the right standard of Christ-like pity. In all this she succeeded didactically. Unfortunately, the moral intention has in some ways stunted the imaginative possibilities. The plot becomes too obvious and the characters too simplified. At the same time, we must recognize that the moral intention also stimulated the imaginative possibilities in the most memorable scenes of the book. How vividly the imagination was stimulated may be measured by a comparison, say, with a work such as Mrs Trollope's *Jessie Phillips*, which is competent but no more. The sympathy that resides in *Ruth* is absent from that book. Mrs Trollope attempts to infuse sympathy, but it never seems very much a part of the book itself. In *Ruth* there is no need for

[1] Vol. XXXIII, 3 Feb. 1853.   [2] *The Leader*, vol. IV, 23 Jan. 1853.

infusion; the sympathy belongs to the situation and the characters, it is generated by the action itself. Mrs Gaskell has concentrated attention on her central character at the expense of developing other figures and possible relationships more fully. She has portrayed her heroine after the seduction with considerable power. Ruth needed, however, to be more convincing, more obviously human, before that event. The failure in this regard lessens the subsequent achievement. Nevertheless, Mrs Gaskell has largely succeeded with this her main character, and by that, rather than by its weaknesses in both plot and character, the success of the book as a whole must be measured. She has written a fable, whose moral emerges unmistakably from the history of its central character.

CHAPTER VI

'NORTH AND SOUTH'

WILLIAM Rathbone Greg, in his severe criticism of *Mary Barton*, had presumed that the lot of the Dorsetshire labourer was probably as bad as, if not worse than, that of the Lancashire mill-hand. In her second novel to deal with industrial conditions Mrs Gaskell took North and South, put them alongside each other, and contrasted them constantly; but she can hardly be said to have shown the full realities of the South. She did, however, avoid the charge of bias in favour of the workers and against the employers, which had been levelled against her previous novel. Indeed, she may well have remembered Greg's strictures specifically, for there is much in *North and South* to suggest that she was trying to redress the balance of the scales which some had felt she had so strongly weighted in one direction in *Mary Barton*. We know that Greg was pleased with the new novel. He wrote to her:

[I] sat up till 1 o'clock, and came to an end, and was sorry when I had done it. I find no fault in it, which is a great deal for a critic to say. . . . I think you have quite taken the right tone, and the spirit and execution of the whole is excellent.[1]

We may note, in passing, that by 1855 he considered *Mary Barton* 'as thorough a work of genius'.[2]

Nevertheless, Greg preferred *North and South* to both *Mary Barton* and *Ruth*, because of 'the spirit and execution of the whole'. He was surely right in this judgment. The

[1] Quoted in Knutsford edition, p. xix.   [2] Ibid.

novel marks a great leap forward in this respect. The management of plot and character, the exposition of theme, the variation in direction of interest, all demonstrate a grasp of the novelist's technique hitherto unsuspected. This is the more remarkable when one considers the conditions under which the book was written. It was the first time that Mrs Gaskell had published a novel in regular serial form. *North and South* appeared in *Household Words* on 2 September 1854 and continued till 27 January 1855. Mrs Gaskell's method and manner were hardly suited to this form of publication. The serial required ability to write in highly coloured episodic blocks, needing far too many climaxes and being altogether too disjointed to suit her ways. She could not accommodate herself, either, to the pace of the serial. Dickens felt that her dialogue was often too long drawn out; and the end of the story she sent to him in a mood of utter weariness. She prefaced the first edition of the book in volume form with a statement which included the words: 'The author found it impossible to develop the story in the manner originally intended, and, more especially, was compelled to hurry on events with an improbable rapidity toward the close' (p. xxix). She therefore altered the latter part of the work by adding the two chapters (45 and 46) dealing with the return of Margaret to Helstone with Mr Bell and by lengthening the original last chapter into four chapters. The addition of the Helstone chapters is interesting, because this is related to another of Mrs Gaskell's differences with Dickens, that about a title. She wished to call the work *Margaret Hale*, and in her letters she referred to it as 'Margaret'. Eventually, however, *North and South* was agreed upon. The difference between title and treatment may not be so great as in *Mary Barton* where John

Barton remains most important because he was meant to be so in the terms on which the novel was originally conceived, but even in *North and South* the subject is Margaret and the process of her enlightenment, what North and South mean to her, rather than any contrast there may be between the conditions in the two areas. This was even more the case in the serial form of the novel where the later Helstone chapters did not appear.

It is part of the strength of *North and South*, not least in its portrayal of the industrial scene in Milton, that Mrs Gaskell has chosen to project events through a character who is at once protagonist and observer. This is a variation of the technique already employed through Mary Smith in *Cranford*. Margaret, and to a lesser degree her father also, are at once involved and detached. As observer she both sees more and understands less than anybody had done in *Mary Barton*. As she learns to understand, she does so with such freshness of mind that she must eventually come to teach her teachers. This is her role within the industrial theme of the novel. She brings both the employer Thornton and the workman Higgins to see as they have never seen before and thereby to understand each other better than they could ever have done before. North and South not only are different, but the inhabitants of the one are able each to see the other differently, and to see moreover not only the place but the people differently. To this extent the contrast that the title implies is fundamental, and Mrs Gaskell employs that contrast with consummate skill throughout the novel.

It is, however, as protagonist that Margaret Hale is most important, and an estimate of this role necessitates, first, a look at Mrs Gaskell's management of the story. For a serialized novel *North and South* is markedly more coherent than many others of its kind, no doubt because Mrs Gaskell had conceived most and written a good portion of it before publication began. She was not at the mercy of her reader's whims, as apparently Dickens was at times. She did, however, consult her confidante, Catherine Winkworth. A letter of 15 October 1854 written from the Nightingales' house at Lea Hurst near Matlock, shows how far she had gone and puts a suggestion for ending the novel which was not, in the event, developed:

What do you think of a fire burning down Mr Thornton's mills *and house* as a *help* to failure? Then Margaret would rebuild them larger & better & need not go & live there when she's married. Tell me what you think. MH has just told the lie, & is gathering herself up after her dead faint; very meek & stunned & humble (211).

We do not know why she did not adopt the idea mentioned here. It may have been a result of Dickens' hurrying her to a close; but surely it was better not to take us beyond the point where the book now ends, and Mrs Gaskell must have realized this herself, for she was perfectly free to have included a fire in the extended ending of the novel in book-form. Margaret is able to re-establish Thornton in business, and this is in a manner symbolic of the return to Manchester. The book ends in the fashionable London house where it began, but Margaret does not belong to that world, indeed belongs to it even less at the end than it was obvious that she did at the beginning. The identity of scene at beginning and end is one means by which Mrs Gaskell shows how far Margaret has moved in the course of the novel. By contrast with *Mary Barton* where Manchester has nothing to offer at the end, where it is a place to leave, in *North and South* it is a place to return to, a place where Thornton will re-establish himself in both private and public life with Margaret at his side.

There was another good reason for not having a fire. Mrs Gaskell had used this device already in *Mary Barton*. Here, again, we may note a contrast with the earlier novel. *North and South* depends far less on sensational incident than its predecessor. There are parallels with that book; both novels have strikes, both show suffering and death among the workmen, but there is less gratuitous violence in *North and South*. Admittedly, the heroine herself is injured in a spectacular strike scene, but Mrs Gaskell seems deliberately to play down the physical suffering. The wound is a slight one. The incident has more important purposes—to develop the relationship between Thornton and Margaret, to cause Mrs Thornton to believe even more vehemently than before that Margaret is in love with her son and is trying to catch him as a husband, to bring Margaret bitterly to blame herself for creating such a scene and leading Mrs Thornton to such conclusions, and to leave Thornton still seriously doubting his chances of persuading Margaret to respond favourably to his affection. In yet another direction Mrs Gaskell seems to play down the possibilities of the sensational. There had been crime and pursuit in *Mary Barton*. They are here, too, in the story of Margaret's brother Frederick, the naval lieutenant who has refused to acquiesce in the tyranny of a repressive captain and, in consequence, has found himself numbered among his ship's mutineers and been forced to live abroad to escape trial in England. In the course of the novel he returns home to see his dying mother and is spotted by an old enemy who tries to arrest him. Frederick escapes by tripping his assailant. Mrs

Gaskell makes little of all this as an exciting incident in itself. The critical encounter is quickly dealt with, and Frederick is gone. The whole affair is strictly subsidiary to the history of Margaret, portraying her anxiety and in the subsequent police enquiries leading to her lie, a lie which Thornton knows she has told and which leads him to conclude that she is shielding a lover, a rival for her love more successful than himself. It is the burden of this knowledge, her awareness that Thornton knows she has told a lie, that Margaret has to carry through the latter part of the novel.

Unlike *Mary Barton*, *North and South* avoids the sensational and the melodramatic. It is also much less patchy, much less dependent on sudden accelerations of excitement. Its pace is more even and purposeful; the whole work is much more unified; the transitions are managed more skilfully and more naturally. The very opening is itself indicative of a greater confidence proceeding from a larger skill and a broader experience. At first, it looks as if it might almost belong to the 'Silver Fork' school of novelists who concentrated on high-society life. The setting is right, a drawing-room in Harley Street and talk 'about wedding dresses and wedding ceremonies; and Captain Lennox, and what he had told Edith about her future life at Corfu, where his regiment was stationed' (p. 1). Even the style assists the impression with such a sentence, for example, as over-written as the following:

If Titania had ever been dressed in white muslin and blue ribbons, and had fallen asleep on a crimson damask sofa in a back drawing-room, Edith might have been taken for her (p. 1).

Of course, the over-writing is for ironic purposes, and

'the back drawing-room' makes that clear. The artificial-ity of Harley Street is a strange way to introduce us to the real world of doing and suffering in Helstone and later in Milton, but Mrs Gaskell constantly refers us back to Harley Street, and with considerable effect, as Margaret makes her progress through the novel.

After Edith's marriage Margaret is to return home to Helstone and to rural happiness. It is 'like a village in a poem—in one of Tennyson's poems . . . There is the church and a few houses near it on the green—cottages, rather—with roses growing all over them.' All very idyl-lic, as Henry Lennox suggests in his reply to Margaret's description: 'And flowering all the year round, especially at Christmas—make your picture complete' (p. 9). Mar-garet is annoyed and insists that her picture is the truth and not a fantasy. Hardly has she returned home when her father announces that they must leave Helstone. He can no longer subscribe to the Thirty Nine Articles as an ordained minister in the Church of England. What the exact nature of his doubts is we never know, but the change that has to follow upon these doubts makes Hel-stone seem more idyllic than Margaret could ever have painted it. Mrs Hale, as well as Margaret, connects the three worlds of London society, rural Helstone and manu-facturing Milton. She is less adaptable than Margaret, more unquestionably adherent to the aristocratic values of Harley Street, and for her, therefore, the move to Milton is repulsive, an incomprehensible and apparently unneces-sary disaster.

Once the action is established in Milton, the book pro-vides three areas of interest—first, the association of both father and daughter, Mr Hale and Margaret, with the manufacturer John Thornton; secondly, Margaret's acquaintance with Bessy Higgins and her millhand father Nicholas Higgins; and thirdly, Mrs Hale's illness and her longing to see her son Frederick once again. Industrial attitudes and relationships must obviously be important in a setting such as Mrs Gaskell had chosen, and much of the dialogue deals with these subjects. The plot also moves towards strike, but at the same time Mrs Gaskell traces very delicately the birth and growth of Thornton's passion for Margaret. As in *Mary Barton*, Mrs Gaskell here also brings the public and the personal themes together. The strike is the climax of the one, and by Margaret's intervention to protect Thornton we come to a crisis of the other with his proposal and her rejection of his offer. The difference as compared with the earlier novel lies in Mrs Gaskell's by now much greater technical finesse. Attention is then moved away from both these themes by the arrival of Frederick to see his dying mother. Our interest in him has been stimulated and sustained by a succession of brief references. The episode of his visit is shot through with an intense pity. He comes on a sad errand, at great personal risk under the shadow of an unjust accusation, and he comes from a world away both in place and time. Helstone is recalled once again, recalled with a poignancy unmatched elsewhere in the novel, as Margaret thinks back over eight years to 'the tall stripling in his middy's uniform'. The lost loved one was a character with tremendous appeal for Mrs Gaskell. We think of Peter Jenkyns in *Cranford*, and there is also the lost lover, Charlie Kinraid, in *Sylvia's Lovers*. It is not extravagant to suggest that Mrs Gaskell's thoughts about her own lost brother, John Stevenson, may well have led to her frequent recurrence to this topic. One may also wonder whether recollections of her own father's scrupulous resignation from the Unitarian ministry and his subsequent activity may have suggested Hale's career in this novel.

The return of Frederick and his adventures in Manchester compose the next phase of the novel. George Leonards, the character who tries to apprehend Frederick, is a thorough villain, reminiscent of a familiar Dickensian type. His meeting with the Hales' servant, Dixon, and his suggestion to her has something of the concentration and macabre caricature of the master:

To plague me to the last, he turned back before he got in [the bus], and said, 'If you can help me to trap Lieutenant Hale, Miss Dixon, we'll go partners in the reward. I know you'd like to be my partner, now wouldn't you? Don't be shy, but say yes.' And he jumped on the bus, and I saw his ugly face leering at me with a wicked smile to think how he's had the last word of plaguing (p. 301).

This perhaps lacks the full Dickensian vividness, but Leonards' villainy as seen through the eyes of the simple, outraged servant is conveyed extremely well. It is all the more effective when one remembers that Dixon is herself a 'character' in her own right, a creature often unconsciously comic. It is inevitable, after this meeting, that Leonards and Frederick will meet, but to this expectation Mrs Gaskell, with her by now thoroughly matured narrative skill, adds the surprise of Thornton's coming upon Margaret and Frederick as they wait for the train which will take the latter away from Manchester. Mrs Hale has just died, and to the strain of this there is suddenly added for Margaret the realization that Thornton will put the worst interpretation on her presence alone in the evening at a remote suburban station with a man he does not know and whom she cannot introduce to him. Then there comes the still further burden of the lie and the knowledge that Thornton knows that she has lied. 'Chaos and night surrounded the one lurid fact that, in Mr Thornton's eyes, she was degraded' (p. 338). The irony is that the lie is unnecessary, Frederick does not need her protection, he is safe; but Margaret does not know it.

The last stage of the novel's course pursues a double movement with contrasting emphases. The industrial story stresses the understanding that has been reached between Thornton on the one hand and Higgins as the workers' representative on the other. Thornton has become enlightened, and the previously considered inevitable opposition has been transformed into reconciliation. Nevertheless, there is much trouble in this part of the story. Thornton is pressed and eventually ruined by economic conditions; and before this Higgins has been brought to work for Thornton only out of a sense of obligation (hardly justified, though nobly assumed) to the family of a fellow-worker, Boucher, who has been driven to suicide by his inability to obtain work after the strike. As a whole, however, the public theme in the novel comes to a satisfactory resolution. By contrast, the reader wonders whether the personal story will ever issue in any kind of happiness. The extended ending which Mrs Gaskell gave to the novel endows it with a persistent quiet, sad tone in its latter pages. The death of Mr Hale, Margaret's nostalgic return-visit to Helstone, the appearance of her settling once more into the purposeless existence of Harley Street, above all, her sense of shame towards Thornton, all these give to the book its dominant sombre note. Then comes the death of Margaret's godfather Bell, her sudden access of wealth, her interview and reconciliation with Thornton and the happy ending. By his convenient death Bell is something of a *deus ex machina*, but Mrs Gaskell manipulates him for the tasks he has to perform in the latter half of the novel with considerable ability. It is the mark of Mrs Gaskell's development as a novelist, of the skill and confidence to which she has now arrived that she can end the book as she does. In two short speeches she shows how the marriage of Margaret and Thornton symbolizes the union not only of two very different people, but also of two different ways of life. The end shows, too, by its reference to the two women of the older generation, Aunt Shaw and Mrs Thornton, how great a distance has been travelled. Gentility has united with commerce, North has become allied to South. Above all else, Mrs Gaskell can trust herself to convey this humorously:

'What will she say?'

'I can guess. Her first exclamation will be, "That man!"'

'Hush!' said Margaret, 'or I shall try to show you your mother's indignant tones as she says, "That woman!"' (p. 521).

Thus ends Margaret's role as protagonist.

We must now examine a little more closely the contrast between North and South. The method of showing industrial conditions in *Mary Barton* depends mainly on intensity of visual impression; hence the memorable descriptions of abject poverty in the workers' houses. There is practically nothing of this in *North and South*. This is not because the novel is principally set on a different social level; it proceeds chiefly from a difference in approach. *North and South* is both less didactic and less dramatized than *Mary Barton*. We are much less conscious of the author's own presence. It is more properly dramatic than its predecessor; much more is left to the characters in the book. The contrasts upon which our impressions depend

are those which strike the characters themselves. For
Margaret Helstone represents the joys of childhood, the
beauty of the countryside and the happiness of tender
associations with her lost brother and her lover. There is
little criticism of Helstone as a place or as an example of
rural society. We may be inclined to draw inferences
about the squatters' cottages and the lone old man left in
them, but Mrs Gaskell does not encourage us to do so.
Even in the inserted chapter forty-six, after Margaret's
experience in Milton, her return to Helstone, though confronting her with many changes for the worse as compared with the time of her father's residence, is not
prominent for much evidence of suffering among rural
labourers. Mrs Gaskell seems not to have had, or at any
rate not to have wanted to use, much experience of the
kind which provided Kingsley with so much of his
material in *Yeast*. The nearest that we get to considerations of this nature comes in Margaret's dissuasion of
Higgins in his desire to go south. Her brief account makes
much of the sheer tedium of agricultural toil:

They labour on, from day to day, in the great solitude of
steaming fields—never speaking or lifting up their poor, bent,
downcast heads. The hard spadework robs their brain of life;
the sameness of their toil deadens their imagination,

whilst Higgins' reply also refers to 'labour's paid at star-
vation prices' at nine shillings per week (pp. 363–5).

In fact, Helstone is there not for itself, but for what can
be said about Milton by those who know Helstone. First
there is Milton as it appears to the Hales on their arrival.
Not unexpectedly, the city is a depressing sight, 'long
straight, hopeless streets of regularly-built houses, all
small and of brick. Here and there a great oblong many-

windowed factory' (p. 66). Then there is the special view which specific characters, being what they are, can bring by their reaction to Milton. There is Mrs Hale, for ever recalling a glory in a past that has gone—for her Milton and her new home produce only 'blank dismay' (p. 74). Her position is at once ridiculous and pathetic—ridiculous because her standard of judgment is so irrelevant, pathetic because, understanding the place so little, she is, in fact, its victim. Then there is the servant Dixon who enjoys her own sort of glory, a reflection of Mrs Hale's which comes from service with her mistress's family over many years; the 'rough independent way' of the Milton girls, prospective servants, batters the image of that glory. Indeed, Mrs Hale and Dixon present to the reader differing possibilities of judgment, the former reminding us of the pathos of the Hales' position, the latter, with her feeling of offence, seeming at times rather comic and helping us to see the independence of Milton as sturdy and admirable rather than merely uncouth. Thirdly, Milton and Helstone are related by what Margaret and her father are able to tell the Higgins family of their life in the south, of conditions of work and of life generally. By this Mrs Gaskell is able to express even more strongly, through the mouth of Higgins himself, the northern feeling of independence.

I have heard say they're a pack of spiritless, down-trodden men; welly clemmed to death; too much dazed wi' clemming to know when they're put upon. . . . We know when we're put upon; and we'en too much blood in us to stand it (p. 156).

The difference in standards of life is seen by Mr Hale in his references to food and furniture, which are signs also of improvidence, for the pawn-shop took over in Milton as soon as work became scarce. The difference is summed up in his comment: 'One had need to learn a different language, and measure by a different standard up here in Milton' (p. 188).

Hale learns to do that and, more especially, so does Margaret; but Mrs Hale does not. She is one of those genteel creatures who live in the faded glories of the past. In this she has her affinities with some of the characters in *Cranford*. In her querulousness she reminds us also, on a different social level, of course, of Mrs Wilson in *Mary Barton*. Mrs Hale is a small-minded character. She must have been in her own youth as empty-headed and frivolous as her niece Edith Shaw. She cannot appreciate that the reasons for her husband's resignation of his orders may have been conscientious and weighty—'Can't the Bishop set him right?' (p. 49); and her 'real suffering' at the prospect of exchanging Milton for Helstone can be dissipated by the idea of a few days by the sea beforehand. 'Her only regret was that Mr Hale could not be with her all the fortnight she was to be there, as he had been for a whole fortnight once, when they were engaged, and she was staying with Sir John and Lady Beresford at Torquay' (p. 57). This Beresford reference is used by Mrs Gaskell repeatedly to link mistress and maid, to show that both rely on by now irrelevant ideas of social status. When Mrs Shaw arrives at Milton with her maid, Dixon has 'visions of former grandeur, of the Beresford blood' (p. 425), and can even dismiss Thornton 'cavalierly'. Mrs Hale shares Dixon's horror of Milton—but at her own level, reproving Margaret, for instance, for using 'factory slang'. The interview in which this rebuke is given contrasts parent and daughter, and shows Margaret's adaptation to her environment. She points out that Edith had 'picked up all sorts of military slang from Captain Lennox'; but, more important, 'if I live in a factory town, I must speak factory language when I want it' (p. 281). Mrs Hale does not belong to this sort of world, but to that of Sir John Beresford long ago. The affinity in this respect between her and Dixon reminds us of another contrast in the novel, between the unified society of squire and dependents in rural areas and the independence in yet another sense, the individualism, of the city. Too many live only for themselves. In *North and South* master and men have to learn something about mutual responsibility and relationship. 'God has made us so that we must be mutually dependent,' Margaret reminds Thornton (p. 143). Sense of relationship is beautifully conveyed in Dixon's attitude to Mrs Hale when she speaks with Margaret of the fatal disease that has attacked her mistress. Comic as Dixon can be in her rigid ideas of social status, her reaction at this point shows an appealing tenderness:

I loved her better than any other man, woman, or child—no one but Master Frederick even came near her in my mind. Ever since Lady Beresford's maid first took me in to see her dressed in white crepe, and corn-ears, and scarlet poppies, and I ran a needle down into my finger, and broke it in, and she tore up her worked pocket handkerchief, after they'd cut it out, and came in to wet the bandages again with lotion when she returned from the ball—where she'd been the prettiest young lady of all—I've never loved any one like her (pp. 152–3).

Inadequate as Mrs Hale is in many ways, she remains the sacrifice offered on the altar of her husband's conscience, the victim of Milton for whose death he never really forgives himself; and Dixon helps to show this.

It has already been remarked that death is generally important in Mrs Gaskell's novels, and certainly in her mature work it is usually deliberately introduced. In fact, of this novel itself she wrote to Dickens, as she approached the end of the work: 'I think a better title than N. & S. would have been "Death & Variations". There are 5 deaths, each beautifully suited to the character of the individual' (220). Two of them are in the section of the novel concerned with social and industrial conditions, namely, those of Bessy Higgins and of Boucher. The plight of Bessy is used to introduce the theme of the workers' suffering to Margaret and to the reader. She would welcome death, and the joy of such life as remains to her is concentrated in the expectations which she derives from the Book of Revelations, 'her Methodee fancies, and her visions of cities with golden gates and precious stones', as her father describes them (pp. 104–5; cf. also p. 118). It is in the light of her description of her illness and its causes, the pulmonary tuberculosis that followed on work in a carding-room amidst the fluff and dust of the cotton, that we make our judgment in the arguments about conditions of work that follow.

North and South in its treatment of this aspect of the novel is much more theoretical, much less realistic, than *Mary Barton*. In the earlier work Mrs Gaskell was avowedly representing only one side of the question. *North and South* takes a more complex view. Mrs Gaskell had therefore to cope with the difficulties she had foreseen in a reply she made to some of Lady Kay-Shuttleworth's criticisms of *Mary Barton*. She had there written:

I can not imagine a nobler scope for a thoughtful energetic man, desirous of doing good to his kind, than that presented to his powers as the master of a factory. But I believe there is much to be discovered yet as to the right position and mutual duties of employer, and employed. . . . I think the best and most benevolent employers would say how difficult they, with all their experience, found it to unite theory and practice. . . . How could I suggest or even depict modes of proceeding (the details of which I never saw), and which from some error, undetected even by anxious and conscientious witnesses, seems so often to result in disappointment? (72*a*).

She was aware of the difficulty of the subject in itself, of the differing views of the social problem. She was aware also of her own ignorance. Nevertheless, in *North and South* she not only accepted the task, but even, as it were, made difficulties for herself. Her employer is not enlightened. At the beginning he is as reactionary as the rest of his fellows. In this we may detect the interest of the novelist over that of the economic theorist in Mrs Gaskell. She was going to describe a progress, to work out change in the character of her choice. At the same time she has, in effect, put aside the economic difficulties mentioned in her letter in order to demonstrate that what matters is not the success of industrial philanthropy but the recognition that it must be attempted. Thornton fails, we must remember.

Because Thornton changes, Mrs Gaskell had to create agents of change. This is one function of Hale and Margaret, representative, for Thornton, almost of reason and passion. Hale's arguments are necessary, but they would never suffice to convince Thornton without his personal regard for Margaret. We need Hale to enable Mrs Gaskell to give us the abstract problem. As he talks with Thornton we learn, for instance, of the cotton industry's history with its effect on the character and outlook of the masters, pioneers often crude and domineering in their attitude, men who led wild lives with fits of unrestrained extravagance. After the initial phase there had followed the period of men and masters more evenly matched, but with no conception of any possible reconciliation of mutual responsibility (pp. 95–6). Hence the frequent strikes, with the masters refusing to explain their case for lower wages. The masters, claims Thornton, have their right to independence (p. 143). This Mrs Gaskell, through Margaret, will not concede; but she never shows any inclination to question the economic theory on which the masters relied. We have no reason to believe that she would have wished to dissociate herself from Hale's views when he speaks with Higgins of the book given by the employer Hamper, which taught 'that wages find their own level, and that the most successful strike can only force them up for a moment, to sink in far greater proportion afterwards, in consequence of that very strike' (p. 272).

Hale goes on to suggest consultation between masters and men. This is Mrs Gaskell's remedy. For her there is no sense in violence. The masters ought not to oppress, but the workers should not strike. Strikes are fomented by unions, but the danger is not necessarily in what the unions do but rather in what, once a strike has begun, the violence so started can run to of its own momentum. Indeed, Mrs Gaskell, whilst pointing out the evil oppression of the Union, for example, in persecuting dissentients, is scrupulously fair in allowing Nicholas Higgins to stick to his point that 'It's the only way working men can get their rights, by all joining together' (p. 347). The strike outruns the union's plans, and issues in the violence by which Margaret is hurt and for which Boucher is tried. Afterwards, he is jobless and as a result commits suicide.

Boucher is a weak character, a parallel to Tom Darbyshire in *Mary Barton*. He is described as 'an unskilful workman with a large family depending upon him for support' (p. 181), a man for the most part listless, but roused to uncontrollable fury by the emotional excitement of the striking mob, a man thoroughly unstable, utterly undependable. He is one of those who break the restraint advised by the union and thereby help to ruin the strike campaign. Mrs Gaskell cherishes no over-simplified, sentimental view of the workers. She sees them as individuals, differing as much from each other as the members of any other class of society. They do not automatically qualify for sympathy. Because they differ so much from one another, she can use one worker to criticize another. The steady, thoughtful workman Higgins regards Boucher with mingled pity and contempt. The contrast works the other way as well. Higgins appears all the better by comparison with Boucher. No man, however, is simply a worker. In recognizing this, Mrs Gaskell is tacitly criticizing the view which regarded men as 'hands'. Boucher is a husband and a father; that is, he has human bonds as well as economic significance. We are reminded of Travers Madge's statement about the origins of *Mary Barton*. After Boucher's death we see him in a good light, when his wife tells of the affection he had for his family and, in particular, for the youngest of their seven children: 'He loved this babby m'appen the best of us; but he loved me and I loved him' (p. 353). Death severs the closest ties, and by its intervention here Mrs Gaskell is able to show that, whatever else a man may be, however he may be regarded, for some he is dear by reason of intimate human associations. It is surely thus that Boucher's death is 'beautifully suited to the character of the individual'.

It is not Boucher, but his neighbour Nicholas Higgins, Bessy's father, who is the most important representative of the workers. He is the direct antagonist of Thornton; he is a leader of the workers as Thornton is of the manufacturers. As with Thornton, so with Higgins we learn much of his side of the case through what he has to tell Margaret and Mr Hale. He also, like Thornton, goes back to the past. Combination has been bred out of the workers' sufferings at the hands of the masters: 'Their fathers ground our fathers to the very dust; ground us to powder!' (p. 276). Higgins' speech possesses a racy vigour, expressive of all his ingrained suspicions and dislikes of men he regards as his natural enemies. His view of Slickson will serve for example:

He'll wheedle his men back wi' fair promises. . . . He'll work his fines out on 'em, I'll warrant. He's as slippery as an eel, he is. He's like a cat—as sleek, and cunning, and fierce (p. 159).

Higgins is a character whose varied emotions Mrs Gaskell captures extremely well. His tenderness for his daughter, his overweening confidence about the strike, his joyful anticipation of the employers' surrender, his downcast pessimism at failure, his later loyalty to the enlightened Thornton, all these are vividly represented. It is not only Thornton who must be enlightened; so must Higgins. In this process of enlightenment Hale is used both as inquirer about the workers' attitudes and counsellor to better views. As Bessy lies dead and the strike has failed, Hale leads Higgins by the latter's belief in the existence of a God who 'set her life' through a long discussion of industrial strife, not to a neat agreement, but to the statement that 'your union in itself would be beautiful, glorious—it would be Christianity itself—if it were but for an end which affected the good of all, instead of that of merely one class as opposed to another' (p. 276). Before Higgins leaves, he joins in prayer. 'Margaret the Churchwoman, her father the Dissenter, Higgins the Infidel, knelt down together. It did them no harm' (p. 277). This, in Mrs Gaskell's view, is combination of the right kind to the right end.

She constantly opposes commendable private virtues and troublesome public attitudes, and in this respect her treatment of Higgins is no exception. He is much more attractive as a father than as a union leader; he is most attractive as foster-father to the Boucher children. Mrs Gaskell does not fail to emphasize this by her references to the way in which he assumes this obligation and by her descriptions of trivial incidents, his pride in the children's precociousness or his amusing them with some little game such as spinning a coin on the dresser (p. 385).

This pleasanter view of Higgins is matched by a similar one towards Thornton in the latter stages of the novel. His vigorous *laissez-faire* attitude gives way to a benevolent paternalism, expressed, for instance, in his setting up a canteen for his workmen. At the end, despite the failure of his own business, he is advising a fellow-manufacturer of the need 'of cultivating some intercourse with the hands beyond the mere "cash nexus" ' (p. 515). 'Behold! supply!—and—demand is not the one Law of Nature; Cash-payment is not the sole nexus of man with man,— how far from it!' Mrs Gaskell still recalled the Carlyle who had been in mind when she wrote *Mary Barton*. 'Deep, far deeper than Supply-and-demand, are Laws,

Obligations sacred as Man's Life itself.'[1] Thornton has seen the need for recognition of, and collaboration with, the workers. His enlightenment is reciprocated by that of Higgins and his fellows in their round-robin, offering to work for him again if ever he should set up in business (p. 516).

Thornton, like Higgins, is more attractive in his private than in his public capacity. The bond between son and mother is very close. That is one reason why the representation of Mrs Thornton is so important. This portrait is, however, a minor triumph in its own right. When we first meet her, Mrs Thornton appears to personify the hard earlier generation, unpolished in manner, outspoken in comment. Her strong purposeful attitude is the more apparent by contrast with the weak, superficial character of her daughter Fanny (cf. p. 109). She is proud of Milton and its manufactures, proud of what her son has achieved, jealous to defend his position and character, quick to take offence at those who would assail him. She is admirable but not particularly attractive. Initial harshness and toughness, however, is later recognized as tenacious affection. Here again we are impressed by Mrs Gaskell's increased skill as a novelist. She now sees much more than in the earlier works the possibilities of portrayal by progressive revelation. Characters change in her previous novels rather as a result of what happens to them. John Barton is the supreme exemplar here. They change, that is, because of the way in which events affect them. Alternately, there are the characters who do not change, who are too strong for life to distort or destroy. With both types, however, it is a matter of the effect of history upon a fully revealed character. In *North and South* characters actually develop

[1] *Past and Present*, Bk. III, c. ix.

for the reader. We do not know all about them at the beginning. We keep on learning. We may even be in part deceived, as we are with Mrs Thornton. Our view may change as the novel progresses and we learn more. In this way the opportunities for surprise are greater. Surprise, however, must convince; it must be consistent with, even though it is an extension of, our previous knowledge. Mrs Gaskell works subtly with Mrs Thornton by a process of what might be called, paradoxically, imperceptible surprise. We hardly realize the stages by which our admiration becomes more spontaneous, but by the end we acknowledge how much it is deserved. Change of this order in a character of this restricted importance helps to make acceptable the vaster change in more major characters, chiefly Thornton himself.

Mrs Gaskell sets off characters who change against those who do not. This is notably evident in the opposition of Mrs Thornton and Mr Hale. She is the person in the novel most fully committed to the existing economic and social organization, he the least. She acts; he observes. She accepts without qualification; he probes, inquires, questions. This is his nature, but it is also his function in the novel. Margaret is not dispassionate enough to act as investigator and commentator simply. Hale himself is meant to act thus. His is a difficult part to portray. He cannot be commentator simply. What he does affects others, what happens to others affects him. In these respects he is not altogether a successful creation. It is perfectly in character that he should have doubts about his faith, but, having in mind the way in which these doubts afflict his family, we may wish that Mrs Gaskell had been more specific in her statement of them. The absence of information contributes to the shadowiness that surrounds Hale. Nor does the representation of his grief and self-reproach at his wife's death seem strong enough. After all, he believes that she has died in consequence of what she has had to suffer by his resignation of his orders. Mrs Gaskell never seems to have gone beyond regarding Hale as a 'decorous, kind-hearted, simple, old-fashioned gentleman' (p. 267). In this sense he is an anomaly in a place of such assertive individualism as Milton, and thus his personal position is no less, probably more, pathetic than his wife's, not least because he has the courage and resilience to try to adapt himself to his new environment. One feels that Mrs Gaskell might have made more of this aspect of Hale's character.

His main role, however, is that of investigator and commentator. He advances the book's thesis by what he says. Others also have a commentary function, not, however, by what they say so much as by what they are. This is especially so with the London characters. They belong to a superficial society, and only Henry Lennox has much regard for others. He is, however, mainly a character required by the structure of the plot, the lover rejected by Margaret, for Thornton the putative rival, and for the story the lawyer who may be able to save Frederick. The other important London characters, Edith and Aunt Shaw, are notable for their complete lack of any sense of human relationships. Aunt Shaw speaks unfeelingly of her own marriage, and Edith considers hers as the conventional climax of a young woman's life. She is shown later as unable (or unwilling) to manage her own children. Her husband seems as vacuous as she is. It is in the world of these characters that the novel begins, and we are constantly reminded of it—as the Hales go through London on their journey north, when they arrive in

Milton and later by letters describing Edith's life in Corfu. The drab November days of Milton and Margaret's new life are contrasted with the gay life of the Mediterranean and 'the house with its trellised balcony, and its views over white cliffs and deep blue sea' (p. 75). Even more telling is the later letter, when Mrs Hale is lying ill, inviting Margaret to come with her mother to Corfu with its 'delicious climate—all sunshine, and grapes as common as blackberries' (p. 277). The poignancy that lies behind Margaret's inability to accept such a desirable invitation is sharpened by what amounts to cruel thoughtlessness in Edith, her inability to realize the circumstances of those to whom she is writing.

Margaret did long for a day of Edith's life . . . even for a few hours to be in the midst of that bright life, and to feel young again. Not yet twenty! and she had had to bear up against such hard pressure that she felt quite old. That was her first feeling after reading Edith's letter (p. 279).

Margaret, however, would not have found such a life satisfying. There is proof enough of that when she stays with the Shaws in London after her father's death. For her the life is one of boredom and triviality, 'frivolous and purposeless' (p. 485), as even Henry Lennox sees it; and for Margaret the cleverness and wit of the latter and his friends is mere 'sparkle and crackle' (p. 486). This is the life that Margaret has escaped, admittedly for one of struggle and trial, but also for one which has a purpose and a reward. These characters live a life which has nothing to teach them, and in any case it is doubtful whether most of them have any capacity to learn.

By contrast, the history of Margaret and Thornton is centred on their re-education. It is therefore appropriate that two such receptive characters, moving in the course of this re-education from almost diametrically opposite positions, should finally express the change that has occurred in each of them by love for one another. The development of the relationship is most skilfully handled by Mrs Gaskell. Their first meeting is hardly propitious. Thornton finds Margaret beautiful and refined but haughty and proud (p. 71), and this impression is confirmed and strengthened by later encounters, such as that on which she bows farewell instead of following the northern custom of shaking hands (p. 99). When they do shake hands on a later occasion, 'he knew it was the first time their hands had met, though she was perfectly unconscious of the fact' (p. 191). Here, as at their first meeting, Mrs Gaskell describes Margaret's beauty in some detail for the effect which it has on Thornton. There follows the superbly managed climax when Margaret is hurt by the strikers as she seeks to defend Thornton. Mrs Gaskell suggests his confused emotions excellently—'a mixture of joy, of anger, of pride, of glad surprise, of panting doubts' (p. 221). He is sufficiently encouraged to make his proposal. Again Mrs Gaskell lays stress on Margaret's beautiful appearance. In the interview she shows Thornton's initial hesitancy, then increases the pace with the fervour of his declaration, only for the whole movement of the scene to come to a full stop with Margaret's reply: 'Your way of speaking shocks me . . . your whole manner offends me' (p. 231). The previous warmth is dissipated by bitterness and harsh words.

Such is the state of their relationship when Thornton sees Margaret with Frederick. In the subsequent scenes Mrs Gaskell again achieves a triumph in the handling of complex emotions in Thornton. There is jealousy of the other man, puzzlement, and even a hint of despising

Margaret, yet unshakable loyalty to her. In Margaret also we see shame for her lie and frustration at her inability to explain herself. The very estrangement leads her to a better view of Thornton, even as she denies having such a view (p. 391). Her increasing sympathy with him is seen in her attempt to divert Bell from his jests at Thornton's expense (p. 399). It is immediately after this that Thornton commits his sudden *faux pas*, a few words which change a light piece of conversational chit-chat into a scene fraught with remorse and suffering. Bell refers to Margaret's truthfulness, and

'Is Miss Hale so remarkable for truth?' said Mr Thornton. The moment he had done so, he could have bitten his tongue out. . . . She sat quite still, after the first momentary glance of grieved surprise, that made her eyes look like some child's who has met with an unexpected rebuff; they slowly dilated into mournful, reproachful sadness. . . . He could have struck her before he left, in order, that by some strange overt act of rudeness, he might earn the privilege of telling her the remorse that gnawed at his heart (pp. 400–1).

This last sentence, in particular, shows Mrs Gaskell's understanding of human psychology and the use she is now able to make of it in her fiction. Her awareness of the way in which characters interact and her representation of this interaction marks the greatest advance in Mrs Gaskell's practice of the craft of fiction in *North and South* as compared with her previous works.

When Margaret is to leave Milton after her father's death, Thornton realizes how much she has meant to him even in the months of their estrangement. For the reader it is now a question of Margaret's becoming more amenable and of the way in which reconciliation will be achieved. The use of Bell as intermediary to explain Margaret's previous conduct to Thornton represents, in fact, a false trail, for Bell dies before he can do so. Thus Mrs Gaskell sustains the uncertainty to the last pages when Higgins is chosen to elucidate the mystery for Thornton. But when all is clear to him, his business collapses, and with it his hopes of Margaret's hand. It is her offer to re-start him in business which leads to his successful declaration in another scene handled by Mrs Gaskell with consummate tact and assurance.

Many of the meetings between Thornton and Margaret originate in his friendship with her father, and many of them involve discussions of the industrial and social problems in which Hale is so interested. Margaret also has her views on these problems, and Mrs Gaskell adds a new level of interest to these discussions through the personal relationship which exists between Thornton and Margaret. Their differences on the personal level give an edge, even a tinge of bitterness, to their divergent attitudes to the subjects under consideration. Mrs Gaskell also gains an effect by the way in which each of the protagonists advances almost unwillingly nearer to the position held by the other. Even here their personal relationship, which at best makes no progress and often seems to deteriorate, acts as a kind of counterpoint to the discussion. In an association of this kind there could be no gradual restorative movement, and Mrs Gaskell is right therefore to conclude the story by a reconciliation that proceeds from a sudden realization, an inrush of enlightenment and understanding. This is why the final touch of humour is so important. Without it the end might have appeared too sentimental, too conventionally romantic in the most hackneyed sense of that word.

The love of Thornton and Margaret symbolizes both

the union of North and South and the completion of their respective individual enlightenments. It is a fitting sign also for the triumph of understanding, humanity and humility. Misunderstanding, misjudgment and estrangement are banished by the recognition on both their parts of a 'deep feeling of unworthiness' (p. 520). This phrase reminds us of another, of Margaret's meditations on her father's book at the time of her furthest separation from Thornton and of the need there spoken of to follow 'the way of humility' (p. 412). This emphasis upon fundamental personal attitudes is important. Mrs Gaskell, of course, had always believed that the solution for the social ills about which she wrote lay not so much in change of organization as in change of attitude. This is the message of *Mary Barton*, and especially of Carson's conversion at the end. That event, however, is too sudden and appears forced and hardly credible. In part this is due to the fact that the action of the novel takes place at a late stage in the deterioration of industrial relationships; in part also because the angle of vision is largely that of the oppressed workers. In *North and South* relationships, though critical, are not irretrievably set for catastrophe, events themselves are less spectacular, and the viewpoint of the masters receives a fuller hearing. Thus it is possible to portray the change in Thornton as a gradual process and by his extensive participation in the story to show it as the result more of personal influences than of theoretical considerations. Mrs Gaskell is again concerned to show that what matters is the way in which people affect each other. Thus the reconciliation of Thornton and Margaret is at once a healing experience in their personal histories and a token of the resolution of the public argument.

Much more, therefore, depends on the principal characters, and particularly upon Margaret herself, than was the case in earlier novels. Both John Barton and Margaret may be described as intensely delineated characters, but between them there is an obvious opposition of simplicity and subtlety. Barton makes his effect by bold, emphatic, sombre colouring. Margaret has depth and complexity. She is the most interesting, because the most difficult, character that her creator had so far conceived. Her personal situation, called upon as she is to bear so much whilst still so young, is full of narrative potentiality. Mrs Gaskell makes the most of this, accumulating trial upon trial until the suffering is cruel and prolonged. We have to admire the manner in which she keeps Margaret at the centre of the story. It would be difficult to name a single character who matters in terms other than his or her relationship to Margaret. This means that Mrs Gaskell herself does not need to be in the novel as much as she appears to be in *Mary Barton*. It means also that, as Margaret looks from the centre at the various characters in the circle around her, we get some idea of the variety and richness of her life—and of its problems. When we think of her, we must immediately take account of the impact made upon her by her father and mother, Thornton and his mother, Nicholas and Bessy Higgins, even by her relatives in the luxury of far-off London and farther-off Corfu. Margaret's soul becomes a crucible not only for refining her own trials but also the mingled and confused experiences of all those with whom she comes in contact. The result is that Mrs Gaskell produces from her delineation of Margaret an intensity previously unparalleled in any of her characters and unique within the range of her creations. She knew what she was doing when she wished to call the book 'Margaret'.

North and South is a didactic work, a *roman à thèse*, like *Ruth* and *Mary Barton*, but the thesis is much less dominant. This is because it is much better worked into the artistic realization of the novel than in the earlier books. The areas of action and character in which it is primarily important are themselves much less important and less central within the work as a whole. Of greater significance, however, is the fact that Mrs Gaskell has achieved a coalescence between personal and public stories in the relationship of the two major characters. That is why I have chosen this relationship as the culmination of my study. In *North and South* Mrs Gaskell has finally decided that a novel must be, primarily, not about things but about people, not just about people but about persons. Before this novel (*Cranford* always excepted) she had been interested mainly in individuals as they were affected by social and economic forces. This interest is still important, but she has now found that what one person means to another is the novel's supreme concern. The technical advance in her powers as a novelist went hand in hand in *North and South* with this new recognition of what her novels must really be about.

CHAPTER VII

'THE LIFE OF CHARLOTTE BRONTË'

IF Lytton Strachey was right when he claimed in the preface to *Eminent Victorians* that biography is 'the most delicate and humane of all the branches of the art of writing', we should not perhaps be surprised that Mrs Gaskell was able to produce one of the finest examples of the genre in English literature. In the novels written between 1848 and 1855 she had already demonstrated her delicate appreciation of life and her humane understanding of her fellow-beings before she came to write *The Life of Charlotte Brontë*. These novels demonstrate, as we have seen, her capacity for fine observation, sensitive appreciation and sympathetic concern for the human condition. To these qualities Mrs Gaskell added an intimate acquaintance with the remarkable woman who formed the subject of her study.

Mrs Gaskell and Charlotte Brontë knew each other for only five years, from 1850 to Charlotte's death in 1855, but it was a friendship of tremendous warmth and attachment on both sides. Charlotte Brontë had sent Mrs Gaskell a copy of *Shirley* in November 1849, but they did not meet until 19 August 1850—at Briery Close, Windermere, the house of Sir James and Lady Kay-Shuttleworth. Charlotte had stayed with them at Gawthorp Hall, Burnley, for three days in March.[1] It is probably to this occasion that Mrs Gaskell is referring in a letter to Lady Kay-Shuttleworth, in which she also

[1] S.H.B., vol. III, 81–2.

mentions her desire to meet Charlotte. This must be quoted at some length:

No! I never heard of Miss Brontë's visit; and I should like to hear a great deal more about her, as I have been so much interested in what she has written. I don't mean merely in the story and mode of narration, wonderful as that is, but in the glimpse one gets of *her*, and her modes of thought, and, all unconsciously to herself, of the way in wh. she has suffered. I wonder if she suffers *now*. Soon after I saw you at Capesthorne I heard such a nice account of her, from a gentleman who went over to see her father, and staid at the inn, where he was told of her doings as well as her sayings and writings. I should like very much indeed to know her: I was going to write to 'see' her, but that is not it. I think I told you that I disliked a good deal in the plot of Shirley, but the expression of her own thoughts in it is so true and brave, that I really admire her. I am half amused to find you think I could do her good. (I don't know if you exactly word it so, but I think it is what you mean.) I *never* feel as if I could do anyone good—I never yet was conscious of strengthening anyone, and I do so feel to want strength and to want faith. I suppose we all *do* strengthen each other by clashing together, and earnestly talking our own thoughts, and ideas (72).

Lady Kay-Shuttleworth seems to have displayed a rare perceptiveness in foreseeing the beneficial influence that Mrs Gaskell might exercise on Charlotte, but our main interest in this extract lies in Mrs Gaskell's attraction thus early to the mind and emotions of the individual behind the novelist.

Mrs Gaskell has left a number of accounts of the first meeting, but for our purpose it is sufficient to quote from only one of these, a letter to Mrs Froude:

Miss Brontë I like. Her faults are the faults of the very peculiar

circumstances in which she has been placed; and she possesses
a charming union of simplicity and power; and a strong feeling of responsibility for the Gift, which she has given her. She
is very little & very plain. Her stunted person she ascribes to
the scanty supply of food she had as a growing girl, when at
that school of the Daughters of the Clergy. Two of her sisters
died there, of the low fever she speaks about in Jane Eyre. She
is the last of six; lives in a wild out of the way village in the
Yorkshire Moors with a wayward eccentric wild father,—
their parsonage facing the North—no flowers or shrub or tree
can grow in the plot of ground, on acct of the biting winds.
The sitting room looks into the church-yard. Her father & she
each dine and sit alone. She scrambled into what education she
has had. Indeed I never heard of so hard, and dreary a life,—
extreme poverty is added to their trials,—it (poverty) was no
trial till her sisters had long lingering illnesses. She is truth
itself—and of a very noble sterling nature,—which has never
been called out by anything kind or genial (78).

It is obvious from this extract that Mrs Gaskell was much
impressed by Charlotte's character and attitude and also
by the version she gave of her life and surroundings, 'the
very peculiar circumstances in which she has been placed'.
Closer acquaintance did little to modify the vivid impression of Charlotte's life which she gave to Mrs Gaskell
at this first meeting.

Mrs Gaskell visited Haworth in September 1853 (*Life*,
II, 305–12). In a letter quoted in the *Life* she refers to the
journey on 'a dull, drizzly Indian-inky day, all the way on
the railroad to Keighley'. She goes on:

The day was lead-coloured; the road had stone factories
alongside of it,—grey dull-coloured rows of stone cottages
belonging to these factories, and then we came to poor,
hungry-looking fields;—stone fences everywhere, and trees
nowhere. Haworth is a long, straggling village: one steep

narrow street ... [and] the church; moors everywhere beyond and above. The crowded grave-yard surrounds the parsonage house (*Life*, II, 306).

This first view of Haworth must have reinforced the impression of Charlotte already received. The very locality in which she lived assisted those other 'very peculiar circumstances in which she [had] been placed'. All around was gloom, harshness and severity. Mrs Gaskell visited Haworth again after she was commissioned to write the *Life*. She was there on 23 July 1855,[1] and in a letter to the Haworth stationer and friend of the Brontë sisters, John Greenwood, she spoke of going over again 'probably from Sir James Kay-Shuttleworth's in August' (258). This was doubtless the famous occasion on which Sir James accompanied her and which she describes in a letter to her publisher George Smith, the visit in which Sir James brusquely bore down all resistance and they left with the manuscript of *The Professor*, the beginning of a new tale and Mr Nicholls (Charlotte's husband)'s reluctant agreement to allow his wife's portrait to be photographed. These later visits do not appear in any way to have modified Mrs Gaskell's first sombre assessment of Haworth and its environs.

Mrs Gaskell thus brought to the task of writing the biography a deep interest in an unusual personality, a tender concern for her friend and a definite opinion about the circumstances and environment of her life. The news of Charlotte's death on 30 March 1855 was given to Mrs Gaskell by John Greenwood. Replying to his letter on 4 April, she wrote:

I cannot tell you how *very* sad your note has made me. My

---

[1] S.H.B., IV, 191.

dear dear friend that I shall never see again on earth! I did not even know she was ill. . . . Strangers might know her by her great fame, but we loved her dearly for her goodness, truth, and kindness, & those lovely qualities she carries with her where she is gone (232).

The letter ends:

I loved her dearly, more than I think she knew. I shall never cease to be thankful that I knew her: or to mourn her loss.

This profound attachment was no doubt a compelling factor in Mrs Gaskell's decision to write a memoir even before Charlotte's father asked her to do so. On 31 May she wrote to George Smith:

If I live long enough, and no one is living whom such a publication would hurt, I will publish what I know of her, and make the world (if I am but strong enough in expression) honour the woman as much as they admired the writer (241).

Less than a week later Charlotte's friend, Ellen Nussey, was writing to Mr Nicholls complaining of an article in *Sharpe's Magazine* and wishing

Mrs Gaskell, who is every way capable, would undertake a reply, and would give a sound castigation to the writer. Her personal acquaintance with Haworth, the Parsonage, and its inmates, fits her for the task.[1]

As a result, Patrick Brontë requested Mrs Gaskell to undertake the task of writing an account of Charlotte.[2]

An authorized biography, however, is a very different thing from what Mrs Gaskell had originally proposed, and it may perhaps be appropriate at this point to consider some of the problems which every biographer must face. Biography is essentially a study of human

[1] S.H.B., IV, 189, 6 June 1855.   [2] S.H.B., 190–1, 16 June 1855.

relationships focused upon a central figure. It is an art that demands truth and candour, and, if Dr Johnson is to be believed, it even requires that the writer should be personally acquainted with his subject. Boswell reports him as saying that 'Nobody can write the life of a man but those who have eat and drunk and lived in social intercourse with him.'[1] Whilst such an acquaintance is likely to provide an intimate knowledge and even understanding of the subject, its very intimacy may lead to bias, to a loss of detachment, a failure or inadequacy in truth and candour. It is obvious from her comments that Mrs Gaskell was concerned to portray Charlotte Brontë in the best light possible, and it is clear also from her reaction to Patrick Brontë's request that she immediately found herself hindered in that task by her inability to say what she would have said about many circumstances of Charlotte's life:

I shall have now to omit a good deal of detail as to her home, and the circumstances which must have had so much to do in forming her character. All these can be merely indicated during the lifetime of her father, and to a certain degree in the lifetime of her husband (245).

Nevertheless, she was determined to be as little inhibited as possible. With what results we shall see later. This letter, however, reminds us that the biographer's consideration is not limited to his or her view of the central subject, but must also include attitudes towards all the other persons referred to. It confronts us with the problem of relevance in various forms—how far, for instance, should an author explore the character and activities of such persons and to what extent should he comment upon

[1] *Life*, ed. Hill and Powell, 1934, II, 166.

them either implicitly or otherwise? Indeed, there is the question as to how far the writer should comment at all. All these questions arise in a criticism of *The Life of Charlotte Brontë*. The Branwell Brontë-Lady Scott affair would provide a test-case here.[1]

Mrs Gaskell's treatment of this episode reminds us of another problem which particularly beset the biographer in Victorian times, that of relation to the contemporary ethos. What did the audience expect? How much might it be prepared to accept? And, as we consider this question, how much is to be expected from the biographer herself? Carlyle, commenting on criticisms of Lockhart's *Life of Scott* for being too indiscreet, too outspoken, remarked:

How delicate, decent is English biography, bless its mealy mouth! A Damocles' sword of *Respectability* hangs for ever over the poor English life-writer (as it does over poor English life in general), and reduces him to the verge of paralysis. . . . The English biographer has long felt that if in writing his Man's Biography, he wrote down anything that could by any possibility offend any man, he had written wrong.[2]

Mrs Gaskell does not spare Lady Scott. Indeed, her daring disregard for respectability here led to her being threatened with a libel action and to the withdrawal of offensive passages. These very passages, however, in their indignant moral condemnation are not free from the effects of Mrs Gaskell's own adherence to Victorian attitudes. As Virginia Woolf remarked, 'the Victorian biographer was dominated by the idea of goodness'.[3]

[1] See below, p. 166 f.
[2] *The London and Westminster Review*, January 1838, p. 299.
[3] 'The New Biography', *New York Herald Tribune*, 30 October 1927.

Though there is no sentimental heroine-worship, Mrs Gaskell is certainly intent on exalting the goodness of Charlotte; and because of Charlotte's goodness amid the greater than normal trials of her life, Mrs Gaskell attacks all the more fiercely the person responsible, as she thinks, for Charlotte's unnecessary sufferings. She did not spare Lady Scott's moral turpitude, especially as this lady was still considered *respectable* and accepted in London society.

To say that Mrs Gaskell was intent upon exalting Charlotte's goodness is to recognize that biography involves an estimate of character, and this reminds us of yet other problems, those of psychological analysis and judgment. In matters of this nature we twentieth-century readers may easily be looking for something which biographers in centuries before our own rarely, if ever, set out to provide. Even though in this case the biographer was a novelist, there is but little effort to interpret the inner life of the subject. Mrs Gaskell, it is clear, began with a firm idea of Charlotte's character based on their friendship and intimacy. She conceived of her task as being to place her subject's character in its setting, to relate Charlotte to those around her, to trace her history and, as far as possible, to do so by letting her speak for herself. There was to be no close or intricate psychological exploration and analysis. Indeed, on the penultimate page of the work Mrs Gaskell explicitly disavows her capacity for such an undertaking: 'I cannot measure or judge of such a character as hers. I cannot map out vices and virtues, and debateable land' (*Life*, II, 335). One may perhaps take leave to question Mrs Gaskell's modesty, but certainly in the *Life* she did not attempt the task which here she says she could not carry out.

She sought to let Charlotte speak for herself. In preparing the *Life* Mrs Gaskell not only tried to visit every place at which Charlotte had stayed—Haworth, London, Cowan Bridge, even Brussels—but also to see and use as many of Charlotte's letters as possible. Writing to George Smith in August 1856, she said: 'Her language, where it can be used, is so powerful and living, that it would be a shame not to express everything that can be, in her own words' (303). Mrs Gaskell thus recognized the point made by a nineteenth-century critic, namely, that

letters, written in the genuine confidence of self-disclosure, offer, certainly, the most important materials to biographical composition . . . letters lay open the communication of [the writer's] very thoughts and purposes.[1]

Ellen Nussey supplied over three hundred and fifty letters, the earliest written in 1832, and the series continued up to a few days before Charlotte's death (271). These form the basic substance of the book. It is interesting to contrast the reliance Mrs Gaskell placed on the letters with her estimate of the recollections of others, assiduously as she sought after and collected these. As soon as Greenwood informed her of Charlotte's death, she wrote to him: 'I want to know *every* particular. Has she been long ill? What was her illness?' (232). This same urgent curiosity extended from her desire for details of the last days to other matters. A month later she wrote: '*Every* thing you can tell me about her and her sisters—of *her* especially is most valuable. . . . When did *you* first know of "Currer Bell"?' (238). This was no doubt in part the response to a ready informant. She sent some of

[1] J. F. Stanfield, *An Essay on the Study and Composition of Biography*, 1813, q. J. L. Clifford, *Biography as an Art*, 1962, p. 71.

Greenwood's letters to George Smith on three occasions in June 1855, but on the last she commented: 'One can see that poor John Greenwood takes things according to the impulse of the moment, from the contradictory accounts of Mr Nicholls that he sends' (244). In fairness to Greenwood one should perhaps say that at this stage, difficult as she felt that Nicholls might be from things that Charlotte herself had said, Mrs Gaskell had not yet entered into the most trying period of her relationship with him. After her visit to Haworth in July 1855 Mrs Gaskell reported to her daughter Marianne that she liked Mr Nicholls (259). The later visit with Sir James Kay-Shuttleworth no doubt sadly enlightened her, and in the letter I have already quoted about the vividness of Charlotte's own letters, she asked Smith not to allow

the letters to assume a prominent form in the title or printing; as Mr Nicholls has a strong objection to letters being printed at all; and wished to have all her letters (to Miss Nussey and every one else) burned (303).

By November she was in despair. H. F. Chorley had informed her that permission for publication rested not with the correspondent, but the executor, and that Nicholls might therefore forbid quotation. She concluded 'Oh! If once I have finished this biography, catch me writing another!' (318).

Even with letters, however, and with the subject's own reminiscences there is the question of credibility. How far is her statement accurate? How far is it coloured by factors for which allowances must be made? Attitudes towards the topic under discussion, attitudes towards the correspondent or interlocutor, the characteristic inclinations and attitudes of the writer herself must all be allowed for. In other words, the biographer must try to read between the lines. Mrs Gaskell tried to do this, for instance, in the Cowan Bridge episode, Were things as bad as Charlotte had said? In July 1855 she told George Smith of her inquiry to the Miss Temple of *Jane Eyre*:

I think that she may give me some particulars of that Cowan Bridge time, & possibly some explanations which may modify that account of the school in Jane Eyre, which took such a strong hold on the public mind (256).

This episode, the Lady Scott incident and Mrs Gaskell's own remarks about heeding the feelings of Mr Brontë and Mr Nicholls remind us of another of her problems. Having collected her material, how was she to use it? How was it to be arranged? What were to be the criteria of selection, and not least of exclusion? The basic arrangement she determined very sensibly was to be chronological. The picture of Charlotte she wished to paint required as little exclusion of material as possible, and her insistence on this brought about the troubles which followed the book's publication. On one subject, however, Mrs Gaskell insisted on omission. This was the matter of Charlotte's relationship with Monsieur Héger, the Brussels teacher, to whom she went in 1843. An article in *The Times* of 29 July 1913, together with four letters of Charlotte's, revealed the full story of her deep but unreturned passion for M. Héger. This stage in Charlotte's life presented difficulties of representation. M. Héger's position had to be protected, but Mrs Gaskell did not want to present Charlotte in a bad light. Yet she had to explain the reasons for the estrangement of Charlotte and Madame Héger. Mrs Gaskell blamed it on Madame Héger's reaction to Charlotte's outspoken Protestant criticism of that lady's Roman Catholicism (*Life*, 1,

311–12). She even goes so far as to say that it was 'a silent estrangement . . . of which, perhaps, the former i.e. Madame Héger was hardly aware'. This scarcely fits in with Madame Héger's refusal to see the friend of Charlotte Brontë when Mrs Gaskell herself visited Brussels.

Did Mrs Gaskell see these letters? Miss Hopkins has discussed this question at some length in her biography of Mrs Gaskell[1] and concludes that M. Héger probably showed Mrs Gaskell the letters and prepared the extracts for her. I am not sure that she actually saw them, because she refers in a letter to Smith to 'hearing' the letters (259). She certainly knew them well enough to know that they were dangerous. This explains her anxiety about the proposal of Sir James Kay-Shuttleworth for publishing Charlotte Brontë's novel, The Professor. She knew this referred to the Brussels era of Charlotte's life, and

dreaded lest the Prof. should involve anything with M. Héger . . . I believed him too good to publish those letters—but I felt that his friends might with some justice urge him to do so (308).

The two passages quoted in the Life (1, 330–1, 336) consist in the first case of two paragraphs, one from the first letter, the other from the second, and in the second of a further passage from the first letter. Was this all that M. Héger allowed Mrs Gaskell to have? Whatever be the answer to that question, we now know more fully than she allowed us to know what lay behind Charlotte's remark in a letter of 23 January 1844: 'I suffered much before I left Brussels. I think, however long I live, I shall not forget what the parting with M. Héger cost me' (Life, 1, 316). It is little wonder that Mrs Gaskell was so

[1] Hopkins, pp. 195–7.

apprehensive about Sir James Kay-Shuttleworth's enthusiasm for publishing *The Professor* which she felt
related more to M. Héger even than *Villette* did. In the
letter to Smith already quoted, she wrote: 'I can not tell
you how I should deprecate anything leading to publication of those letters of M. Héger's' (299). Her fears about
what *The Professor* might reveal were stilled when she
read the book (301) and realized that nothing in it would
compel M. Héger to publish the letters. It is difficult to
know exactly what course Mrs Gaskell ought to have pursued, but I am unable to go as far as Miss Hopkins in
believing that 'she was entirely right in protecting both
Charlotte and her correspondent' (p. 194). Even if Mr
Brontë and Mr Nicholls were hanging on every word she
wrote (p. 197), it seems to me that the utmost brevity and
even omission of reasons would have been preferable to
the distortion that results from the deliberate exclusion of
the real cause and the consequent exaggeration of what
at best must have been a subsidiary reason for Charlotte's
estrangement from the Hégers.

Though the circle of Charlotte Brontë's life was narrow,
her experience ran deep and all the more intense because
of her own nature. In addition to this, her life was surrounded by an almost unrelieved tragic aura. 'All her life
was but labour and pain,' wrote Mary Taylor (*Life*, II,
336) who, next to Ellen Nussey, was her closest friend.
Her mother dying when she was five, Charlotte was left
one of six children with a remote and eccentric father in a
bleak moorland village. Going to a school whose conditions and discipline seem hardly credible to us to-day,
she there saw her two elder sisters decline and shortly
afterwards die. Her second school (Roe Head) was a

better one and brought her the acquaintance of the two people who were to become her most intimate friends. Thereafter, however, there were two unsuccessful governess-ships, the failure of the attempt to start a school with her sisters, the sad culmination of her stay in Brussels, and, as literary fame was developing, the terrors of the dissipated Branwell and the deaths of Emily and Anne, her two remaining sisters. Finally, after a brief nine months of marriage, came Charlotte's own death. There could be no better rhetoric to conclude the history of such a life than the simple, bare description, the controlled understatement with which Mrs Gaskell ends her account of Charlotte:

Early on Saturday morning, March 31st, the solemn tolling of Haworth church-bell spoke forth the fact of her death to the villagers who had known her from a child, and whose hearts shivered within them as they thought of the two sitting desolate and alone in the old grey house (*Life*, II, 333).

Mrs Gaskell ended her story where she began it, reminding us of the child who grew up in this place and among this people. I have referred above to the letter which she quotes describing her visit to Haworth in 1853. The *Life* begins with a similar account, first describing Keighley and the view of Haworth one gets approaching from that direction,

on the side of a pretty steep hill, with a background of dun and purple moors . . . wild, bleak moors—grand, from the ideas of solitude and loneliness which they suggest, or oppressive from the feeling which they give of being pent-up by some monotonous and illimitable barrier.

Here, incidentally, is that economy of means which always served Mrs Gaskell so well in her pithily suggestive passages of description. Next, she gives us a picture of the village, the steep, cobbled street, the stone-houses, the church and the parsonage, then the interior of the church, and finally the Brontë memorial tablet, with its record of so many premature deaths, the mother in her thirty-ninth year, the children, eleven, ten, thirty, twenty-nine, twenty-seven, and nearby the tablet to Charlotte herself, like her mother, in the thirty-ninth year of her age. Thus ends Chapter One. Mrs Gaskell goes on with a racy account of the independence and, even, rebelliousness of the Haworth populace, telling of the rough treatment they meted out to Redhead, Patrick Brontë's predecessor, who, as they thought, had been wrongly thrust upon them. This with other anecdotes establishes that sense of place, which Charlotte herself described as one of 'barbarism, loneliness and liberty'. In this way Mrs Gaskell as bio-grapher is doing what only Lockhart for Scott had done before her, namely, indicating the possible influence of environment upon character.

A chapter is devoted next to the Brontë parents and the children's early life. Thus due prominence is given to the strangeness of Patrick Brontë, though later, and perhaps in the circumstances understandably, Mrs Gaskell does not seem to notice explicitly enough the possibly here-ditary influences in the children's temperaments. Enough, however, is implicit for us not to regret this omission overmuch. The next chapter deals with Cowan Bridge and the searing impression that that experience left on Charlotte. Then on to a chapter about the juvenile writings, which are described in a letter to Smith as 'the wildest and most incoherent things. . . . They give one the idea of creative power carried to the verge of in-sanity' (297). Mrs Gaskell compared them with the work of Blake. This shows her recognition of their literary power. It is a pity that she did not spend more time upon them, for she would, I think, have recognized their importance. As it is, one must agree with Miss Hopkins that, with the *Life* as we have it, it appears that Mrs Gaskell 'probably did not understand their full significance' (p. 172); or if she did, she recoiled from something she did not like. Is this the meaning behind the reference to 'the verge of insanity'? The next two chapters conclude the story of Charlotte's girlhood on a more tranquil note, with the accounts of Roe Head and her return home to Haworth.

The second half of the first volume covers the period from 1835 to 1846. It deals with Charlotte's two spells as governess, her stay in Brussels, the increasing difficulties caused by Branwell's behaviour and the advent of the curates to Haworth. It is concerned also with the family's literary attempts, their letters to Wordsworth and Southey; and the volume ends with an account of the publication of Poems by Currer, Ellis and Acton Bell. The letters in which Charlotte describes her governess-experiences illustrate particularly well that vividness, which led Mrs Gaskell to want to allow them to tell their own tale. A brief sentence or two will illustrate the point:

I will only ask you to imagine the miseries of a reserved wretch like me, thrown at once into a large family, at a time when they were particularly gay. . . . In that state I had charge given me of a set of pampered, spoilt, turbulent children. . . . At times I felt—and, I suppose, seemed—depressed. To my astonishment I was taken to task by Mrs [Sidgwick] with a sternness of manner and a harshness of language hardly credible (*Life*, 1, 201).

Charlotte was not made to be a governess, and she knew it:

No one but myself can tell how hard a governess's work is to me—for no one but myself is aware how utterly averse my whole mind and nature are for the employment (*Life*, I, 234).

Mrs Gaskell seeks some explanation in the motherless childhood, but it would seem better to trace it to that delicate and hypersensitive nervous and emotional organization, which is evident at every stage of Charlotte's history. Mrs Gaskell knew how sensitive Charlotte was, and one can sense the effort of restraint which was necessary when she introduced this phase of Charlotte's life, with the declared resolution 'carefully to abstain from introducing the names of any living people, respecting whom I may have to tell unpleasant truths, or to quote severe remarks from Miss Brontë's letters' (*Life*, I, 197).

With the single exception of the Héger episode Mrs Gaskell refused to shirk the unpleasant duty of telling unpleasant truths. Early in the second volume she describes the last days of Branwell's ill-starred career. Apart from the need to explain the sisters' suffering at his hands, she adduces another reason:

It is well that the thoughtless critics who spoke of the sad and gloomy views of life presented by the Brontës in their tales, should know how such words were wrung out of them by the living recollection of the long agony they suffered (*Life*, II, 50).

Mrs Gaskell was throughout intent on explaining the writers by the individuals who lay behind them. Hence Cowan Bridge, hence the governess episodes, hence even the description of Haworth's bleak environs, though

Mrs Gaskell seems signally to have failed to appreciate Emily's sombre vision.[1]

The second volume begins with the account of Charlotte's first adventure into fiction with the writing of *The Professor*, and thus it covers the effective career of Charlotte as a writer. It is therefore devoted mainly to her novels, the impact they made and the introduction to the great world which they brought her. There is more of Currer Bell than Charlotte Brontë, but, to say truth, the vivid moments of the second half of the *Life*, with the exception only of the visit to London and the stay at the Chapter Coffee-House, belong to the private life of the family circle rather than the public world of the novelist. Even the Chapter Coffee-House episode derives most of its appeal from its quaintness of situation—ignorant provincial young ladies on a visit to London, staying at the only place they knew about, and that an out-moded tavern, once the resort of booksellers, later of country clergymen. The whole incident is one of comedy and pathos. Here were the two young sisters in a strange place,

a place solely frequented by men. . . . Few people slept there. . . . The old 'grey-haired elderly man', who officiated as waiter . . . touched from the very first with the quiet simplicity of the two ladies, . . . tried to make them feel comfortable and at home in the long, low dingy room up stairs, where the meetings of the publishing Trade were held (*Life*, II, 72–3).

These lines show Mrs Gaskell's capacity to capture and represent the essence of a situation in a few strokes. This

[1] Cf. letter of 9 December 1857, 'I cannot say I agree with you in preferring "Wuthering Heights" to their other works—notwithstanding its wonderfully fine opening' (385).

same ability shows itself also in the comparatively rare instances on which she was able to use dialogue. In one short scene she manages to suggest the remoteness, condescension and pleasurable surprise of Patrick Brontë. The occasion was the publication of *Jane Eyre*:

'Papa, I've been writing a book.'
'Have you, my dear?'
'Yes, and I want you to read it.'
'I am afraid it will try my eyes too much.'
'But it is not in manuscript; it is printed.'
'My dear! You've never thought of the expense it will be! It will be almost sure to be a loss, for how can you get a book sold? No one knows you or your name.'
'But, Papa, I don't think it will be a loss; no more will you, if you will just let me read you a review or two, and tell you more about it.'
So she sate down and read some of her reviews to her father; and then, giving him the copy of 'Jane Eyre' that she intended for him, she left him to read it. When he came in to tea, he said, 'Girls, do you know Charlotte has been writing a book, and it is much better than likely?' (*Life*, II, 36–7).

Both these incidents and that which I describe next come from the long second chapter of the second volume, covering the years 1847 and 1848. These were eventful years, both happy and sorrowful. Mrs Gaskell's resources were more than sufficient for the task of covering such extremes of emotion. Her handling of the paragraphs describing Emily's illness and death is a masterpiece of arrangement and emphasis. She begins with a quotation of Charlotte's biographical notice of her sisters:

My sister Emily first declined. . . . Day by day, when I saw with what a front she met suffering, I looked on her with an anguish of wonder and love. I have seen nothing like it; but, indeed, I have never seen her parallel in anything. Stronger than a man, simpler than a child, her nature stood alone. The awful point was, that, while full of ruth for others, on herself she had no pity; the spirit was inexorable to the flesh (*Life*, II, 80).

A brief comment by Mrs Gaskell, then quotations from two of the letters giving details of Emily's weakness and Charlotte's anguish:

A more hollow, wasted, pallid aspect I have not beheld. The deep tight cough continues. . . . She resolutely refuses to see a doctor. . . . God only knows how all this is to terminate (*Life*, II, 81).

This is from a letter of 23 November 1848. There is another of 10 December, from which Mrs Gaskell cleverly includes a second paragraph about visitors and estrangements, thus suggesting Charlotte's anxiety to turn to some other subject; but in vain, for the letter returns to Emily at the end: 'If Emily were but well, I feel as if I should not care who neglected, mis-understood or abused me,' and Emily's thanks for a cheese—'I wish she were well enough to eat it' (*Life*, II, 83). Mrs Gaskell takes up the story again, describing Charlotte's visit to the moors in wild December 'for a lingering spray of heather—just one spray, however withered—to take in to Emily', and doing so, Charlotte 'saw that the flower was not recognized by the dim and indifferent eyes' (*Life*, II, 83). This incident suggests in its brevity and concentration the deep attachment of the sisters, Emily's affinity with the wild heathland, the terrible pathos of her indifference to its beloved flower and the consequent poignancy of Charlotte's suffering on seeing such indifference. Then, by sudden contrast, Mrs Gaskell speaks about Emily's independence to the last, her insistence on getting up and trying to sew; 'the servants looked on, and knew what the catching, rattling breath, and the glazing of the eye too surely foretold; but she kept at her work' (*Life*, II, 83–4). She died that same day, before two in the afternoon. Then there is a letter of Charlotte's, expressing the relief and the calm: 'the anguish of seeing her suffer is over. . . . No need now to tremble for the hard frost and the keen wind. Emily does not feel them.' A final paragraph tells of Keeper, 'Emily's fierce, faithful bulldog', following her to her grave, and then lying at her bedroom-door and howling for days afterwards. The last sentence of the chapter reads with laconic matter-of-factness: 'Anne Brontë drooped and sickened more rapidly from that time; and so ended the year 1848' (*Life*, II, 85). Anne's last days are described in contrast with those of Emily. They were quiet and touching; she slid into death.

In one sense the *Life of Charlotte Brontë* was an intentional piece of hagiography. As its author said, her aim was to 'show what a noble, true and tender woman Charlotte Brontë was' (*Life*, II, 277). This aim is intermingled with the continual indication of Mrs Gaskell's sorrow for Charlotte's lot and regret for what in better surroundings she might have become. Mrs Gaskell considered that Haworth and Charlotte's home exercised an influence both strong and baneful. In a letter to Lady Kay-Shuttleworth on 7 April 1853 she wrote:

What would have been her transcendent grandeur if she had been brought up in a healthy and happy atmosphere no one can tell; but her life sounds like the fulfilment of duties to her father, to the poor around her, to the old servants (154).

Yet this was in the years of Charlotte's literary fame, those years of contact with the great world, of visits to London and meetings with celebrities such as Thackeray. These years indeed supplied something of that 'craving for keen enjoyment of life' mentioned by Mrs Gaskell in this same letter, and mentioned disapprovingly as being excessive. Such craving was no doubt a reaction to the general dullness of life, but it was probably also accentuated by the extreme excitableness and sensitive nature of Charlotte's own temperament. We see this, for instance, in her response to rebuke as a governess. This excitableness may also have affected and exaggerated her passion for M. Héger. It may also have determined that settled pessimism, the 'absence of hope' (*Life*, I, 134) which Mrs Gaskell found even in the early correspondence. Surely it manifested itself again in Charlotte's exhaustion, headache and sickness after her first interview with her publisher, George Smith, during the Chapter Coffee-House visit. Here it assumed the form of nervous shyness as it did during Charlotte's stay in Manchester with the Gaskells (*Life*, II, 296–7). Greater intercourse with the world at large did nothing to reduce this affliction.

Charlotte's concern about her appearance is another reflection of her exaggerated sensitiveness. She thought herself extremely ugly, but if people were struck by her appearance, it may well have been by its peculiarity rather than its ugliness. Mrs Gaskell describes her features as 'plain, large and ill-set . . . the crooked mouth and the large nose', but she mentions these to say that they were forgotten by reason of the fact that the eyes 'large and well shaped; their colour a reddish brown' with the iris composed of a greater variety of tints, and the 'power of the countenance over-balanced every physical defect' (*Life*, I, 104–5).

The interplay between heightened expectation and frustrating actuality may have been a determining influence in Charlotte Brontë's writings, out of which arose that uncontrollable, spontaneous, self-directing power to which she refers in a letter to Lewes about *Jane Eyre*:

When authors write best, or, at least, when they write most fluently, an influence seems to waken in them which becomes their master—which will have its own way—putting out of view all behests but its own, dictating certain words, and insisting on their being used, whether vehement or measured in their nature (quoted *Life*, II, 53).

Mrs Gaskell did not fully understand such a concept of authorship, and this may explain her attempts at times to apologize for Charlotte, as, for example, in the lines in which the sisters' experience with Branwell is used to excuse some of the more violent passages of the novels (cf. II, 288–9). This same attitude reveals itself again in remarks to Lady Kay-Shuttleworth: 'I am sure she works off a great deal that is morbid *into* her writing, and *out* of her life' (154). Charlotte probably did, but Mrs Gaskell seems to see it as altogether too deliberate, almost as an act of psychotherapy rather than, as Charlotte herself saw it, the outworking of overpowering inspiration.

We associate this phenomenon among the Brontë sisters most closely with Emily and with *Wuthering Heights*. Mrs Gaskell speaks of 'the immature, but very real powers' of that book (*Life*, II, 49), and in introducing her reference to it, she quotes Charlotte's preface to the second edition at some length, stressing Emily's isolation from human contact and her sombre imagination. Mrs Gaskell did not understand Emily's literary power, and though she tried to describe her accurately and without repugnance as 'that free, wild, untameable spirit, never happy nor well but on the sweeping moors that gathered round her home—that hater of strangers doomed to live among them' (*Life*, I, 168) she did not really like her. Indeed, an awed fascination permeates the narrative as Mrs Gaskell describes Emily, that strong strange character, beating her fierce bulldog and beloved pet, Keeper, into cringing submission for his repeated disobedience in sleeping on the beds (*Life*, I, 318–21). Keeper was the model for the bulldog Tartar in *Shirley* and Shirley herself was based on Emily. Presenting this fact, Mrs Gaskell makes the most forthright statement of her own view of Emily: 'All that I, a stranger, have been able to learn about her has not tended to give either me, or my readers, a pleasant impression of her' (*Life*, II, 116).

There were others also in the Brontë circle that she did not much like, but she could not always say so. I have mentioned some of the difficulties she had with Mr Nicholls and, before that, she had feared from what Charlotte told her that their friendship might well be affected by his Anglican hatred of Dissenters. In the *Life*, however, she pays tribute to his love for Charlotte and to his conscientious work as a minister of religion, though not without one or two oblique references of another sort, such as: 'He was not a man to be attracted by any kind of literary fame' (*Life*, II, 278). The qualification in the opening paragraph of the chapter from which this quotation comes may also be intended to speak more than appears; in writing the biography, Mrs Gaskell states that she resolved to withhold 'nothing, though some things from their very nature, could not be spoken of so fully as others' (*Life*, II, 277).

Elsewhere, however, she was not so reticent, not even about Patrick Brontë. Mary Taylor saw what should be said and the difficulties of saying it. In a letter to Ellen Nussey she spoke of the 'gloomy anger' with which she contemplated 'Charlotte's sacrifices to the selfish old man'. She went on:

But how on earth is all this to be set straight! Mrs Gaskell seems far too able a woman to put her head into such a wasp nest, as she would raise about her by speaking the truth of living people.[1]

Mary Taylor was speaking particularly about Patrick Brontë's original opposition to Charlotte's marriage. Because of this, Nicholls departed in June 1853, but returned within less than a year. Mrs Gaskell is careful to conceal the reasons for Patrick Brontë's change of mind, and there is only oblique reference to his selfishness as an important factor determining Charlotte's acquiescence in his refusal. 'Thus thoughtfully for her father, and unselfishly for herself, [she] put aside all consideration of how she should reply, excepting as he wished!' (*Life*, II, 279). The degree of Charlotte's self-sacrifice is ubiquitously evident; practically every letter includes some reference to her father's health, her concern for him, her efforts on his behalf.

But if Mrs Gaskell was discreet here, she was not discreet enough in her original description of him (*Life*, I, 56-9). There, drawing on the accounts of villagers and servants, she spoke of his 'strong passionate Irish nature', his long, lonely walks, his 'strong and vehement prejudices'; but she did not confine herself to these. She also described his eccentricities and harsh behaviour. A short paragraph in the third edition (*Life*, I, 56) refers to his

[1] S.H.B., IV, 198.

attempts to make the children hardy, but the first edition contained more detail. It described the servant's putting coloured shoes by the fire to warm in readiness for the children's return from the moors in the rain and Mr Brontë's burning the shoes because they were 'too gay and luxurious for his children'. Other incidents excluded from the third edition include the slashing of one of his wife's dresses, his custom of firing pistols out of the back-door when he was annoyed, his burning the hearth-rug and sawing up chairs (*Life*, 1st ed., I, 51–2). All this, with the exception of the slashing of the dress, Mrs Gaskell had, she says, from 'a good old woman who came to nurse Mrs Brontë in her last illness' (*Life*, I, 54). The dress-cutting episode she attributed to Charlotte's telling (368). In a letter of 25 August 1850 to Catherine Winkworth she referred to 'an old woman at Burnley who nursed her at last' (75), going on to give details of the kind mentioned above, but concluding 'All this Lady K. S. told me'. George Smith must have been worried about stories such as these, for in a letter to Ellen Nussey of 9 July 1856 Mrs Gaskell indicated that he had objected to certain passages, but she commented: 'I thought that I carefully preserved the reader's respect of Mr Brontë, while truth and the desire of doing justice to her compelled me to state the domestic peculiarities of her childhood' (294). Patrick Brontë at first expressed himself satisfied with the *Life*. His letter of 2 April 1857 contains only congratulations, no complaints, just a reference to 'a few trifling mistakes' (S.H.B., IV, 220–1); but within a few days he was complaining, and the work of excision had to begin.

There were numerous objectors, from Martha Brown, the Brontës' servant, to Harriet Martineau. The former complained of a reference to a story told to Mrs Gaskell by Patrick Brontë of the grief of a young village girl who had been seduced and whom Charlotte had befriended (S.H.B., IV, 194). Mrs Gaskell altered the word 'seduced' to 'betrayed' (*Life*, II, 335). Harriet Martineau complained of a statement made by Charlotte in a letter that is quoted to explain the misunderstanding that arose between them over Harriet's criticism of *Villette*. She is pacified by a footnote (*Life*, II, 289–90). Patrick Brontë had to give the sisters Sarah and Nancy Garrs, his former servants, a signed testimonial that they had been kind to the children, honest and not wasteful (S.H.B., IV, 226). John Stuart Mill objected to quotation of Charlotte's comments on an article about the emancipation of women written by the woman he was to marry and published in *The Westminster Review* which he edited (*Life*, II, 233–234). He too had to be allotted a footnote. G. H. Lewes resented the suggestion that his review of *Shirley* had been disrespectful to women, and so the third edition inserts the clause: 'Now although this review of 'Shirley' is not disrespectful towards women . . .' (*Life*, II, 143).

These were some of the objections. There were still others, some indeed which Mrs Gaskell anticipated, for in a letter of 2 October 1856 she wrote to Smith:

Do you mind the law of libel—I have three people I want to libel—Lady Scott (that bad woman who corrupted Branwell Brontë), Mr Newby & Lady Eastlake—the first and last not to be mentioned by name, the mean publisher to be gibbeted (314).

The mean publisher was T. C. Newby, who brought out *Wuthering Heights* and *Agnes Grey* and in what amounted to sharp practice sold the American rights of *The Tenant of Wildfell Hall* as being another book by Currer Bell

(*Life*, II, 66). (The Chapter Coffee-House visit was undertaken to prove both to Newby and to Messrs Smith and Elder that Currer, Ellis and Acton Bell were not, as Newby conveniently alleged, one and the same person.) Lady Eastlake was attacked for her cruel review of *Jane Eyre* with a veritable flurry of rhetorical questions and emotion-charged phrases, of which the following is a sample:

Has he [the reviewer], through trials, close following in dead march through his household, sweeping the hearthstone bare of life and love, still striven hard for strength to say, 'It is the Lord! let Him do what seemeth to Him good'—and sometimes striven in vain, until the Kindly Light returned? If through all these dark waters the scornful reviewer passed clear, refined, free from stain,—with a soul that never in all its agonies, cried 'lama sabachthani',—still, even then let him pray with the Publican rather than judge with the Pharisee (*Life*, II, 88).

This attack did not bring retaliation, but there was a vigorous reaction against Mrs Gaskell from the defenders of Lady Scott and the Rev. William Carus Wilson, founder of Cowan Bridge School. The third edition's sentences on the Branwell-Lady Scott affair: 'Of the causes of this [Branwell's] deterioration I cannot speak' (*Life*, I, 326) and the paragraph: 'Whatever may have been the nature of Branwell's sins. . . . Let us read of the misery caused to his poor sisters in Charlotte's own affecting words' (*Life*, I, 336–7) are but the poor relics of the extensive and unmitigated attack in the first edition. There one reads:

The story must be told. If I could, I would have avoided it; but not merely is it so well-known to many living as to be in a manner, public property, but it is possible that, by revealing the misery, the growing, life-long misery, the degrading habits, the early death of her partner in guilt—the acute and long-enduring agony of his family—to the wretched woman, who not only survives, but passes about in the gay circles of London society, as a vivacious, well-dressed, flourishing widow, there may be awakened in her some feelings of repentance (*Life*, 1st ed., I, 316–17).

Mrs Gaskell goes on to refer to this 'mature and wicked woman', Lady Scott (then Mrs Robinson)'s making love to Branwell in front of her children. She speaks about Branwell's lingering of conscience which caused him to reject her suggestions of an elopement. Then she moves on to a veritable crescendo of denunciation:

The case presents the reverse of the usual features; the man becomes the victim; the man's life was blighted, and crushed out of him by suffering, and guilt entailed by guilt; the man's family were stung by deepest shame. The woman—to think of her father's pious name—the blood of honourable families mixed in her veins[1]—her early home, underneath whose roof-tree sat those whose names are held saintlike for their good deeds,—she goes flaunting about to this day in reputable society; a showy woman for her age; kept afloat by her reputed wealth. I see her name in County papers, as one of those who patronise the Christmas balls; and I hear of her in London drawing-rooms. Now let us read not merely of the suffering of her guilty accomplice, but of the misery she caused to innocent victims, whose premature death may, in part, be laid at her door (*Life*, I, 328).[2]

---

[1] She was Lydia, daughter of Thomas Gisborne and Mary Babington, grand-daughter of Thomas Babington and great-niece of Zachary Macaulay, and thus descended from prominent Evangelical families of the 'Clapham Sect'.

[2] Cf. letter to Smith, 29 December 1856 (328): 'About Lady — (did I tell you the name?) I see you think me merciless,—but details

What the truth of the relationship was we shall never know. Some like Sir James Stephen rejected the whole thing as a figment of Branwell's diseased imagination, but then he was Lady Scott's cousin by marriage. Others like Margaret Lane think that 'there *was* a love affair, and that Mrs Robinson's denials covered a skilful retreat from a dangerous position'.[1] The family certainly believed the story. Patrick Brontë applauded Mrs Gaskell's pictures of 'my brilliant and unhappy son, and of his diabolical seducer'[2] and Charlotte wrote: 'A worse woman, I believe, hardly exists.'[3] Mrs Gaskell's account derived from information presumably supplied by Charlotte on the basis of letters said to have been found in Branwell's pockets at his death, but this was hardly evidence enough on which to make such an outspoken attack. Not only were Mrs Gaskell's words unbalanced; they were also

---

of her life (past & present) which I heard from her own cousin when I was staying at Sir C. Trevelyans & which were confirmed by Lady Trevelyan (also a connection) showed her to be a bad heartless woman for long and long,—& to think of her going about calling, & dining out etc. etc.—(her own relations have been obliged to drop her acquaintance) while those poor Brontës suffered so—for bad as Branwell was,—he was not absolutely ruined for ever till she got hold of him, & he was not the first, nor the last. However it is a horrid story, & I should not have told it but to show the life of prolonged suffering those Brontë girls had to endure; & what doubtless familiarized them to a certain degree with coarse expressions such as have been complained of in W.H. & the Tenant of Wildfell Hall. However, I will not name that she was a clergyman's wife—nor that she is a *Lady* anybody. But you see why I wanted to contrast the two lives, don't you?'

[1] *The Brontë Story*, 1953, p. 170.

[2] 2 April 1857, quoted W. Gérin, *Branwell Brontë*, 1961, p. 241. The last phrase is not printed in S.H.B., IV, 221.

[3] July 1848, S.H.B., II, 240.

unwise, and not even necessary. She was prompted by her feeling for the Brontë sisters' suffering beyond her usual discretion. She may also have been affected by the view she derived of Branwell's misspent talents. The end of it all was that, threatened by a libel action, Mrs Gaskell instructed her solicitors to insert a public retraction in *The Times* of 30 May 1857 of every statement 'which imputes to a widowed lady, referred to but not named therein, any breach of her conjugal, her maternal, or of her social duties, and more especially of the statement contained in chapter 13 of the first volume and in chapter 2 of the second volume, which imputes to the lady in question a guilty intercourse with the late Branwell Brontë'.

The Cowan Bridge controversy began in April 1857 with W. W. Carus Wilson (the son of the founder)'s letter to *The Daily News*. It continued until August, with Mr Nicholls taking a notable part on Mrs Gaskell's side. This was, to some extent, the result of the attack's being directed more against Charlotte than against Mrs Gaskell. Changes, however, were made in the text of the *Life*. Mrs Gaskell suppressed passages such as that in which Carus Wilson is said to have replied to complaints about the food 'to the effect that the children were to be trained up to regard higher matters than dainty pampering of the appetite, and . . . he lectured them on the sin of caring over-much for carnal things' (*Life*, 1st ed., 1, 72). Another deleted passage referred to his possessing 'so little knowledge of human nature as to imagine that, by constantly reminding the girls of their dependent position, and the fact that they were receiving their education from the charity of others, he could make them lowly and humble' (*Life*, 1, 77). Here, however, Mrs Gaskell might have drawn on supporting testimony from many of Charlotte's contemporaries at Cowan Bridge. She was thus in a stronger position than in the Lady Scott affair.

Mrs Gaskell had been warned that she was stirring up a hornet's nest; but, anxious as she was to be out of England when the book was published, she appears to have desired this mainly to escape the reviews, favourable or otherwise, rather than because she anticipated such an outburst of criticism and controversy. On 16 June 1857, less than three weeks after her return, she gave Ellen Nussey an account of the various objections (352). Then in lines instinct with feeling, she continued:

I am writing as if I were in famous spirits, and I think I *am* so *angry* that I am almost merry in my bitterness, if you know that state of feeling; but I have cried more since I came home than I ever did before; and never needed kind words so much —& no one gives me them. I *did so try* to *tell the truth*, & I believe *now* I hit as near the truth as any one *could* do. And I weighed every line with my whole power & heart, so that every line should go to its great purpose of making *her* known & valued, as one who had gone through such a terrible life with a brave & faithful heart.

Mrs Gaskell amply succeeded in her purpose. However distressing the contemporary circumstances may have been, she had the satisfaction of knowing that she had tried to tell the whole truth. As the ever forthright Mary Taylor put it in a letter to Ellen Nussey on 28 January 1858: 'As to the mutilated edition that is to come, I am sorry for it. Libellous or not, the first edition was all true' (S.H.B., IV, 229). Mrs Gaskell's biography presents a strange sad life amid strange sad surroundings. It delineates a peculiar genius with a most sympathetic and

understanding pen. Small errors of fact and graver errors
of judgment there were, as Miss Hopkins has very sagely
remarked (p. 199). Even in emphasis and interpretation
we may now feel that Mrs Gaskell was sometimes wrong;
but when all has been said, *The Life of Charlotte Brontë*, in
its sustained and acutely perceptive evocation of a person
and a place, is worthy to be ranked with the great bio-
graphies of English literature. Charles Eliot Norton aptly
remarked of it: 'I know of no biography that has so deep
and touching an interest as this of Miss Brontë—none
other written so tenderly, sympathetically and faith-
fully.'[1]

[1] *Letters of Charles Eliot Norton*, 1913, I, p. 172.

CHAPTER VIII

SHORT STORIES AND SHORT NOVELS

No one who has read *Cranford* will be surprised to find that Mrs Gaskell practised extensively in the genre of the short story, for despite the connexions which exist between the various chapters of that book, there is a self-sufficiency within the separate episodes that helps to make them reminiscent of the short story. Indeed, as I have mentioned, *Cranford* took its origin from a short story, 'The Last Generation in England'.

Four stories had preceded this one, three of them in 1847, later gathered under the title *Life in Manchester*. They were 'Libbie Marsh's Three Eras', 'The Sexton's Hero' and 'Christmas Storms and Sunshine'. These latter two, together with the fourth story 'Hand and Heart', are very slight pieces indeed, and even 'Libbie Marsh's Three Eras' is not very elaborate. It deals with Libbie Marsh's kind ministry to a crippled and dying boy and of the effects of this kindness upon his widowed mother, hitherto an embittered creature. Libbie is one of Mrs Gaskell's good young women, and the tale points its moral very obviously. Good young women and obvious morals are fairly common in these short stories. 'Libbie Marsh's Three Eras' is set in Manchester, and so is the next tale, 'Lizzie Leigh', the first fruits of Mrs Gaskell's long literary association with Dickens. This story was contributed to three numbers of *Household Words* in March and April 1850. By contrast with 'Libbie Marsh's Three Eras', it concerns one of its author's bad young women, Lizzie, who leaves home and declines into prostitution in Manchester.

Mrs Gaskell's mind around the period 1847 to 1850 was concentrated upon life in Manchester, and it is not surprising to find tales like these written almost concurrently with *Mary Barton*. *Cranford* was the next major work, and it, too, is accompanied by its own short story, 'Mr Harrison's Confessions', in *The Ladies' Companion*, February–April 1851. Mrs Gaskell was not, in fact, attracted by tales of Manchester very much after 1850. The Knutsford life which lies behind the inspiration of *Cranford* was much stronger. She returned to it at the last with *Cousin Phillis* (1863), and there are elements in other tales, *The Moorland Cottage* (1850) and *My Lady Ludlow*[1] (1858), which seem suggestive of the locale and way of life of Cranford and its neighbourhood. It is perhaps indicative of the appeal of this setting that these three tales and 'Mr Harrison's Confessions' are among the longest of the minor works, *nouvelles* or short novels rather than short stories. Moreover, with the exception of *The Moorland Cottage*, they do not depend remarkably upon plot; they are much more tales of atmosphere and feeling than of action. *The Moorland Cottage*, however, gives us two portraits, those of Mrs Browne and Maggie, which anticipate characters in Mrs Gaskell's last novel that is also set in an imaginary Knutsford, *Wives and Daughters*. With the single exception of *Sylvia's Lovers* (and even that was inspired by strong associations arising from a visit to

[1] I am indebted to Lady Bromley-Davenport of Capesthorne Hall near Macclesfield, Cheshire, for the information that there is a family tradition that the character of Lady Ludlow was based upon that of Mrs Davenport (later Lady Hatherton), one of Mrs Gaskell's intimate friends.

Whitby), the major works are set in areas familiar to Mrs Gaskell, in Manchester and Knutsford. What she does at length in *Sylvia's Lovers*, she does more frequently in more limited compass in the short stories. She imagines events and histories in places which she knew only from visits. Thus 'The Doom of the Griffiths' (1858) is set in North Wales, 'Half A Lifetime Ago' (1855) in the Lake District, and 'Six Weeks at Heppenheim' (1862), as its title indicates, in Germany.

Much more striking, however, is the extent of the totally unfamiliar in the short stories. 'Lois the Witch' (October 1859), for example, is a story of the New England witch-hunts of 1692. This tale reminds us that Mrs Gaskell often moved back rather further in time in her short stories than she did in her novels. There it was usually no more than half her lifetime ago, to Cranford in the years before or just after the railway came. Among the short stories, one readily recalls some such as 'The Poor Clare' (1856) set in the mid-eighteenth century and 'The Grey Woman' (1861) in the early years of the French Revolution. *My Lady Ludlow*, too, contains its tale within a tale centred upon the Revolution. All these tales are concerned with violence, and in this respect also the short stories differ from the novels. Time after time Mrs Gaskell deals in these narratives with the mysterious and the spectacularly criminal. In 'The Grey Woman' she links her story to the activities of the *Chauffeurs*, a gang of bandits who terrorized whole areas of Eastern France and Western Germany, and in one of her slight pieces 'The Squire's Story' (1853) she constructs her tale around the life of the highwayman Higgins. 'The Poor Clare' is based on a terrible curse which works itself out on the offspring of the woman who uttered it, and 'The Old

Nurse's Story' (1852) is likewise the outworking of a revenge, but in this case with the added refinements of ghostly appearances.

   The short story, it could doubtless be claimed, has been in existence ever since the first anecdote was told, and yet it has also been argued that as an art-form it is a child of this century. Certainly the possibilities that lay within the eighteenth-century essay do not seem to have been developed, and what happens in the nineteenth century really represents a new start. The more extensive reading public of the last century was catered for by numerous periodicals, which provided opportunities for the short-story writer. Because of the custom of serialization, however, a short story did not have to be confined within strict limits. It might be complete in one issue or it might run through as many as ten or even a dozen. Mrs Gaskell wrote both short and long short stories. Hence it is difficult to criticize her achievement as though it represented a body of work in a single manner. I propose therefore to say something about those pieces whose length is more conformable to our notions of the short story and then to consider the longer ones later. Because there was no precise idea of the short story in the nineteenth century the really short story often tended to be too slight not so much in length as in the importance of its subject and theme, and because the form was insufficiently defined the author did not always realize the need for proper emphasis at the various stages of the tale, and especially at the beginning and the end. Time and again Mrs Gaskell is much too leisurely in her introduction. This shows itself, for instance, in tales which depend on the fulfilment of prediction. The beginning represents a move backward in time—over nine generations in 'The Doom of the

Griffiths' and two centuries in 'Morton Hall' (1853), for example; and too much space is given to describing the original prediction. A similar failure in a tale of longer scope is to be found in 'A Dark Night's Work' (1863), where far too much attention is given to the history of Ellinor Wilkins' father's career. What matters for the tale is his downfall and the murder he commits; his social pretensions and the importance of Corbet at the beginning might have been much more succinctly conveyed.

Besides the shortcomings which arise from the working out of what is predicted, there are those which stem from what is predictable. Sometimes inadequacy of this kind does not matter much, because the strength of the tale lies in aspects other than those of plot. Events, however, sometimes turn out almost too good to be true. Thus in 'Six Weeks at Heppenheim' we are not surprised that Thekla eventually marries her employer, nor in 'Lizzie Leigh' that Lizzie is found, nor again in 'The Crooked Branch' (1859) that the worthless son returns to rob his parents' home; but whereas in the first two cases absence of narrative surprise does not matter much, in the last it is more serious, since 'The Crooked Branch' has fewer resources to rely upon once its plot has come under criticism. 'Right at Last' (1858) is inadequate in another way. Admittedly the really short story is limited in opportunity to establish character, but in this tale Mrs Gaskell, after the manner of many a modern detective-story writer, ultimately convicts the least likely character, about whom we have not only not had the smallest hint of suspicion but we have also been told of his extreme reliability. Lest it should be thought that Mrs Gaskell cannot do right in this regard, let it be said that what is really required is what I would call appropriate surprise, that is, an outcome not foreseen but yet in character with what has gone before. This she achieves in 'Half a Lifetime Ago' in which Susan Dixon finds her love of long years ago dying, and then comforts and protects his widow and her family. Of course, surprise is not always necessary. Sometimes it is the sheer inevitability of the predictable that gives a tale its force. This happens, for example, in the career of Edward Browne in *The Moorland Cottage* and, better still, in 'Lois the Witch'. There Mrs Gaskell develops the history of a mass hysteria in such a manner as to keep the reader's attention fascinatedly, almost shudderingly, upon the events. Then when all the terror is over, she brings the tale to a quiet close on a sardonic note about the uselessness of posthumous acquittals and belated confessions of judicial error.

The short tale was, generally speaking, too short for Mrs Gaskell; she needed room in which to spread herself. There was, however, another source of trouble. Too many of her short stories were written to order, usually from Dickens. She provided twenty-four contributions for *Household Words* between 1850 and 1858 (including *Cranford* and *North and South*), and seven of these appeared in a single year (1853). She herself knew how much her work varied in quality, and after the initiation of *The Cornhill Magazine* (published by George Smith) in 1860 she reserved her best work for that and gave the rest to Dickens. She told Smith in a letter of 23 December 1859 of the work she had on hand. Besides *Sylvia's Lovers* there was 'a story of perhaps 40 (of my pages) long. Begun & I think good; intended *for C. M.*' and 'a story, 120 pages of which are written & have been this year & a half; *not very good*, & that would not be above 1 vol. in length.

It is not good enough for the C. M. . . . but might be good enough for *H. W.* [Household Words]. This was the story I once thought of finishing for Mr C. D. [Charles Dickens]' (451*a*). This latter story was 'A Dark Night's Work' (cf. 517, 518), and the other was probably 'Curious if True'.

'A Dark Night's Work' was serialized in five numbers of Dickens' *All the Year Round* in January and February 1863. It is inadequate, as Mrs Gaskell herself thought it to be, and it will serve well for considering the insufficiencies of plot as they are exemplified in her longer works. Others of the *nouvelles* are deficient in plot-structure. *My Lady Ludlow* would not suffer for the excision of the whole of the Crequy incident in revolutionary Paris. *The Moorland Cottage* has one of those spectacular incidents at the end which are not altogether convincing. The ship's fire is difficult enough to accept, but when to this are added the quite unexpected appearance of Maggie's lover, Frank, and the convenient death of her wastrel brother, the strain on credibility becomes too great. This happens in a *nouvelle* which depends closely upon plot. Others much less reliant upon narrative interest—'Mr Harrison's Confessions', *Cousin Phillis*, the main sections of *My Lady Ludlow* are more successful. 'A Dark Night's Work', however, is more like *The Moorland Cottage*. I have already noted its initial long-windedness. After Wilkins' decline has been described at length, the critical event occurs; in a state of drunkenness he strikes his partner Dunster, who falls badly and is killed. Incidentally, when one considers how much has gone before, this character is much too shadowy. There follows next a long tract of story in which nothing of special note occurs. Then at the end, with the finding of Dunster's body and the wrongful condemnation of the faithful servant Dixon, Ellinor has her chance to rescue him by pleading with his judge and her own former lover, Corbet. The end is quite vivid, once one has accepted some glaring unlikelihoods and far-fetched coincidences. 'A Dark Night's Work' has its qualities, but they are not those of plot. Its pace is in general too slow and uneven. Too much is made of too little. Above all, it conveys no sense of internal necessity, no sense that it has to be what it is. Its virtue consists in just those qualities which represent Mrs Gaskell's strength elsewhere, in evocation of atmosphere, understanding of characteristic behaviour and demonstration of her kindly philosophy of life. The same basic fault, flabbiness in plot-structure, is found again in both 'The Grey Woman' and 'The Poor Clare'. The former has the materials for an exciting story—a brigand who appears to be a *grand propriétaire*, married to a girl, who on discovering the truth, deserts him with her maid, an older woman, and is then pursued by her husband. Mrs Gaskell instils some sense of excitement into the latter half of the tale with the chase and its accompanying deeds of terror and moods of fear, but the introduction is altogether too leisurely and the method of narration, allegedly, by letter is both long-winded and retrospective and as a result lacks some of the vividness it might otherwise possess. 'The Poor Clare' is again one of those tales that take so long to start that the reader is puzzled about its direction. Striking characters such as Bridget Fitzgerald (later the poor Clare) and Squire Gisborne attract attention, but there is too much uncertainty about their ultimate purpose.

It lies in the logic of the short story that its very brevity requires economy, the fullest significance for every sentence. By contrast with the tales referred to in the previous paragraph, three may be singled out for their achievement —'Lizzie Leigh', 'Half a Life-time Ago' and 'Lois the Witch'. The scope and method of each is different. The first is the shortest. It begins in an atmosphere of suffering and mystery, a dying father forgiving his absent daughter. The little farm where he dies contrasts with the Manchester whither Lizzie has gone and her mother will shortly go to seek her. The story is of a mother's love which is ultimately rewarded, but the daughter is not so simply wicked as she at first appears. The mother's anxious search is paralleled by Lizzie's no less anxious watch over the daughter that as a prostitute she could not keep but had left to be found and cared for by Susan Palmer. The coincidence of the latter's engagement to Will Leigh is acceptable within the story, and even if the baby's death may seem a moral imposition on the tale, it does not detract from the structural unity and neatness of organization. The use of an obviously moral ending is displayed in many of Mrs Gaskell's tales; acceptance of its presence is almost a necessary condition in reading her work. Critically speaking, we need to question not its presence, but its appropriateness, the way in which the moral arises from the ending and the way in which that ending proceeds suitably from what has gone before. The criterion, that is, is related to the degree of imposition. Thus part of the trouble with the end of *The Moorland Cottage*, quite apart from the extreme narrative unlikelihood, is that it disposes of Edward Browne too conveniently. Three other tales demonstrate varying measures of success. Bridget in 'The Poor Clare' expiates the curse by saving the man who had caused her to utter it. The narrative here assists the moral, for after a predominantly slow-moving and disjointed story the end is vivid and full of action. The moral conclusion of 'The Heart of John Middleton', in which the hero forgives his great enemy when he is at his mercy, may seem more plainly imposed, but in fact it is in accord with the later history of Middleton who has undergone a Methodist-type conversion. The end of this story is, however, by no means so natural as that of 'Half a Life-time Ago' where the moral arises from and is fully incorporated within the action.

For unity of tone and structure, this tale is wellnigh perfect. Everything fits—the place, the character, the events. Like 'Lizzie Leigh', it catches our attention at once with a reference to what life has done and to the unspoken pity that those who have known Susan Dixon long enough have for her. They remember that 'that tall, gaunt, hard-featured angular woman—who never smiled and hardly spoke an unnecessary word—had been a fine-looking girl, bright-spirited and rosy';[1] but whereas 'Lizzie Leigh' goes forward into the future, this tale explains the past that has made this woman what she is, skilfully demonstrating the oppositions of Susan's love for Michael Hurst and her responsibility for her half-wit brother, and giving its history of a broken engagement, a long illness and longer years of caring for her brother. The story is neatly divided into a three-act drama, as Mrs Gaskell herself describes it, consisting of Susan's early happiness, her long sorrow, and her final years. At the

[1] Vol. v, p. 280. In referring to the short stories it is necessary to indicate the volume in which they occur in the Knutsford edition. The titles of the relevant volumes are:

Vol. i, *Mary Barton and Other Tales*; Vol. ii, *Cranford and Other Tales*; Vol. v, *My Lady Ludlow and Other Tales*; Vol. vii, *Cousin Phillis and Other Tales*.

end she finds Michael, now a dissipated and unsuccessful farmer, dying in a snowstorm almost on her doorstep. She goes to tell his wife, her victorious rival of those years ago, the mother of children who might have been hers. They all go to live with Susan, and a sad life's latter days find not joy, for that is impossible, but a purposeful consolation. The end is moral, but it is also completely at one with what has gone before. In a harsh world the firm and resolute nature of Susan Dixon flinches neither in youth nor age from the responsibilities placed upon it. The success of this tale depends crucially upon its central character, but others also fit perfectly, for Mrs Gaskell knew the place and the people. It is not fanciful, surely, to think that, as she wrote it, she had in mind people like the Prestons, with whom she sometimes stayed at their home near Skelwith, the exact area in which this story is set. It is not inappropriate either to recall that the original version of this tale was entitled 'Martha Preston'. Of the family she wrote to Charles Bosanquet that Mrs Preston was a 'Stateswoman',

. . . a fine true friendly sensible woman. . . . Wordsworth once said of the Prestons that they were a 'Homeric family'. I am sorry to say the father sometimes drinks. . . . Mrs Preston's family have lived in that house and on that land for more than 200 years, as I have heard. They have no ambition but much dignity (439a).

Setting, plot and character coalesce with even greater aptness in the quite different tale of 'Lois the Witch'. Salem is a place both of repressions and exaggerations. Its atmosphere even in the initial period of comparative normality is full of foreboding, and when Lois refers to the old crone back in England who had predicted that none would save Lois herself when she was brought up for a witch (vol. VII, p. 122), we feel that we hardly need to be told by Mrs Gaskell beforehand that 'all present had reason, before many months had passed over, to remember the word which Lois spoke' (p. 121). By little details of behaviour and speech we learn at the outset of the intense religious fervour and unbalanced psychological condition of the community in which Lois finds herself. All its passions are abnormal, Faith Hickson's hatred of Pastor Tappau for banishing a rival pastor whom she loves, Manasseh Hickson's half-mad love for Lois herself, the young Prudence Hickson's petulant dislike of Lois which later, stimulated by jealousy of Hester Tappau's notoriety in exposing the first witch, is to bring about the denunciation of Lois. It is an insane society, breeding hate in the name of Christianity. It is a society helpless to do any other, and events, once they have begun to move, go forward in relentless and ever-increasing acceleration to catastrophe. Lois's balance, happiness and human dignity are anomalies in Salem. She has to die. It is a neat touch on Mrs Gaskell's part to use the poor crazed Manasseh to deflate the gargantuan pretensions to divine agency which characters such as Tappau and Cotton Mather assume. He puts these Calvinistic Puritans in a fine theological dilemma by arguing that the whole witchcraft episode 'must have been foredoomed in the counsels of God. If so, why punish her for doing that in which she had no free-will?' (p. 188). After the frenzy that reaches its climax in the trial, the mood becomes solemn in the quiet days before Lois's execution. It would have been easy for Mrs Gaskell simply to pit the nobility of her heroine against the insane wickedness of Salem, and, so far as characters like Tappau are concerned, this seems in fact to be the case. In their authoritative and self-righteous persecution such figures are nauseating examples of a repressive, death-directing creed. Other characters, however, are not so simplified. In particular, Lois's aunt, Mrs Hickson, stern as ever Puritan was made, really believes in her niece's sin, and there is something plainly pathetic as well as tragically ridiculous in her bidding Lois to release Manasseh from his infatuation for her. 'Lois the Witch' possesses an intensity unusual in Mrs Gaskell's short stories. There is little relaxation of narrative pressure, and even what there is is usually there to provide a prelude by which to impress us the more strongly by what follows. Realization of environment, disposition of incident, control of pace, opposition of characters, all go to make this one of the most convincing of her short stories.

Much of the power of this piece and of 'Half a Lifetime Ago' derives from characterization. Indeed, Mrs Gaskell never seems to have much trouble with plot when she is able to imagine her characters fully and precisely. The longer tales obviously give her fuller scope, but among the shorter ones the appeal of Mrs Leigh, briefly but firmly sketched, gives force to 'Lizzie Leigh' and in their opposite ways the delineation of Openshaw and Thekla make 'A Manchester Marriage' and 'Six Weeks at Heppenheim' respectively memorable. Most of Mrs Gaskell's eccentrics are women. She imagined the characters of women far better than those of men, and the eccentric is a type which makes great demands upon strength. The distortion of caricature, if unsuccessful, can easily become a more resounding failure than inadequate portrayal of more rounded characters. Openshaw is as near eccentricity as any of Mrs Gaskell's male characters, with his comically brusque proposal of marriage and his decisive views on most subjects. He is neatly balanced by his quite ordinary wife; and his love for her child develops an appropriate sympathy for him in the reader. When his wife's first husband Wilson returns after being thought dead (in a variant of the *Sylvia's Lovers* situation), the mood of the tale turns from comedy and tenderness to potential tragedy. Wilson resolves the situation, after looking his last upon his child (again we note the comparison with *Sylvia's Lovers*), by going away without letting his wife know of his return and drowning himself. Mrs Gaskell quietly records that from that day Openshaw was 'curiously changed' and she concludes by telling of his taking his stepdaughter to her father's grave and recounting the story to her. 'For the fate of that poor father whom she had never seen he shed the only tears she ever saw fall from his eyes' (vol. v, p. 523). It is the mark of a good story that it should seem to possess the ability to reveal more than it does, and when it does reveal, that its revelation is as exact as we would expect it to be. This is what happens in 'A Manchester Marriage', and it happens largely because Openshaw contains within him resources that never seem extended to their limits.

In 'Six Weeks at Heppenheim' with its restrained delineation of Thekla, the kindly maid-servant, deeply but very unwisely in love with a worthless acquaintance of her girlhood, we encounter another precisely imagined character and condition. It is a quiet tale, of the kind in which Mrs Gaskell excelled, not without its pathos nor its comedy. We are engaged in the events through the presence of a narrator, for whom Thekla is doing her part in bringing him back to health after a sudden illness whilst on a walking tour in Germany. The story is set in the idyllic days of the vine-harvest and no doubt owes much in this respect to Mrs Gaskell's reminiscences of holidays in the area. This effect is increased by the sense of the narrator's own enjoyment of the time and the place. The autobiographical standpoint is forcefully employed on a number of occasions elsewhere and is particularly suitable for the establishment of an intimate atmosphere. (This is especially exemplified by *Cousin Phillis*.) The sense of participation in suffering helps us better to understand the sufferer, and the nearness of the narrator to Thekla in 'Six Weeks at Heppenheim' helps to make her sympathetic. Her goodness to him, his understanding of her position, the expression of the reader's own hopes and fears by the narrator himself all contribute to this effect. He is also useful as a means of extracting information from Thekla that otherwise might have to be reported by the omniscient author, with consequent loss of the expression of her feelings as she gives the information. The principal success of the characterization of Thekla derives then not so much from what she is, for she is quite a simple character, but rather from the way in which she is regarded.

Thekla, however, also belongs very much to the circumstances and environment of the tale. The interaction of individual and surroundings is evident in all of Mrs Gaskell's best work. Sometimes atmosphere and environment, ways of life and attitudes to life, give a sense of solidity to character as in the Lake District tale of Susan Dixon. At other times the effect is almost directly opposite, an alienation of character from environment, producing a sense of instability and crisis as in 'Lois the Witch'. The worlds of both these tales are hard and trying in their different ways. Those of other stories are quieter, more serene, in the popular mind perhaps more typical of Mrs Gaskell. This is the case, for instance, with *My Lady Ludlow*, *Cousin Phillis* and 'Mr Harrison's Confessions', which together with *The Moorland Cottage* we may consider now as representing their author's broad achievement in the realm of the *nouvelle*.

The Moorland Cottage was a work about which Mrs Gaskell herself had reservations. She told Eliza Fox: 'I have been writing a story for Xmas; a very foolish engagement of mine—which I am angry with myself for taking' (79). It is really a simple story of a family in which the worthless boy, Edward Browne, is favoured by his mother at his sister Maggie's expense. Mrs Gaskell skilfully exploits the contrast in character and treatment between brother and sister. The tale goes on to tell of Edward's self-indulgence eventually bringing him into trouble with the law and of the difficulties in the way of Maggie's love-affair with Frank Buxton. The crisis is powerfully presented as a dilemma for Maggie, who must decide for her lover or her brother when Mr Buxton offers not to prosecute Edward if she will renounce her love. The development of the plot shows how Mrs Gaskell can rely quite adequately upon the most economical resources. The end is therefore all the more unsuitable. It is out of accord both from the point of view of plot-structure and tone. It is both melodramatic and improbable. Mrs Gaskell adopted a desperate device at once to save Maggie and to get rid of Edward. It brought into the open a danger that lurks throughout the story, but which up to this point she had managed to confine within bounds, namely, that Maggie appeared too good and Edward too bad. With Edward there is some sense of development, of increasing moral deterioration. Thus when he returns home desperately fleeing from arrest, the sensation is not outrageous. The event has proceeded from the history of the character. By contrast, the fire on the ship is just a convenient device, an accident whose arbitrariness is only made more evident when to it is added the further arbitrariness of saving Maggie and Frank and killing Edward. Maggie herself succeeds as a character because of the manifest sincerity with which she has been imagined, but like Molly Gibson, for whom she looks much like a trial sketch, she does seem occasionally almost too good-tempered, too self-sacrificing, too long-suffering, too forgiving. It is only almost, because she is saved by the juxtaposition of her character both to the good group (the Buxtons) and more especially to the not so good. Her mother's criticism, for instance, is of such a kind as to make us sympathize so much with Maggie that it makes her more readily acceptable. Mrs Browne is the greatest success of the work, and she too was to be a predecessor for a fuller portrait, probably the greatest of all Mrs Gaskell's creations, that of Mrs Gibson in *Wives and Daughters*. Another way in which the air of convincing verisimilitude is maintained in this tale is by its use of dialogue; Mrs Browne's criticism is particularly well done with its suggestions of her petulance, partiality and small-mindedness. The more Mrs Gaskell seems at home with her characters, the more she is prepared to rely on dialogue to convey her effects. Despite its imperfections, *The Moorland Cottage* is probably a better tale than its author thought it was at the time she wrote it.

'Mr Harrison's Confessions' belongs to the same period. It is almost as episodic as *Cranford* and its world is much the same. It is allegedly the story of Surgeon Harrison's wooing of his wife, but all Duncombe comes into it with its rounds of visiting, picnics, dinners and illnesses. All the fuss and the goodwill of small-town society is conveyed, and there is plenty of variety in the incidents. There is the sadness of little Walter's sudden illness and death, the pathos of Miss Bullock, victim of her parents' mania to marry her off, and the light satire of a group of spinsters who obviously belong to Cranford, no matter by what other name it may be called. Harrison himself tells the story, and he does so as a newcomer from a larger world, able to assess the affairs of Duncombe at less than its inhabitants are accustomed to do. Mrs Gaskell aptly opposes him to his partner, the old-established doctor Morgan, the modern against the ancient; and there are some conflicts about treatment in which the town is on the side of Morgan, as we might expect, but also in which Harrison proves to be right. Mrs Gaskell, however, is not content with such a simple opposition. There is a laugh for Duncombe as well as a triumph for Harrison. She shows with exquisite touches how, even as he feels himself different from, more modern than, Duncombe, Harrison is also being moulded by the town and its ways. He never does the hunting he had proposed for himself, and when the loud-spoken practical joker Jack Marshland arrives, by his talk we are made to mark the contrast between the lively pranks of the medical students (albeit in Harrison's case by no means so bad as his friend suggests) and the decorous parlour-games that the young doctor is now playing. In fact, far from hunting, much of the book's comedy arises from Harrison's being hunted. Almost every spinster in the village, eligible and not so eligible, seems to want him. The notable exceptions are Miss Bullock, who is thrust upon him, and Sophy Hutton, with whom he is in love. In this story the autobiographical standpoint adds to the comedy and to the pleasantness of the work. Harrison is able to laugh at himself. At the same time, by the variety of situations in which she places him and the sense of his learning from the experience with which she endows him, Mrs Gaskell is able to produce a fully rounded character.

In evoking the atmosphere of place in 'Mr Harrison's Confessions' she relies considerably upon the group of women characters she creates—the imperious Miss Tomkinson, the simpering and affected Miss Caroline, the spiteful Miss Horsman. *My Lady Ludlow* also depends much upon its chief women characters, Lady Ludlow herself principally, of course, but also Miss Galindo, one of the best of Mrs Gaskell's minor characters. Margaret Dawson, who tells this tale, claims that it is 'no story; it has . . . neither beginning, middle, nor end' (vol. v, p. 9). This is not strictly true, but one might well argue that the events hardly matter in themselves, and that their sequence is only minimally necessary. Character is what matters, and what people say and do, and think of what other people say and do. Lady Ludlow herself is a kind of aristocratic anachronism, a benevolent autocrat and a lovable reactionary. Like Miss Jenkyns in *Cranford*, she opposes all change, but when she sees the good it has done, she readily accepts it. She is one of Mrs Gaskell's mildly satirical and attractive characters. Miss Galindo is markedly eccentric, but, like Lady Ludlow, she is endowed with extreme kindliness and enjoys the golden opinions of others. In *My Lady Ludlow* Mrs Gaskell creates a whole village-society from the lady of the manor down to the poacher Gregson. She shows how each regards the other, delineating the relationships of parson and lady of the manor, agent and mistress, lady of the manor and other independent ladies in the village, parson and labourer and so on. Altogether, a sense of depth is given to the circumstances of the story. It does not therefore matter that so little seems to happen. She is re-creating the very being of the society she describes.

In the last and best of her shorter works, *Cousin Phillis*, Mrs Gaskell focuses interest upon a single family. The story is told by Paul Manning about events which took place when he and Phillis were in their teens. It is really quite slight, a matter of Phillis's falling in love with Paul's superior, Holdsworth, of her breakdown after hearing of his marriage in Canada and of her slow return to health. The setting again is Knutsford (here called Eltham) and its neighbourhood, the time the coming of the railway. Not least of the work's qualities is its loving description of the countryside and its evocation of rural ways of life. The narrative standpoint is again cleverly placed. Paul at the time of the story is young, old enough to appreciate the attractions of Phillis, but not so sophisticated as the slightly older Holdsworth. Paul is unlearned enough to marvel at the intellectual attainments of Phillis and even more of her father, the remarkable minister-farmer Holman. Paul's apparent inferiority contributes to the sense of helplessness before events, a sense that is accentuated in that this is a book without any wickedness in it. Holdsworth does not trifle with Phillis's affections; her hopes are raised only by Paul's simply reporting something that he has said. As Paul describes him, 'Thou wast a delightful fellow! Ay, and a good one too; though much sorrow was caused by thee!' (vol. VII, p. 53).

The degrees of importance of the various characters are excellently realized. There is much that is missing from Holdsworth, but we never regret the omissions. He is sufficient for his role. Even better is the distinction between the relative importance of the mother over against the father and the daughter. She is there much more for the setting of the household than for herself. By contrast, the individuality of Holman is strongly suggested by his distinctive and unusual characteristics. That, however, could have been done if he had been just a static character. He is, in fact, much more than this, and Mrs Gaskell uses his qualities of character excellently to give pace to the sequence of her events, verisimilitude to his encounters especially with Holdsworth, and then at the end to show how this formidable man is really as tender as we have often previously suspected him of being, when all his bustle and purposefulness is put aside for his care of and deep anxiety about his sick daughter. Phillis, by contrast, is more passive, but the qualities of the good girl— maidenly affections, modesty, gentleness—are suggested without any hint of sentimentality or insipidity.

The world of *Cousin Phillis* is, on the whole, a happy one; critics often describe it as idyllic. It is marred by the heroine's illness, but even then we have to admire the goodness, tenderness and concern of all around her. Mrs Gaskell's achievement here has the appearance of that perfect spontaneity which marks the consummate artist. Setting is lovingly and attractively drawn, characters are exact even down to the farm-labourers who make but two or three appearances, plot is scanty yet sufficient, tone is perfectly modulated throughout, the author's own attitude is generous and kindly without any hint of deliberate moralizing. The whole work has about it the perfection of a delicate piece of china, but it has also abundant human warmth. It crowns its author's achievement in the realm of the short story and the short novel. This achievement came at the end of a long and sometimes uneven progress. It shows that here too, as in her novels, Mrs Gaskell appeared to have become endowed with new energy and new vision in her last years.

The overall achievement is so mixed, the degree of her own interest so varied, that it is difficult briefly to estimate Mrs Gaskell's work as a writer of short stories and *nouvelles*. What can be said is that, generally speaking, her powers of plot-construction were not strong enough to make her a predominantly successful author in these kinds. Where a simple plot will suffice, she does quite well. Often, however, she finds herself trying to do too much with too little. Her strength lies rather in her ability to create character, to evoke mood, to establish a sense of place. In her best tales her success derives from the fact that her characters belong to the atmosphere and environment in which she has set them. Usually they are found in surroundings which she knew well herself, but occasionally, as with 'Lois the Witch', an alien world is powerfully imagined. What remains lastingly memorable is the succession of characters Mrs Gaskell created—Susan Dixon, Lois, Maggie Browne, Thekla, Holman, Phillis and a host of others—characters as sympathetic as she herself was. They represent aspects of their creator's own moral vision of life. Because of this, deficient though many of the stories may be in one way and another, we would not easily forgo the best of them.

CHAPTER IX

'SYLVIA'S LOVERS'

MRS Gaskell's contemporaries were quick to realize what a difference there was between her last two and her earlier novels. In the concluding remarks which Greenwood, the editor of *The Cornhill Magazine*, appended to *Wives and Daughters*, her last novel which lay unfinished at her death, we read: 'Mrs Gaskell had within these five years started upon a new career with all the freshness of youth.' He seems, however, to have placed too much emphasis upon what may be called a moral transformation. He talks about 'a mind which seemed to have put off its clay and to have been born again' and of a 'purer intelligence that prefers to deal with emotions and passions which have a living root in minds within the pale of salvation, and not with those that rot without it'. This seems a peculiarly narrow way of looking at the matter, and perhaps arises from the Victorians' too exclusively and deliberately ethical mode of considering literature which at times resulted in distorted judgment. Greenwood does, in fact, concede by exception that *Sylvia's Lovers* would not quite fit his pattern. He talks of 'this spirit [being] more especially declared in "Cousin Phillis" and "Wives and Daughters"'. He also accepts that the world of these last novels is 'one where there is much weakness, many mistakes, sufferings long and bitter, but where it is possible for people to live calm and wholesome lives'. In the first part of this last quotation he must have had *Sylvia's Lovers* clearly in view, but the latter part is not wholly true about this book. Greenwood's statement rightly notes that a change has taken place in Mrs Gaskell's work, but it fails perfectly to recognize the nature of that change. The movement is not towards 'the purer air of the heaven-aspiring hills', it is not making everything simpler, not a journey into the serene. Mrs Gaskell was too much aware of the human condition to take such a facile direction. The really significant change that has taken place is shown in her new realization and grasp of the complexity that underlies the apparently simplest lives; there has been a growth in imagination. This growth was fortunately matched by an advance in her technical powers as a novelist, with the result that in *Sylvia's Lovers* she can tell a story of primal passions reminiscent at times of *Wuthering Heights*, and then within two years she can give us a very different and quieter tale whose delicacy and subtlety invites occasional comparison with Jane Austen.

Sylvia's Lovers did not appear until 1863, some eight years after her previous major novel *North and South*, but it was commissioned by Smith, Elder at the end of 1859. Mrs Gaskell took a holiday at Whitby in November of that year, and those few days must have brought to birth what she called 'the saddest story I ever wrote'.[1] Dean Liddell thought it 'like a Greek tragedy, for power'.[2] It is, indeed, Mrs Gaskell's most massive attempt at treatment of the passions, and the more impressively so for its choosing the simplest of people to convey the conflicts of the drama. In this saddest of her stories she shows suffering inexplicable, inescapable, relentless, destroying. It may, of course, be said that it is all perfectly explicable, and indeed, it is as a sequence of events, of result inevitably

[1] Knutsford edition, p. xii.   [2] Ibid., p. xxvi, note.

proceeding from cause, but it remains inexplicable on the deeper metaphysical level. Why does it have to happen? Why is so much visited for so little? One is even left asking questions still more baffling, asking them as Hardy often asks them, but Mrs Gaskell never betrays anything like the feeling of supernatural contrivance, the postulation of a malign deity, which is found in Hardy's novels. Why do the life-paths of some of these characters have to cross at all? Once they have crossed, there is then only a sense of helplessness. Philip cannot help falling in love with Sylvia, nor can she help her inability to return that love nor even the readiness of her response to Kinraid. No more can Philip help not being able to return the love of Hester Rose, whose temperament is so much more like his own than that of Sylvia. Sylvia and Hester speak of this, and Mrs Gaskell summarizes the whole tragic confusion thus: 'Sylvia was thinking how strange life was, and how love seemed to go all at cross purposes; and was losing herself in bewilderment at the mystery of the world' (p. 469). Happiness is so ineluctable and, when found, so fragile; and our efforts to find it may well result in our obtaining the opposite of what we seek.

Sylvia's Lovers is a passionate story. Passion opposes apparent prudence. On the one side, there is the common sense and reliability, the deep affection and care of Philip, associated with town and trade, encouraged by Sylvia's mother; on the other, there is the dashing Kinraid, linked with the danger and adventure of the sea, supported by Sylvia's garrulous father. Herein lies the conflict of the book. Prudence is so much sounder, but also so much less exciting. Passion is preferable, and Sylvia therefore chooses Kinraid. For the same reason Philip chooses

PLATE II

Mrs Gaskell, 1864–5, from the portrait by
Samuel Laurence

Sylvia when he might have had Hester. Philip, that is, is only apparently prudent. But prudence itself may not be a sure guide. Sylvia leans too far in the direction of prudence when she decides to accept Philip. Passion cannot be denied, and in its absence she has to suffer. This is the bewildering misery. Can one do right? Suffering seems inevitable. This is one of the themes of the book. It is about the pathos of life. But whereas prudence may involve suffering that arises from denial or requires quiet endurance, passion brings pain as violent in nature as itself. This is illustrated in the contrast of Sylvia and Hester Rose. The latter loves in silence and prudently restrains her passion, but she suffers long and quietly; Sylvia, on the other hand, is more expressive and more storm-tossed. She and Philip in their different ways are each the victims of passion, and yet they are not represented as totally helpless creatures. They choose to do what they want. And thus Miss Hopkins can rightly claim that 'the catastrophe is the logical outcome of faults of character: self-seeking, sexual passion, fierce independence, relentless hatred, the spirit of revenge'.[1] They each allow their passions rein. Philip's passion leads him to an implicit lie, to the concealment of Kinraid's survival by his failure to convey his message to Sylvia. He then has to live with his lie, to acknowledge the fraud of his success, to fear the exposure of his deceit and to face the collapse of his happiness. His fall is spectacular, and his latter days so different from his former that we may well have difficulty in recognizing the soldier in the erstwhile draper.

The history of Sylvia displays a more constant vividness. She seems always capable of the unexpected. Her

[1] Hopkins, p. 261.

youthful vivacity is embittered, but not extinguished, by sad experience. It is transformed into a mainly submerged and smouldering, but nevertheless settled, ferocity of spirit that seems always liable to burst forth in violent explosion. This is demonstrated in her great unwillingness to forgive. The hatred that has led her father to seek revenge on the press-gang is reproduced in his impulsive daughter in her refusal to forgive Simpson whose information has betrayed her father and, above all, in her terrifying rejection of Philip on Kinraid's return—'I'll never forgive yon man, nor live with him as his wife again' (p. 404). Eventually she does forgive—when she also sees her own need to be forgiven. In the great last scene of the book we read:

'My wife! Sylvia! Once more—forgive me all.'
She sprang up, she kissed his poor burnt lips; she held him in her arms, she moaned, and said—'Oh wicked me! forgive me —me—Philip.'
Then he spoke, and said, 'Lord, forgive us our trespasses as we forgive each other!' (p. 528).

Forgiveness is possible because each realizes his own responsibility, just as a little before they have realized also that there is an element in the catastrophe beyond their responsibility because it lies outside their control:

'You and me have done wrong to each other; yet we can see now how we were led to it; we can pity and forgive one another' (p. 524).

Mrs Gaskell knew the tragic essence, that men and women work in blindness to their own destruction, that neither fate nor character alone constitutes tragic inevitability but that both together work an end beyond all contriving. She knew too that tragedy requires that, whatever the suffering and whatever its causes, the human spirit must emerge triumphant over all calamity. In Philip's and Sylvia's mutual forgiveness this is shown. Philip dies redeemed from his faults. Sylvia is left to live on, her experience sadder than before but no longer embittered, enriched rather by a love that she had failed to recognize when she might have enjoyed it, but which will now sustain her to a nobler purpose in the years that are left to her. What a concentration of human experience Mrs Gaskell distils into the story of Sylvia Robson! This is her triumph in this novel. By comparison with what had gone before this work enters new realms of dramatic intensity. The setting is simple, the characters few, the action straightforward, but the thematic richness is displayed in a variety of situations, the variations upon the fundamental passions of love and hate, revenge and forgiveness, illustrated in all their complexity and power. There is nothing theoretical about *Sylvia's Lovers*; the reader's gaze is mercilessly concentrated upon the cruel and bewildering realities of life, cruel and bewildering because each moment is infinitely rich. 'The old life lives for ever' (p. 414). It cannot be forgotten or disowned. Here again we see Mrs Gaskell demonstrating that the past is the most tragic of the tenses. She knew, however, that, though there is much that we cannot do with the past, we can forgive it, and that by this alone we may redeem the time and enable the present to overcome, and the human spirit to discover a new nobility.

How then is this thematic richness expressed in the terms of fiction? Something must be said first about the setting against which the drama is acted out. Mrs Gaskell marks its importance by devoting the whole of the first

chapter to a description of Monkshaven in 1793 and to
the visit of the press-gang. She gives a brief but accurate
picture of town, moor and sea, of the ancient whaling
port hemmed in by hills, of the bare farmhouses behind
the town inland with their 'small stacks of coarse poor
hay' and of the sea, the dominating element of the area—
'in this country sea-thoughts followed the thinker far
inland' (p. 5). Mrs Gaskell's accuracy is vouched for by
the way in which readers who knew Whitby were able
to recognize the various places she described. Her precision is attested by the sense of place which is established
in the reader's mind so that in later scenes he readily
recognizes the locality in which different events take
place. This is particularly noticeable in the description of Philip's wanderings on his return to Monkshaven.

One feature to which Mrs Gaskell especially calls attention is the church. Set on its hill, it is there that one of the
first public events of the novel takes place, the funeral of
the sailor Darley killed by the press-gang. A couple of
paragraphs are devoted to the church's importance, as it
looks down over the town and sea, 'types of life and
eternity'. It beckons the sailor home and sustains him
with solemn thoughts as he sails away. In its yard lie
the dead of many generations, and this first mention is
associated with death. It next appears 'flooded with silver
light, for the moon was high in the heavens' as Daniel
Robson and his fellows prepare their death-bringing retaliation against the press-gang. It is to the church that
Sylvia climbs after she has told Philip that their marriage
has been a mistake. The characters see the church as
symbolic of enduring values and spiritual comfort. Yet
it seems signally to fail in giving much spiritual comfort.

Mrs Gaskell remarks on the inadequacy of the good old vicar's sermon at Darley's funeral. The very use of the churchyard as the venue for conspiracy against the press-gang is its own commentary, and Philip's decline in personal integrity is paralleled by a movement away from the primitive Quakerism of his youth and his employers, the good Foster brothers, to allegiance to the Established Church and the ambition of churchwardenship as marks of his material advancement. At the end, however, we receive the lesson of forgiveness in specifically Christian terms. Mrs Gaskell may have meant by this to show that, though institutions may fail, the basic Christian values remain and will triumph in the end.

The church looks down over what in normal times is a happy community, prosperous and purposeful, but disaster invades from the sea. *There* is struggle and adventure, and this makes Kinraid so attractive in the eyes of the young girl that Sylvia is at the beginning of the novel. Kinraid's is a specialized and in some ways dangerous employment as specksioneer; and to this is added, as further cause of attraction to Sylvia, his valiant defence of his fellow-sailors against the press-gang. Disaster from the sea falls upon personal relationships. Kinraid disrupts the quiet flow of Philip Hepburn's affections and stirs them to deeds at discord with his nature. The sailor's later re-appearance marks the doom of the precarious relationship between Philip and Sylvia. Disaster from the sea, in the form of the press-gang, overwhelms communal happiness. Mrs Gaskell begins with a straightforward description of the tyrannous work of the gang (p. 6 f.), but she quickly dramatizes the account with her narration of the gang's attack on the returning whalers. The sudden change from hope and joy to sorrow and despair is very effectively conveyed in the reactions of the expectant women-folk:

Their wild, famished eyes were strained on faces they might not kiss, their cheeks were flushed to purple with anger or else livid with impotent craving for revenge. Some of them looked scarcely human; and yet an hour ago these lips, now tightly drawn back so as to show the teeth with the unconscious action of an enraged wild animal, had been soft and gracious with the smile of hope; eyes that were fiery and bloodshot now, had been loving and bright, hearts, never to recover from the sense of injustice and cruelty, had been trustful and glad one short hour ago (p. 31).

To this is added the vivid tale of the attack on *The Good Fortune* and the killing of Darley. Mrs Gaskell indicates not only the personal, but also the public sufferings consequent upon the activities of the gang—the suspicion and fear, the enforced idleness and the economic stagnation ('No fish was caught, for the fishermen dared not venture out to sea; the markets were deserted . . . prices were raised and many were impoverished'—p. 264), and the communal hatred and desperation ('Fierce men drank and swore deep oaths of vengeance in the bar'—p. 265). The gang's malevolent influence is pin-pointed at maximum concentration in the incident of Kinraid's capture and impressment. The gang is the agent of fate, and twice its tyranny proves advantageous to Philip—once in Kinraid's kidnapping and the second time in the gratitude evoked from Sylvia for the part Philip plays in Daniel Robson's trial for his attack on the gang's headquarters. Advantage that comes from such a quarter can only prove a chimera, and like Macbeth's witches, the gang brings hope that sours into deep damnation. In fact, the gang brings ill to Sylvia's love, death to her father and doom to her marriage. In contrast with what would have been her earlier practice, Mrs Gaskell here launches into no condemnation or moralizing. Straightforward account and dramatization is left to do its own work.

It is perhaps a mark of her confidence as a novelist that in 1859 she felt that she had reached the point where she might depart from the familiar scene and the more or less contemporary, or at any rate the personally recollected, setting and embark on a major work which both in place and time took her into new areas. As far as place was concerned, it was easy for her with her skill in observation and description to provide a picture of Monkshaven. She goes further than that, however, in her creation of environment. She enables us to understand how the way of life of the inhabitants is conditioned by the place and by the occupations they have to pursue. She gives us the sense of a people constantly at odds with natural forces, making earth and sea yield up their harvest. From this she establishes the idea of local character, endowed with such qualities as rugged strength, endurance, patience and independence. These people are capable of suffering much, but when they are provoked beyond their patience, their wrath is terrible to behold. It is this which makes the action of the rioters in general and of Daniel Robson in particular so much at one with the ethos of the place.

To demonstrate this feeling Mrs Gaskell chooses the activity of the press-gang. It was here with the move back into history and the need to create a sense of a special time that she had to engage in some research. Ward[1] has provided us with evidence in this particular. She consulted Young's *History of Whitby* (1817) and she made inquiries in the town itself. The picture of what happened

[1] Knutsford edition, pp. xxiii–iv.

on 23 February 1793 was amplified by the copy which she obtained from the Admiralty of a letter in which the Keeper of the Whitby Rendezvous set out in some detail the story of the attack on the house. She entered into correspondence and inquired at the British Museum to ensure that her account of the manner in which the gang worked was correct. She got a copy of the Assize Calendar at York for 18 March 1793, when three of the Whitby rioters were tried. She spared no pains in her quest for accuracy, but when all is said in this regard, the triumph lies not in the fullness or faithfulness, but in the imaginative transmutation, of the record, above all in the effect that she suggests the events have upon the lives of those who suffered them.

This helps to explain the way in which the book begins. First we are given the description of Monkshaven in socio-geographical terms. In similar generalized reference we are told of the time, of war and the press-gang; that is, we receive some sense of the economic, military and political situation. What can individuals matter amidst all this? And what especially can the first characters we meet have to do with all this, two carefree country-girls setting off from their homes to sell butter and eggs at Monkshaven market? Then suddenly the pattern is poignantly revealed. The great warring world beyond bursts in upon the peaceful time-honoured routine of life in Monkshaven in the form of the press-gang. The great warring world invades the private lives of individuals, and the closest human bond is severed by arbitrary public action. It is not hard to guess that even the life of the carefree girl we have met will not remain unscathed by the forces that have revealed themselves in such ugly and devastating fashion.

The novel indeed pursues a twofold course. It works out a private drama constantly in the shadow of a possible public intervention. Because this shadow is always there, there seems to be no chance of happiness. A feeling of foreboding broods over the novel, and even in periods of tranquillity we are not allowed to forget that disaster may quickly descend. Catastrophe seems always inevitable, and the onward progress to destruction differs in one place and another only in the pace at which it proceeds. This is shown most succinctly at the birth of Philip's and Sylvia's child. One chapter ends with the sentence 'Perhaps on that day Philip reached the zenith of his life's happiness'; the next is entitled 'Evil Omens' (pp. 372–3). Even the first major event of the novel, the sailor's funeral, is as ominous as it is in itself deeply moving. If the poor old gardener, father of the murdered sailor, a mere incidental character, can be described as 'full of indignation and dumb anger [with] the unwonted longing for revenge' and the questioning of divine disposition (p. 73), may not, we think, other and more important characters be brought to comparable dilemma and despair? We do not miss the significance of those first thoughts of eternal things which Sylvia shortly afterwards ponders upon. The pathos of the gardener with his metaphysical doubts is representative of much that happens later. These are all of them simple people in a great world.

Mrs Gaskell suggests the ominous in yet other ways. She makes use, for example, of analogous situation. Bell Robson warns Sylvia about trusting a runaway sailor by her tale of poor crazy Nancy Hartley (p. 199). The story fails as a caution, 'though it touched [Sylvia] strangely to imagine the agonies of forsaken love' (p. 200). Similarly, in the story of Alice Rose's husband, the dissolute whaler Jack Rose who had won the hand that the industrious John Foster failed to win, Philip envisages a repetition in the possible future history of Sylvia, Kinraid and himself (p. 254). Though there is no exact repetition and the detail in the pattern varies, Mrs Gaskell fastens our attention upon the abiding sorrows that human relationships inescapably stir up. Another means of conveying the ominous is illustrated by the use of dream, especially in the married life of Philip and Sylvia. Philip wonders 'whether it [is] not all a dream that he [calls] Sylvia "wife"' (p. 362), but he is troubled by a real dream—of Kinraid's return; and we are told that Sylvia has 'like most of her class at that time, great faith in their prophetic interpretation' (p. 363). 'But Philip never gave her any truth in his reply' (p. 363). He has to stick to his deception, even in telling his dreams. Sylvia, too, has her dream at this time—of Kinraid as still alive. She tells her dream and is rebuked by Philip thus: 'And what kind of a woman are yo' to go dreaming of another man i' this way, and taking on so about him, when yo're a wedded wife, with a child as yo've borne to another man?' (p. 374). It is in just such terms that she has to consider the situation when Kinraid returns. In the meantime, the words recur often to her memory (cf. p. 380); and playing like another theme in the music is the recurrence of some of her words to Philip, the words by which she had refused to comfort her father's betrayer: 'It's not in me to forgive' (pp. 376, 377). She does not forgive Philip for his rebuke at this time; but the reader looks beyond this and asks himself what chance there can possibly be of her forgiving Philip when Kinraid inevitably returns. That is, the ominous operates yet again in this way also.

The ominous derives its power from its direction of our

attention to the future, from what the reader feels sure
will happen. The irony, on the other hand, works through
the past, through the reader's knowledge of events of
which one or more characters are unaware or wrongly
informed. Mrs Gaskell relies strongly upon this in the
middle section of the novel. In particular, it is employed
against Philip to ensure that the reader is not misled into
believing, as Philip tries to do, that the course of his life
may flow smoothly along now that Kinraid is out of the
way. After the novel's broad survey and somewhat slow
start Mrs Gaskell narrows down the interest to an intense
central emotion, the jealousy of Philip and Kinraid over
Sylvia. We can understand Sylvia's not being attracted
by Philip, and yet he is a sympathetic character. The
reader must admire many qualities in him, and perhaps
with him fear the apparent superficiality of Kinraid. It
is necessary for Mrs Gaskell to show the alloy in the metal,
to portray the baseness that Philip's passion can produce.
This she does in the single incident of the deception, the
failure to convey Kinraid's message at the time of his
capture by the gang. That single failure is enough to
make Philip unworthy; he gains so much by it. Justice
requires, however, even as he enjoys his success, that
retribution shall follow; and the reader knows that it will.

Even before Kinraid leaves, the irony is at work. It
operates mainly as dramatic irony. In this section of the
story Philip's complex passions are adroitly manipulated
by Mrs Gaskell. His jealousy of Kinraid stimulates his
hatred, and over against these any sign of the latter's
departure provokes a magnified and immoderate sense of
relief. On the eve of Kinraid's going relief becomes
elation: 'This night his prayers were more than the mere
form . . . they were a vehement expression of gratitude

to God for having, as it were, interfered on his behalf, to grant him the desire of his eyes and the lust of his heart' (p. 187). This passage is pithily suggestive of Philip's selfishness, with its wrong emphasis in devotion, stressed by the biblical associations of the final words. Then the irony appears. Wrong emphasis is soon seen to have been utter delusion. 'Philip little knew how Sylvia's time had been passed that day' (ibid.). She has had a visit and a virtual proposal of marriage from Kinraid. On the next day Philip and Kinraid meet when the latter is being taken by the press-gang. Philip is bidden to tell Sylvia what has happened and to assure her that Kinraid will return to marry her. Philip's presence might be judged contrivance, for the novelist a happy coincidence. It is a coincidence, but it is not contrivance. The whole sombre, ill-fated atmosphere makes his presence acceptable. It is a coincidence, but it is the sort of tragic coincidence with which this book abounds. Philip himself recognizes the coincidence and curses his ill-fate in 'having been chosen out from among all men to convey such a message' (p. 234). He elects to prosper by an implicit lie.

The capture and the return exemplify one of Mrs Gaskell's main narrative effects in this novel, her reliance on the great scene. She constantly works on contrast between ordinariness and excitement, the ordinariness of lives in their dull pedestrian round (the quiet courses of the minor peripheral characters such as the Foster brothers contribute to this effect) and the sudden violent crescendo of usually ominous or disastrous import. The long quiet periods give a sense of the prolongation of Philip's anxiety. *Sylvia's Lovers* is a book in which we are constantly uncomfortably expectant of one thing or another.

This suspense is periodically transformed into realization of horror, suffering and pathos by disastrous event, event moreover which leaves us in redoubled suspense, feeling that yet worse will follow. The capture of Kinraid is just such an example; the attack on the *randy-vouse* is another. It is at these times when the individual comes into conflict with public authority that one gets the sense of the helplessness of these simple people in a great world. With the attack on the *randy-vouse* Mrs Gaskell excellently conveys the idea that the past has proved too much but that the future will impose demands yet heavier still. The decoy of the fire-bell is the breaking-point; Robson and his fellows can stand no more. We sympathize with their sense of outrage, and yet we realize, as they do not, that there will be a costly consequence of their recklessness. And for this we pity them the more. We pity them not only for what they are driven to do, but also for what they are—so pathetically helpless. Philip, looked upon as capable and by Monkshaven standards sophisticated, a man who has been to London, is used by Mrs Gaskell to show how pathetic they all are. When disaster falls, they must look to him; he has to handle the defence of Daniel Robson. He realizes what may happen to Robson as Sylvia and her mother at first do not, but even he in his naïveté takes the assize sermon at its face value. As he listened, 'his hopes rose higher than his fears for the first time'. The text was 'Execute true judgment and show mercy' (pp. 327, 328).

Kinraid's return marks the highest crisis of the book, and the whole scene has a nightmare quality about it. The chapter in which it appears is entitled 'An Apparition' and the re-appearance is a frightening, horrifying experience for both Sylvia and Philip. Mrs Gaskell uses the dialogue skilfully to suggest their mental and emotional confusion. At first Sylvia's speech is brief as she asks Philip to explain his concealment of the truth from her. This is followed by Kinraid's violent outburst first against Philip, then against Sylvia for marrying Philip. At this accusation Sylvia's previous brevity changes to voluble and somewhat disjointed explanation. Meanwhile, Philip has been standing in stunned silence 'with bitterest shame and self-reproach' (p. 402). His first words on finding speech are like all his words in this scene, simple and forced as it were out of the depths of his being: 'Would God I were dead!' (p. 402). Sylvia is weeping wretchedly in Kinraid's arms, and neither pays any heed to Philip. He comes 'to pull her away; but Charley held her tight, mutely defying Philip' (p. 403). Philip also grasps her tight and implores her: ' "Listen to me! He didn't love you as I did. He had loved other women. I yo'—yo' alone" ' (p. 403). Kinraid bids Sylvia leave with him, claiming the oath she has sworn, but Sylvia remembers also her oath to Philip, symbolized in the child she has borne him. To two oaths she adds a third and it reminds us of what she had said before:— ' "I'll never forgive yon man, nor live with him as his wife again" ' (p. 404).

After this there follows the last section of the book, in many ways a disappointment after what has gone before. Philip's departure from home and enlistment in the army, the battle of Acre at which he saves Kinraid's life, his return home crippled and his stay at St Sepulchre's hospital, the necessary reference to Kinraid's marriage to a fashionable but shallow woman, all this is too remote, lacking in the strong sense of actuality which marks all that goes before. There is also too much description and report, and the coincidence, whilst limited in extent, is too far-fetched to accept.

Nevertheless, one can endure all this for the deeply moving last scene, surely the greatest in all Mrs Gaskell's work. It links directly back to Sylvia's last words in the Kinraid return scene. Philip, back in Monkshaven, dying after rescuing his child, is alone with Sylvia. The theme is the same as at the end of *Mary Barton*, but it is here related to a more intimate and a more poignant sorrow. Again it is 'Forgive us our trespasses'. Both of them realize that they speak in the presence of heavenly judgment. It is a long scene, conducted with magnificent control. No summary and selective quotation can do it justice, but we must try.

'I did thee a cruel wrong,' he said at length. 'I see it now. But I'm a dying man. I think that God will forgive me—and I've sinned against Him; try, lassie—try, my Sylvia—wilt not thou forgive me? . . .'

She lifted up her head; and asked wildly, 'Will He iver forgive me, think yo'? I drove yo' out fra' yo'r home and sent yo' away to t' wars, where yo' might ha' getten yo'r death; and when yo' come back, poor and lone, and weary, I told her [Widow Dobson] t' turn yo' out, for a' I knew yo' must be starving in these famine times. I think I shall go about among them as gnash their teeth for iver, while yo' are where all tears are wiped away.'

'No!' said Philip, turning round his face, forgetful of himself in his desire to comfort her. 'God pities us as a father pities his poor wandering children; the nearer I come to death the clearer I see Him. But you and me have done wrong to each other; yet we can now see how we were led to it; we can pity and forgive one another. I'm getting low and faint, lassie; but thou must remember this: God knows more, and is more forgiving than either you to me, or me to you. I think and do believe as we shall meet together before His face; but then I shall ha' learnt to love thee second to Him; not first, as I have done here upon the earth.' . . .

Once more he spoke aloud, in a strange and terrible voice that was not his. Every sound came with efforts that were new to him.

'My wife! Sylvia! Once more—forgive me all.'

She sprang up, she kissed his poor burnt lips; she held him in her arms, she moaned and said—'Oh wicked me! forgive me—me—Philip!'

Then he spoke, and said, 'Lord, forgive us our trespasses as we forgive each other.' And after that the power of speech was conquered by the coming death (pp. 523, 524, 528).

Mrs Gaskell had thought of calling the book 'Philip's Idol', and the word with its religious associations is obviously in mind when Philip speaks of loving God first in eternity and Sylvia only second. Here is irony of a new kind, that in the moment of reconciliation which is also the moment of final separation in this life he can say, and Sylvia can accept, that she should be only second in his affections. Yet as he says this, there seems to be a tenderness in his speech, and especially in the use of the address 'lassie' (and this takes us back to their earliest days together), that we have never seen before, never seen because Sylvia's attitude has never permitted such spontaneity and such intimacy. We notice also that, realizing God's pre-eminence, Philip has at last put matters in the perspective which, despite his religious beliefs, Mrs Gaskell has earlier so often and so pointedly shown him not to possess. The whole of this last scene, that is, is related to and proceeds from what has gone before. There is nothing abrupt, nothing imposed, nothing avowedly didactic. In all these ways the comparison with the close

PLATE III

Water-colour drawing of Mrs Gaskell,
by her daughter, Meta, 1865

of *Mary Barton* is instructive. We are now in the presence of a consummate artist.

The same may be said of Mrs Gaskell's characterization in this novel. Each character has his place, beautifully positioned and for the most part sufficiently developed, in the pattern of the whole. In the forefront are Philip and Sylvia, and subsidiary to them Kinraid; and then, in lesser degree, Daniel Robson and his wife Bell; and in the background a host of minor characters—Hester Rose, Molly Corney, Kester, old Alice Rose, Coulson, the Foster brothers and many more. Some of these last are excellently portrayed, but one or two must suffice for illustration. Often as in the case of Molly Corney and Hester Rose they serve as foils for Sylvia. Molly is a coarse, vulgar young woman who chooses to marry for money a man twice her age. Before that she has shown herself to be a flighty girl, and her cousinship to Kinraid is not lost upon us when he is described in similar terms. Hester, by contrast, is deeply serious, and in love with Philip. She has none of Sylvia's fresh beauty and she knows it. There is a pathetic little incident as she looks from the Fosters' shop at Sylvia and admires her; then 'Hester, half ashamed, stole into [a] corner, and looked at herself in the glass. What did she see? A colourless face; dark, soft hair with no light gleams in it; eyes that were melancholy instead of smiling; a mouth compressed with a sense of dissatisfaction' (p. 125). She watches the courtship of Philip and Sylvia sadly but with resignation. Philip, however, is quite oblivious of her feelings, and his insensitivity reaches its nadir when he asks her to be bridesmaid at the wedding.

There is one minor character of whom special mention must be made. The delineation of the Robsons' farm-labourer Kester is a fine vignette. He is the simplest of men; he cherishes a deep love for the Robsons and especially for Sylvia. He, above all, personifies the dumb distress that we know afflicts the whole community after Robson's arrest. Kester's loyalty and affection is shown in his night-long walk to York to pay his last visit to Daniel Robson. Kester has no love for Philip, and hence he is a staunch supporter of Kinraid. He chides Sylvia for allegedly forgetting Kinraid, for which in return she rebukes him. The relationship between these two provides the opportunity for Mrs Gaskell to show something more of Sylvia and the theme of forgiveness: 'If thou wasn't Kester, I'd niver forgive thee . . . but thou're dear old Kester after all, and I can't help mysel', I mun needs forgive thee' (p. 325). When Sylvia is deserted, Kester remains, and he is there, at the end, by Sylvia's side in her last and greatest distress, type of the devoted, faithful, simple soul.

Daniel and Bell Robson serve a number of purposes. First, they contrast so much with one another in their approach to life, the wife careful, prudent, industrious, the husband impulsive, given to boasting, garrulous and rather idle. There is a perpetual tension between them in their home life. The conflict of passion and prudence, which in their prosaic marriage is a long contest of attrition, is destined to flash out more dramatically and decisively in the lives of Sylvia and Philip. Secondly, the impulsiveness of Robson brings terrible retribution in his execution, with consequent reflection on public tyranny and the provocation of simple men. The execution leads also to the breakdown, suffering and ultimate death of Mrs Robson. Bell Robson has had much to endure in her marriage, and not least the last mad deed, but the final days show how much she cares for her erring husband. There is no word of reproach. The lesson of her faithfulness and forbearance is not wasted when we read of her daughter's troubles in her marriage.

It might be said that Kinraid is hardly individualized enough to carry the weight of the part he is given, and there is, of course, a sense in which he can be regarded as conventional, as the dashing young man who engages the heart of the immature girl. It might also be argued, however, that being conventional, he is all the less worthy of Sylvia's love by comparison with the more substantial Philip. The first words about him come from the lips of a silly girl. The next we know is that he had played the conventional part of the hero in the struggle with the press-gang. He is glamorous, and Philip is prosaic. That is exactly how Sylvia—and her father—regard them both. Philip tries to teach an unwilling pupil to read and write; Charley Kinraid fascinates her with his sailor's yarns. The difference comes out again at the New Year's Eve party, at which Kinraid shines. Mrs Gaskell hints at his success with the girls, and at the same time she describes the growth of his serious affection for Sylvia; but this latter is always by report. She never tells us what Kinraid is thinking or feeling. Thus the reader is never sure about him; never approving, yet never able to condemn. Kinraid rises in the reader's estimation after his capture, not by what he does but by Philip's concealment of the message and consequent advantage for himself. On Kinraid's return there seems to be a certain inadequacy in his response, a conventional theatrical quality, for instance, in his behaviour towards Philip; but this may be a necessity of his subservient role, that thus we may the better appreciate the depth and tumult of Philip's and

Sylvia's emotions. Finally, however, he shows that he really is just conventional. By marrying the superficial woman we hear about, he is shown to be superficial himself, as superficial as some people said he was and the reader has at times suspected. Thus Sylvia's mistaken choice and much of the ill that follows is made sadder still.

The equivalent role of the two main characters is shown by the presence of their names in the title Mrs Gaskell at one time proposed ('Philip's Idol') (501) and in that which she ultimately adopted. Theirs is a history of pre-destined incompatibility, and of suffering different for each in its duration and relative intensity at different periods of its affliction, but soul-searing in the lives of both. Sylvia grows from a carefree young girl to a mature disillusioned, deeply wounded woman in all too short a time. At first she is shown as just a happy farm lass, but then at the funeral of Darley we hear about her first serious thoughts, of her arriving at the church thinking about her new cloak and of her leaving 'with life and death suddenly become real to her mind' (p. 79). The next stage of her life as the beloved both of Philip and Kinraid is quite simply told. It is the attraction of a young girl to the more glamorous rival at the expense of the steadier suitor. Kinraid is associated with play, the party and the dance, and with adventure; Philip belongs to the world of trade, religion and education. ' "Mother!" said Sylvia, bursting out, "what's the use on my writing 'Abednago', 'Abednago' all down a page?" ' (p. 98). By such simple but vivid means Mrs Gaskell expresses Sylvia's repulsion. There is no analysis of her feelings, perhaps wisely so, for Mrs Gaskell's point is to stress that Sylvia is really quite an ordinary adolescent girl, less

216

vulgar certainly than Molly Corney but not essentially different. The ordinariness is important, for this book is about the effects of extraordinary incursions upon the lives of ordinary people.

Sylvia's life is changed by two traumatic experiences, Kinraid's disappearance and presumed death and her father's imprisonment and execution. Mrs Gaskell describes the change in her appearance and manner after Kinraid's departure—'Her face was wan and white; her grey eyes seemed larger, and full of dumb tearless sorrow' (p. 247). One notices the skill with which the novelist has selected her moment to reveal the change in Sylvia. This sentence occurs in the scene in which Philip has just returned from London full of news of the great city. The bustling curiosity of mother and father heightens by contrast the sad, depressed, listless appearance of Sylvia. It is a mark of the world's disillusioning effect upon her that she realizes before her mother does what will be the likely consequence of Daniel Robson's rash rioting. When Philip brings news of the verdict, Sylvia collapses into a swoon, but both before and afterwards her behaviour is sternly stoical. Her sternness expresses itself in her first great refusal to forgive. We have heard her speak in these terms before, as when Kester reports the linking of her name with that of Philip. He is right when he says: 'Here's a pretty lass; she's got "A'll never forgi'e" at her tongue's end wi' a vengeance' (p. 338). (This, incidentally, comes in a passage which illustrates extremely well the nice gradations of dialectal expression which Mrs Gaskell introduces into the speeches of different characters.) Up to this time, however, the words have often been at her tongue's end as a manner of speaking. Very soon they will come from her heart's core. In this she is her father's child, for his unwillingness to forgive the press-gang has led to his undoing. There is a frightening harshness and exultant cruelty in her response to the news that Simpson, who informed against her father, is dying. Not all Philip's pleadings can prevail upon her, and for the reader there is a dire foreboding in such words as 'Thee and me was niver meant to go together. It's not in me to forgive' and 'There's some things as I know I niver forgive; and there's others as I can't—and I won't, either' (p. 352).

It is shortly after this that she marries Philip, thus fulfilling the predictions of some whom she has said she will not forgive. She marries out of gratitude and a sense of duty rather than for love; and for the reader the actual marriage is marked by yet more foreboding. Sylvia resolutely determines to remain in black, and after the wedding they return home to Mrs Robson's semi-delirious cries of sorrow. Mrs Gaskell points the significance with a direct comment:

Did it enter into Philip's heart to perceive that he had wedded his long-sought bride in mourning raiment, and that the first sounds which greeted them as they approached their home were those of weeping and wailing? (p. 360).

The marriage, entered upon without joy, is endured rather than enjoyed. Mrs Gaskell briefly but deftly suggests the essential incompatibility of the two temperaments. There is an obvious, deliberately cultivated detachment on the part of Sylvia. She still dreams both by day and night of Kinraid. Her disillusionment and settled pessimism is exemplified in her plea to Philip to recognize that their marriage has been a mistake but at any rate to keep up appearances before her mother. Then Kinraid returns, the marriage collapses and we are faced with the greatest unwillingness to forgive of all.

Everything happens too late in this novel. Indeed, Mrs Gaskell suggested 'Too Late' as another possible title. It is not until after the catastrophe with the discovery of Philip's deception and his disappearance that Sylvia, mature though she had been made by extraordinary experience and suffering, comes to appreciate his sterling qualities in contrast to the shallowness of Kinraid. It takes the news of the latter's fashionable marriage to make her 'for the first time in her life . . . recognize the real nature of Philip's love' (p. 461). By carefully disposed repeated references Mrs Gaskell impresses the reader with Sylvia's increasing realization of what she has failed to appreciate until it is too late. The last such reference comes just before the final reconciliation when the recurrence of 'Forgive us our trespasses' takes our mind back to that earlier scene about Simpson when Philip's reminder of these words of the Lord's prayer had fallen on such stony ground. The reconciliation scene also is too late. The title of the chapter is 'Saved and Lost'. If Philip had but revealed himself a little earlier, the reconciliation might have been at once more difficult and less dramatic, but the end would have been happiness instead of tragedy. Happiness, however, is not a condition we are to look for in the overcast world of *Sylvia's Lovers*.

Philip seeks happiness and finds it, but only for a brief spell. At the beginning he is shown as a young man who has done well and is likely to do even better. He is respectable and potentially prosperous. He is engaged in trade with the best-established firm in Monkshaven; he is fairly well educated; he is devout. It is not surprising that a lively young girl such as Sylvia does not find him particularly attractive. Even the most minor incident illustrates the difference between them. She chooses the red cloth for her coat in preference to the grey her mother advises and Philip dutifully seeks to press upon her. The relations of Philip and Sylvia are developed by the narration of little incidents such as this and by the insights which Mrs Gaskell gives into Philip's reactions, his hesitations, suppressions and fears, his occasional sternness and ready tenderness. Philip loves anxiously; and Mrs Gaskell displays the varied nuances of feeling and the sustained conflict of emotions within him. To take but one example, when Kinraid visits Foster's shop and Philip learns that he will return to his ship on the following day, we are told that Philip watches him with 'a kind of envy of his bright, courteous manner, the natural gallantry of the sailor' (p. 174). Philip, relieved of his jealousy, is almost ready to praise Kinraid; but then as they shake hands, there is hesitation; 'a cloud came over his face . . . taking light and peace out of his countenance' (p. 174). With such touches Philip is treated in a manner quite different from that of any other character in the book. We know far better the interior working of passion and conscience within him.

Of conscience, as well as passion, because passion leads him to the lie with which he has to live. His passion is idolatrous. His 'passionate prayer [is] "Give me Sylvia, or else I die"' (p. 136). Mrs Gaskell exploits the self-seeking bias which distorts Philip's devotions. Reference has already been made to his prayers and mistaken thanksgiving after he has heard of Kinraid's forthcoming departure. Underlining the importance of this, Mrs Gaskell goes on to moralize on the tendency to egocentric orisons. It is not surprising that Philip should exclaim of Kinraid's imminent capture by the gang: 'It is God's providence' (p. 228); and after it is complete, should think that his 'prayer is granted. God be thanked!' (p. 235). This, after he has just arranged with his conscience, 'the dread Inner Creature', that he is not bound to carry out his promise to carry Kinraid's message to Sylvia because Kinraid may not have heard his reply!

Philip is possessive and jealous, but the tragedy of his deceit proceeds also from the virtue behind his affection for Sylvia, his desire to protect her from a notoriously fickle lover. After the capture he rationalizes this desire into a justification for his concealment of the truth. At the same time, however, he wrestles with the conviction that, fickle though Kinraid may have been, his love for Sylvia is sincere. With her accurate perception of a character so chronically conscience-burdened and confused Mrs Gaskell shows him at one stage almost compelled to reveal what he knows. When Bell Robson tells of Daniel's speculation about Kinraid's possible abduction by the gang, Philip compulsively asks: 'An' who knows but what it's true?' (p. 267). Philip prospers from his deceit; he marries Sylvia. 'The long-desired happiness [is] not so delicious and perfect as he had anticipated' (p. 363); Sylvia's love does not match his own. The irony lies not only in the fact that the reward for his deceit is not what he hoped that it would be, but also in that his love, the greater and the more tender, meets no comparable response. The intrusion of Kinraid is but the final destruction of something that had always been fragile and had already, in effect, collapsed.

There is another side to Philip besides his self-seeking. He possesses a nobility that is always evident to the reader but which Sylvia does not see, or at any rate sees only partially and belatedly. The expression of this nobility reaches its height first in the crisis of the Robson fortunes with Daniel's arrest, trial and execution, and afterwards soars beyond that in the way that Philip faces the situation when his deceit is known and his marriage has been shattered. Kinraid may impress outwardly, but it is always obvious, even in his disgrace, that Philip is a far finer figure. The rich depths of feeling with which he is endowed make Kinraid look a mere stage-character by contrast. This feeling is exhibited in concentrated expression as Philip prepares to leave his home for ever. He looks on his sleeping child and recalls the happiness he has enjoyed with her. 'Then he rose, and stooped over, and gave the child a long, lingering, soft, fond kiss' (p. 409). As he leaves, he takes but one thing with him from his home, a silhouette of Sylvia. He enlists as a 'reckless recruit', and whatever we may think of that, his experience as a soldier enables him both handsomely to redeem his previous injustice towards Kinraid and to make a heavy payment in return for the short-lived and incomplete happiness he had enjoyed. Then comes the end, in which the child re-unites the estranged husband and wife, in which indirectly the sea claims its last victim, but also in which Philip's tragic nobility wins through to a victory over all external forces, even death itself. Love proves stronger than death, more precious than life. Philip Hepburn is not the most complex of Mrs Gaskell's characters, but he is unsurpassed in nobility of conception and portrayal.

Seen as a whole, *Sylvia's Lovers* represents Mrs Gaskell's nearest approach to epic proportions. In its bleak and ominous atmosphere, its fundamentally simple conflict, its terrible basic emotions and its tragic outcome it is not without its reminiscences of the literature of that earlier race of Northern men who battled with the sea to find a settlement in the real Monkshaven and its neighbourhood. For Philip and Sylvia, as for those others a thousand years before, 'lif is læne'. Mrs Gaskell shows that, though life is short, there is yet so much to suffer. In showing this, she reveals her understanding of the essential tragic vision. Thereby the success of *Sylvia's Lovers* is explained.

CHAPTER X

'WIVES AND DAUGHTERS'

AFTER Smith had published *Sylvia's Lovers*, Mrs Gaskell agreed to write another novel for him. Her first thoughts ran to something which she called 'Two Mothers'. This, she told Smith in September 1863, was 'in my head very clear' (532). By May 1864 it had been rejected in favour of *Wives and Daughters*. A long passage in a letter to Smith is worth quoting because it shows how fully Mrs Gaskell had worked out the plot of her last novel:

I threw overboard the story of the 'Two Mothers' because I thought you did not seem to like it fully—and I have made up a story in my mind,—of country-town life 40 years ago,—a widowed doctor has one daughter, Molly,—when she is about 16 he marries again—a widow with one girl Cynthia,—and these two girls—contrasting characters,—not sisters but living as sisters in the same house are unconscious rivals for the love of a young man, Roger Newton, the second son of a neighbouring squire or rather yeoman. He is taken by Cynthia, who does *not* care for him—while Molly does. His elder brother has formed a clandestine marriage at Cambridge—he was supposed to be clever before he went there—but was morally weak—& disappointed his father so much that the old gentleman refused to send Roger, & almost denies him education—the eldest son lives at home, out of health, in debt, & not daring to acknowledge his marriage to his angry father; but Roger is his confidant, & gives him all the money he can for the support of his inferior (if not disreputable) wife & child. No one but Roger knows of this marriage—Roger is rough, & unpolished—but works out for himself a certain name in Natural Science,—is tempted by a large offer to go round the world (like Charles Darwin) as naturalist,—but stipulates to be paid *half* before he goes away for 3 years in order to help his brother. He goes off with a sort of fast & loose engagement to Cynthia,—while he is away his brother breaks a blood vessel, & dies—Cynthia's mother immediately makes fast the engagement & speaks about it to every one, but Cynthia has taken a fancy for some one else & makes Molly her confidant. You can see the kind of story and—I must say —you may find a title for yourself for *I* can not (550).

This seems to anticipate everything that is important in the plot with the possible exception of the part played by the land agent Preston. What it does not even hint at is the superb characterization, as a result of which external action and events are less important in this novel than in any that preceded it. Even *Cranford* needed such things as railway accidents, visits by entertainers and bank failures. The sub-title of *Wives and Daughters* is 'An Every-Day Story'. In this novel Mrs Gaskell has entered a world that reminds us of writers like Jane Austen and Henry James. Nothing much happens, but the very inter-play of character upon character has a moulding, and sometimes a blighting, effect.

Nothing much happens, and yet this is the longest of Mrs Gaskell's novels, and it lay unfinished at her death. In view of this, it may be useful to look first at the struc-ture of the work. In this every-day story it is not easy to indicate the exact emphasis which Mrs Gaskell develops at its various stages, for paradoxically, while nothing much happens, everything is happening all the time. This is because so much depends rather upon what the char-acters are than upon what they do. Mrs Gaskell has given us her outline of the story, but the novel does not pursue a straight narrative course. Because everybody matters all the time, there are a number of lines of interest to be kept constantly in mind, interweaving with each other, forming new patterns, at times puzzling patterns, for the reader to contemplate. As they move towards, across and away from each other, first one line of interest, then another, appears most prominent. Mrs Gaskell is always aware of the way in which the lives of the members of any community impinge upon each other, but this awareness is nowhere else allied with the feeling of depth so fully as it is in *Wives and Daughters*. The lives of the characters are seen here not only to impinge upon, but to interpenetrate, each other.

It has been remarked that Mrs Gaskell here makes a rare incursion into the life of the aristocracy;[1] and descending in the social scale she includes the squire, the professional man, the impoverished but genteel spinsters, and even at one stage briefly enters the labourer's cottage. Hollingford is Knutsford yet again—after Cranford, Duncombe ('Mr Harrison's Confessions'), Barford ('The Squire's Story'), Hamley ('A Dark Night's Work') and Eltham ('Cousin Phillis'). As elsewhere, the day-to-day activities of the little town assume the inflated importance that such events do in such places, but now they are used much more to reveal character than they had been in earlier works. As before, the rigid, even one might say the ossified, standards of such a society are seen in their effect upon the central character. This is evident in the judgment of Molly, for example, as illustrated by the comments made on her being seen with Preston. The contrast with earlier work, and especially with *Ruth*, is instructive. The situation in that book is altogether sim-

[1] Knutsford edition, pp. xxvi–vii.

pler, much more a matter of bold differences. Ruth's 'crime' was more heinous than anything that Molly Gibson might be accused of, but Molly is in some ways under a more delicate and severer standard. Ruth's goodness is straightforward and simple; Molly's is more complex and in a more complex situation. In *Ruth* there are two possible reactions, those of Benson and Bradshaw; Molly is exposed to more angles of observation and comment. Ruth is a stranger in Eccleston; Molly is part of the society which has found occasion to criticize her, born in it, occupying a well-defined and comparatively important position in it, aware of its strict standards and all the more severely judged for that awareness.

The Molly-Preston incident illustrates in detail what happens on a larger scale in the novel. The characters are aware of standards, of the need to behave in certain ways and to stand in any one of a series of predetermined attitudes to other members of the community. They know how they are expected to act. To achieve such ends some of the characters take courses of action which it is an important part of the novel's irony to show producing results other than those intended. Thus Gibson would protect Molly as she grows into womanhood. The standards expected of her must be fostered and developed. The guide he chooses for her, however, his second wife, is about the most unfortunate person he could have seriously chosen for the task. This is one irony; that of Squire Hamley, fearing lest one of his sons should fall in love with Molly, is another. In the first place, much though he might have regretted it, he would have preferred this to the alliance which Osborne has contracted but which he, the father, knows nothing about; secondly, Roger is to become enamoured of the much less worthy

Cynthia; and thirdly, after being jilted by Cynthia, he is to fall in love with Molly, and his father is to be glad of it. As another example of the book's complexity it is interesting to note how in the early stages of the book Mrs Gaskell runs three fears in parallel, Gibson's for Molly, Hamley's for his sons, and Molly's for her father's re-marriage. The emergence of Clare, Mrs Kirkpatrick, as Mrs Gibson affects all three. Her malevolence, which is so important, is the one major feature of the book which, though perhaps inferred, does not come out clearly from Mrs Gaskell's summary in the letter quoted above.

Nothing much happens. We are not to look for the spectacular in *Wives and Daughters*, but this is not to say that there are no large, public scenes. The book may be said to begin with one, with the garden party for the Hollingford folk at Cumnor Towers, but even this occasion is strictly centred upon the young girl Molly and the fact that she is left behind by the Miss Brownings and falls into the hands of Clare. Much more various in its uses is another public scene, that of the charity ball (chapter XXVI), in which Mrs Gaskell, first of all, conveys the sense of public excitement, not without plenty of humour. The old maids 'aired their old lace and their best dresses' (p. 325); and, as the townspeople wait for the coming of the county-magnates and their parties, 'the aristocratic ozone being absent from the atmosphere, there [is] a flatness about the dancing of all those who considered themselves above the plebeian ranks of the tradespeople' (p. 331). The 'plebeians' wait for the coming of the Duchess of Menteith wearing her famous diamonds:

In came Lord Cumnor with a fat, middle-aged woman on his

arm; she was dressed almost like a girl—in a sprigged muslin, with natural flowers in her hair, but not a vestige of a jewel or a diamond. Yet it must be the duchess; but what was a duchess without diamonds? (p. 336).

But besides the comedy there are the serious implications in the reactions of the other characters—Mrs Gibson's dislike, for example, of Cynthia's dancing with people she considers inferior and her anxiety lest by this Cynthia should miss the opportunity of dancing with the young men staying at the Towers—'and who could tell to what a dance might lead?' (p. 331); or Preston's anger at Cynthia's disregard of his request for the first dance after nine o'clock. Lesser characters also have their distinctive role—Lady Harriet, often more candid than gracious, but now aware, with an election in the offing, of the need to notice the burgesses; or, almost at the other social extreme, the crabbed Mrs Goodenough uttering her disappointment in the occasion. Even in minor respects such as this Mrs Gaskell shows us the encounter of convention and individuality, responsibility and inclination.

These oppositions are what the book is about, and that is why it begins with the three parallel fears. These fears represent responsibility arising out of love. We may begin with Gibson, Molly's doctor-father. The affection of father and daughter is excellently implied in the casual playful tone of their conversation (pp. 27–8). An ill-considered and hardly more than adolescent passion on the part of one of Gibson's apprentices, a passion, Mrs Gaskell infers, not unlike one through which Gibson himself had passed, stampedes him into considerations of marriage in order to protect Molly. Even before the marriage takes place, however, he seems to recognize that his move is not so simply correct as he had calculated. In a scene between him, Molly and his future wife, we read of Molly's feelings, of the jealousy she cannot suppress at being excluded from her father's confidence.

She was positively unhappy, and her father did not appear to see it. . . . But he did notice it, and was truly sorry for his little girl. . . . It was his general plan to repress emotion by not showing the sympathy he felt (p. 152).

It is sentences like these that are unique to this book within Mrs Gaskell's whole achievement. They show her recognition of subtlety of feeling and response unmatched elsewhere in her work. In a sense Gibson has by this time played his part. He recedes into the background, and only rarely do we find father and daughter alone together at later stages in the book. When we do, we are often made to feel the poignancy of their relationship, a poignancy deriving from the mistake Gibson had made when his intentions were so laudable. On one such occasion Gibson hints at his fear of a possible alliance between Molly and Osborne Hamley, and on her denial he expresses his relief: ' "I should miss her sadly." He could not help saying this in the fulness of his heart just then' (p. 463). The significance of this last phrase comes out in Mrs Gaskell's comment on Gibson's reaction to Molly's statement of her supreme happiness in being alone with her father. 'Mr Gibson knew all implied in these words, and felt that there was no effectual help for the state of things which had arisen from his own act' (p. 464). Gibson suffers, but he makes the best of things. If there is an inadequacy in the characterization of Gibson, it relates to Mrs Gaskell's claim that 'his whole manner had grown dry and sarcastic' (p. 476), but his wife 'had no great facility for understanding sarcasm'. He is too much in the background for this to be very impressive. Gibson would doubtless have been a match for Mr Bennet in *Pride and Prejudice*, but Mrs Gaskell keeps him in his place. Gibson suffers the consequence of his choice. Mrs Gaskell is showing us that life is like that, and especially marriage. A deed is done and there must be a long contrition. People are what they are, and being brought together, will work irritatingly and wearingly upon each other if there is no harmony between them. It does not need enmity, only incompatibility. It does not need evil, only lack of sensitivity. Thus Gibson and his wife exist together.

Others suffer, however, not for what they have done, but by what others do or fail to do. Gibson's daughter, Molly, is one such suffering heroine, one of those good, but not simply good, young women of whom the Victorians were fond. There is no priggishness about her; she is too natural for that. In her life there are two loves, each amounting to a devotion, the first to her father, the second to Roger Hamley. Her father fails her, and the consequence is tremendous sorrow and even jealousy, but her loyalty to him remains unshaken. Her attitude to her father has, by the nature of events, to be one mainly of endurance, of acceptance of what has happened. For the greater part of the novel it looks as though her love for Roger Hamley must also be mute and unrewarded. After their early acquaintance, his comforting her in the face of Gibson's approaching marriage (p. 129), the evidence of his interest in her (p. 167), the establishment of Roger as a standard ('What would Roger say was right?'—p. 200), all seems set fair; but Roger is attracted by Cynthia, and we encounter a situation not unlike that

which Jane Austen presents in *Mansfield Park* where
Fanny loves apparently hopelessly as Edmund Bertram
and Mary Crawford draw nearer together.

There is no acrimony between Molly and Cynthia,
only a persistently exposed difference of breeding, manners and standards of behaviour. The contrast between
the straightforward integrity of the one and the arti-
ficiality of the other resides even in their names, as Mrs
Gaskell makes Gibson point out when he mentions that
his wife has 'perpetuated her own affected name by
having her daughter called after her. Cynthia! . . . I'm
thankful you're plain Molly, child' (p. 137). On another
occasion in the garden, Cynthia herself remarks on a
contrast: 'Molly, you see, devotes herself to the useful,
and I to the ornamental' (pp. 377–8). In appearance they
differ also. 'Molly's sweet, merry smile . . . the gleam of
her teeth, and the charm of her dimples' (p. 73) cannot
compete with the more striking brilliance of Cynthia.
Molly, however, has standards of behaviour which
Cynthia knows and admits that she herself has not.
Gibson hoped that his daughter will grow up a lady
(p. 28), and he hoped to forward his aim by his re-
marriage. This aim, however, is attained in spite, rather
than because, of Mrs Gibson. At the end Molly admin-
isters to her stepmother the monumental snub that lady
has deserved throughout, when, horrified at Mrs Gibson's
suggestion that the thought of the advantages to accrue
from his young nephew's death must have crossed Roger
Hamley's mind, Molly replies: 'All sorts of thoughts
cross one's mind—it depends upon whether one gives
them harbour and encouragement' (p. 744). Long-
suffering and exploited though Molly is, there comes the
point beyond which she will stand no more. By this Mrs

Gaskell keeps her convincing enough, more convincing perhaps than Jane Austen's Fanny Price.

Molly, whose standards are so firm, must be content through most of the novel to be corrected and rebuked by her stepmother. Here again *Mansfield Park* comes to mind with Mrs Norris's persecution of Fanny. If anything, however, the treatment in *Wives and Daughters* suggests a more subtle form of torture. It issues from a more apparently benevolent intention, concealed beneath Mrs Gibson's pervasive 'affectation and false sentiment' (p. 461). One must agree with Miss Rosamond Lehmann that Mrs Gibson and her daughter Cynthia are masterpieces of portraiture. The former she declares to be 'one of the most devastating portraits of a stupid, vulgar, destructive woman ever drawn this side of wickedness'.[1] It is here that Mrs Gaskell's characterization moves into Jamesian dimensions. It is an achievement such as this that makes us regret so much that death did not permit her to move yet further in her art.

There is much in the earlier stages of the portrait that makes Mrs Gibson (Clare) rather pitiable. As former governess at the Towers she still comes under the Cumnor patronage; she is a widow, and now with difficulty she runs a private school. Even, however, as we learn these facts, Mrs Gaskell so colours Clare's language as to bring out her vacuity, snobbery and selfishness with such expressions as 'I don't look as if I was married, do I? . . . And yet I have been a widow for seven months now; and not a grey hair on my head' (p. 19), 'If three of his [Kirkpatrick's] relations had died without children, I should have been a baronet's wife' (p. 20) and 'Marriage is the natural thing; then the husband has all that kind of

---

[1] *Wives and Daughters*, Chiltern Library edition, 1948, p. 14.

dirty work to do, and his wife sits in the drawing-room like a lady' (p. 110). Mrs Gibson's language is more subtly evocative than that of the characters in earlier novels. Mrs Gaskell is able to suggest simultaneously a satirical response to her character's sheer vacuity of attitude and a pathetic one as we realize how this empty-headed woman is shortly to affect the lives of people far more responsible and attractive than herself. After the last remark quoted above events move fast to Gibson's proposal of marriage. When he does so, 'it [is] such a wonderful relief to feel that she need not struggle any more for a livelihood' (p. 120). Here too one notices the richness of suggestion in Mrs Gaskell's prose. The statement is at once plain matter of fact, a reflection of Mrs Kirkpatrick's character ('such a wonderful relief' might have been her own words), and an ominous introduction to the marriage.

Two among Mrs Gibson's galaxy of shortcomings are seen in the marriage and its preliminaries—her materialism and her calculation. Once she finds that Lord Cumnor thinks of the match as suitable (p. 117), she is quick to see its advantages and to bring Gibson to a proposal; and when he does not approve of the hasty marriage she really desires, she is quick also to simulate her approval of his views (p. 140). Her calculation does not show itself in its most scheming and repulsive guise until later, however, in her manœuvring for Cynthia's advantageous marriage. Gibson's discovery of her eavesdropping in pursuit of her plan provides one of the book's great scenes. As his wife tries to evade his ruthless inquiry, his anger mounts and she dissolves into the predictable self-pity. Finally, utterly routed, she confesses what she has done under his severe cross-examination (p. 443). Gibson sums up the situation in terms which his wife just does not understand: 'You cannot do a dishonourable act without my being inculpated in the disgrace' (p. 445). We are brought face to face with the contrast between honour and self-seeking, between the code of the Gibsons and that of the Kirkpatricks.

The self-seeking is, not surprisingly, accompanied by deception and hypocrisy. Such is her distorted approach to life that even in the smallest things Mrs Gibson cannot help deceiving. Mrs Gaskell illustrates this early on when Clare mentions Lady Cumnor's desire to see Molly, 'my future daughter, as she calls you'; only for her to be shortly afterwards rebuked by Lady Cumnor: 'Now, Clare, don't let me have any nonsense. She is not your daughter yet, and may never be' (pp. 146, 147). We are told later of Molly's anxieties about 'the webs, the distortions of truth which had prevailed in their household ever since her father's second marriage' (p. 420). We read this just after a dialogue between Lady Harriet and Mrs Gibson:

'Tell me, Clare; you've told lies sometimes, haven't you?'

'Lady Harriet! I think you might have known me better; but I know you don't mean it, dear.'

'Yes, I do. You must have told white lies, at any rate. How did you feel after them?'

'I should have been miserable, if I ever had. I should have died of self-reproach. "The truth, the whole truth, and nothing but the truth", has always seemed to me such a fine passage. But then I have so much that is unbending in my nature' (p. 417).

Mrs Gibson's language is nauseatingly convincing. It speaks the utter hypocrisy of the whole woman.

Mrs Gaskell appropriately associates sentimentality with Mrs Gibson's hypocrisy, since the two qualities are often found together. We find it in her embarrassingly unsuitable affectionate speeches to Gibson in front of other people before the marriage (p. 151). We see it again in her reminiscences of her days with her first husband Kirkpatrick:

When I look back to those happy days, it seems to me as if I had never valued them as I ought. To be sure—youth, love— what did we care for poverty! I remember dear Mr Kirkpatrick walking five miles into Stratford to buy me a muffin, because I had such a fancy for one after Cynthia was born. ... If Mr Kirkpatrick had but taken care of that cough of his. ... It really was selfish of him. Only, I daresay, he did not consider the forlorn state in which I should be left. It came harder upon me than upon most people, because I always was of such an affectionate, sensitive nature (pp. 519–20).

Nostalgia and stock attitudes of sentimentalism give way in the latter half of this speech to crassly unconscious declaration of plain egotism. The whole statement is so exasperatingly false. The fact that the reader can be moved to exasperation illustrates the intensity of Mrs Gaskell's writing by this stage. It is in this last novel, moreover, that she depends most extensively upon dialogue. The characters themselves tell us, for the most part, what they are.

Sentimentalism is part of Mrs Gibson's falsity. The shallowness of her feeling is revealed, not masked, by the extravagance of her pretence. The pretence is egocentric, concerned to convince herself and, thereby she hopes, other people as well. The sentimentalism is demonstrated also in self-pity whenever she is thwarted or discomfited. Molly's invitation to Hamley Hall evokes an outburst of querulousness (p. 216). When Mrs Gibson's scheming in connexion with Cynthia's prospects with Roger Hamley is discovered, she retreats into references to her 'poor fatherless girl', who 'might have died if she had been crossed in love' (pp. 444, 445). Reactions such as these point also to an underlying vulgarity. This often comes to the surface, especially when it finds opportunity to ally itself with Mrs Gibson's materialism. She would have Cynthia accept her newest suitor Henderson with quite disgusting alacrity, regardless of the previous understanding with Roger Hamley (p. 696), presumably because he is 'such a fine young man, and such a gentleman . . . [and] he had a very good private fortune besides' (p. 623). Even more crudely, she questions a visit by Gibson to a dying patient, asking sarcastically: 'Does he expect any legacy, or anything of that kind?' (p. 198). The sarcasm does not conceal the lines along which Mrs Gibson's mind is accustomed to run. Indeed, as Mrs Gaskell full well knew, it reveals them all the better.

Mrs Gaskell emphasizes Mrs Gibson's unpleasantness in her behaviour towards Molly. There is, for instance, her petulance and jealousy at Lady Harriet's speaking to Molly; 'almost like shaking a red rag at a bull; it was the one thing sure to put her out of temper' (p. 338). There are countless incidents of petty restrictions and rebukes. They may be aptly represented by reference to one of the last. She is asking Molly, who has just returned from Hamley Hall, about Roger's reaction to Cynthia's engagement to Henderson. Molly defends Roger against lack of feeling in terms that are rather warm. Mrs Gibson's response is typical: 'My poor head! . . . One may see you've been stopping with people of robust health, and —excuse my saying it, Molly, of your friends—of un-refined habits: you've got to talk in so loud a voice' (p. 742). A little later she rebukes her for using the phrase 'the apple of his eye'—'such vulgar expressions. When shall I teach you true refinement—that refinement which consists in never even thinking a vulgar, commonplace thing!' (pp. 743–4). This incident is illuminating. It shows Mrs Gibson's 'refinement' for what it is, a matter of convention and appearance rather than of conduct and character. At the end of the book she is entering what must surely have been a prolonged and querulous old age (p. 753). Her whole character is 'superficial and flimsy' (p. 159). She is vulgar, calculating, materialistic, sentimental, petulant, hypocritical and egotistic; but blighting as her influence is, the reader never feels that it will ultimately prevail. She personifies all the qualities which are opposed to that integrity of character which Mrs Gaskell exalts in Molly.

Mrs Gibson embodies an accumulation of faults, but she is intrinsically a much simpler character than Cynthia, whose complexity, however, owes much to the fact that she is her mother's daughter. It is she on whom the blighting influence has acted most damagingly, but Mrs Gaskell shows also how the girl has developed a protective reaction against her mother. At one point Cynthia remarks: 'I think, if I had been differently brought up, I shouldn't have had the sort of angry heart I have now' (p. 638). Certainly there seems to be a logic in her development that goes far to explain her behaviour. It is not until after her mother's re-marriage that she appears in the book. Mrs Gaskell is quite unequivocal in introducing her; she remarks on her beauty and attractiveness, commenting that this latter is perhaps 'incompatible with very high principle; as its essence seems to consist in the most exquisite power of adaptation to varying people and still more various moods—"being all things to all men". At any rate, Molly might soon have been aware that Cynthia was not remarkable for unflinching morality' (p. 250). What interests about Cynthia, however, is her remarkable degree of self-knowledge and self-understanding, which leads her to appreciate the dilemma of her situation with the Gibsons and with Roger Hamley. 'I've never lived with people with such a high standard of conduct before; and I don't quite know how to behave' (p. 475).

This is not just a matter of ignorance, but also of inability—if she had only been differently brought up! She is her mother's daughter, and can be no other now. 'I'm not good, and I told you so. Somehow, I cannot forgive her for her neglect of me as a child, when I would have clung to her' (p. 257). This explains Cynthia's behaviour towards her mother, for whom she has an ill-concealed contempt, most often demonstrated in the deflating satire which she directs against the more outrageous of her mother's affectations and hypocrisies. It explains also her antipathy to 'the great family . . . as in some measure the cause why she had seen so little of her mother' (p. 410, cf. p. 253). It is a small touch of this kind that shows Mrs Gaskell's mastery of her art in this novel. She seems aware of every one, even the least, of the relationships and attitudes of her characters. Finally, her mother's neglect, as Cynthia tells us, explains the development of the compromising association with Preston.

From the moment that Cynthia is introduced there are portentous indications both in speech and comment. When she remarks, for instance, that perhaps she has grown in wisdom whilst away at school, ' "Yes! That we will hope," said Mrs Gibson, in rather a meaning way. Indeed, there were evidently hidden allusions in their seemingly commonplace speeches' (p. 247). Then there is Cynthia's fierce passion as she asks Molly what Preston may have revealed of her past at Ashcombe (p. 253), and there is her deliberate disregard of him when he visits the Gibsons (p. 261). It becomes evident that Preston exercises some hold over Cynthia, and when Molly comes upon them and the secret of their engagement is revealed, Molly's intervention is characterized by Mrs Gaskell as 'the fearlessness of her perfect innocence' (p. 534). It is this which shows up the stained characters of the other two.

Mrs Gaskell makes much of the contrast in the characters of the two girls. What Cynthia is, we may accept from the girl herself as truth, is in an important measure what her mother has made her. In a sense, it is also what Molly might have become if she had been more pliable in Mrs Gibson's hands. That is, the novel shows the danger to Molly, the strength of her character in resisting it, and the cost in terms of emotional and spiritual attrition. It is not, however, just a conflict between Molly and Mrs Gibson. Even the kindly disposed Cynthia must inadvertently trouble Molly at times. It is these latter occasions which often in our less morally firm and more psychologically candid age provide glimpses of what may seem to us the greater humanity of Cynthia. When, for instance, Molly stoutly rebukes Cynthia for not valuing Roger as she ought, Cynthia replies: 'Don't be so dreadfully serious over everything, Molly' (p. 473). This appears so refreshingly natural, even if not particularly laudable. Cynthia is so much more mature. On the same subject of Roger, with her own engagement hardly over, she forecasts his marriage to Molly, who reacts 'with a sudden violence of repulsion . . . crimson with shame and indignation', asking 'What do you take him for?' To this Cynthia replies: 'A man! . . . And, therefore, if you won't let me call him changeable, I'll coin a word and call him consolable!' (p. 639). This may sound cynical, but it is part of Cynthia's ruthless candour. She turns this quality upon herself and then it becomes a very critical self-awareness. Her rejection of Roger comes from her recognition of his much higher standard and of her inability to allow her past to be judged by that standard and then to be 'graciously' forgiven. She knows that her nature cannot stand that (p. 638). She is obsessed (that is not too strong a word) by, but resigned to, her lower moral standard. 'I have grown up outside the pale of duty and "oughts". Love me as I am, sweet one, for I shall never be better' (p. 257). Thus the whole history of her short engagement to Roger is for her an uncomfortable expectation of having 'to be always as good as he fancies me now, and I shall have to walk on tiptoe all the rest of my life' (p. 508).

Cynthia finds herself incapable of absolute truth and absolute love. She is attractive to men, but cannot love them. Her understanding with Preston had been based apparently, like that of Sylvia with Philip Hepburn, on gratitude (p. 537). Her engagement to Roger is undertaken with little or no enthusiasm on her side. Her alliance with Henderson comes from the superficial world of London society. One remembers the beginning and end of *North and South*. Mrs Gibson is used at the very end of the book to emphasize this fact with her reference to life in Sussex Place and keeping a man and a brougham (p. 753). Cynthia's self-knowledge leads her to see that Preston is 'as much too bad for [her] as [Roger] is too good. "Now," she says, "I hope that man in the garden is the *juste milieu*—I'm that myself; for I don't think I'm vicious, and I know I'm not virtuous" ' (p. 700). Yet in Cynthia's self-knowledge there is also at times an unfair humility. She can be too rigorous with herself. Above all, Mrs Gaskell makes us recognize her ready and sustained love for Molly; and there are more ways than this for her deserving Gibson's praise: 'You're a good girl, Cynthia' (p. 682). Mrs Gaskell makes us see that Cynthia is her mother's daughter, but at the same time she insists on the contrast between her sincerity (if not profundity) of feeling and her mother's affectation and superficiality. The characterization of Cynthia has tragic overtones; she might have been so much better, but the damage has been irreparably done.

A word may perhaps here be said about Preston. He is, in the strictest sense, subsidiary. He exists for the purposes of the plot. He is the nearest to melodrama that Mrs Gaskell ever gets in this book, but even this is not very near, because he is so little of a character in himself. We read of his 'underbred' manner (p. 214) and of his 'affability, and sociability, and amiability, and a variety of other agreeable "ilities",' and his predecessor as land agent, Sheepshanks, has to say: 'Preston's not a man to put himself out for nothing. He's deep' (p. 399). All this, however, is merely the necessary sketchy elaboration of his part as blackmailer, first implicitly in pressing his suit with Cynthia and then openly in his threats to show her letters to her fiancé (pp. 558-60). He is the agent of Cynthia's suffering rather than being in any sense an independent character. Mrs Gaskell, however, fits him neatly into the social pattern by showing his unwilling but unavoidable deference to his employers and especially by indicating how Lady Harriet, the outspoken but upright and basically good-natured daughter of Lord Cumnor, has the measure of him. This integration even of minor characters' attitudes and comments into the pattern of the piece as a whole is yet another mark of Mrs Gaskell's achievement in *Wives and Daughters*.

Life at the doctor's house is matched by life at the squire's hall. The mother and two daughters are paralleled by the father and two sons. The secret engagement has its counterpart in the secret marriage. Just as the two 'sisters' contrast with each other, so also do the two brothers. Yet between the atmospheres of the two houses there is a vast difference. This derives from character. Mrs Gaskell has not visualized the men at Hamley as precisely as the women at Hollingford, but there is a sufficient particularity. The qualification is necessary, because the distance between author and character is greater than with the women. Lord David Cecil has commented on Mrs Gaskell's inadequacy in portraying her men-characters. 'Her elderly men are not so bad. . . . As for her young men, they are terrible.'[1] This is, generally speaking, too severe, but it is essentially right in noting the difference in her achievement as between the old and the young. This judgment can be most clearly traced in *Wives and Daughters*, because this novel depends less upon event and more upon people than the earlier works.

Even here, however, Mrs Gaskell shows her skill by keeping her men-characters in markedly subordinate roles. It has been noted that Gibson's participation grows less as the novel proceeds. With the Hamleys Mrs Gaskell adopts a variety of methods. Osborne Hamley is more talked about than seen; Roger is promptly despatched to the other side of the world when he looks like becoming

[1] *Early Victorian Novelists*, 1960 ed., p. 233.

important; and the father is deliberately portrayed as a simple, uncomplicated character. He is a type of his race, the bluff, blunt yet warm-hearted country squire, proud of his line, attached to his house and his land, somewhat at a loss with anything beyond the horizon of his own estate. He might easily have become a caricature; in fact, he has many of the attractive facets of a caricature, without the distortions. Because of his limitations, he is a man of prejudices, but they are the prejudices of his kind in general and his own family in particular. There is something incongruous, yet also appealing, in his marriage to the 'delicate fine London lady' (p. 44). Mrs Gaskell's psychological shrewdness comes out, as so often in this book, in a single-sentence comment on this 'perplexing' marriage—'They were very happy, though possibly Mrs Hamley would not have sunk into the condition of a chronic invalid, if her husband had cared a little more for her various tastes, or allowed her the companionship of those who did' (pp. 44–5). Hamley's simplicity makes him appear almost comic at times, as, for example, in his dislike of the Cumnors (p. 350). It also endows him with great pathos as he mourns for his son Osborne and is filled with remorse for his severity which had prevented his son from revealing his secret marriage. 'He might ha' known my bark was waur than my bite' (p. 671).

Osborne is shadowy. He is a worthless creature, weak and lacking a sense of responsibility, but with a reputation for supposed intellectual brilliance. His university career disproves this. He has been presented in un-masculine, if not actually effeminate, terms as beautiful (Mrs Gaskell repeatedly applies this adjective to him), languid and immaculate, a sort of *fin-de-siècle* dilettante almost a century before his time. This impression is heightened by

contrast with the plain, even rough, appearance of Roger.
Osborne contracts his unfortunate marriage with the
French governess Aimée and falls into the hands of
moneylenders. It is a nice structural move on Mrs Gaskell's part to let us know of the marriage, and then immediately to switch to Cynthia's arrival. What is a secret to
all but Roger is revealed accidentally to Molly, but neither
she nor the reader is allowed to know details. The whole
matter remains, that is, a virtual secret. In a passage of
interior monologue, not so good as, say, in Henry James,
but good for Mrs Gaskell, Osborne ponders his need for
money to support his wife. It demonstrates his effete dis-
taste for anything like hard work, and concludes with an
unconvincing assertion of his unrepentant feelings in having married Aimée. The monologue then gives place to a
characteristically unpractical decision, namely, to try to
make money out of his poems. Mrs Gaskell does not fail
to remind us that 'he was essentially imitative in his poetic
faculty' (p. 299). It is typical of his morally irresolute
nature that he is content to take money from Roger to
keep his wife. In this there is another parallel with the
sisters; Cynthia is willing to endanger Molly's reputation
so long as she gets the accusing letters from Preston.

Like others of Mrs Gaskell's good characters, but
nothing like so much as Molly, Roger is in danger of
being too good. He is saved in part by his subordinate role
and in part by the extent of his infatuation for Cynthia. Of
all her victims 'he fell most prone and abject' (p. 275).
Not much of this, however, is shown. We are told of it
and have to accept it. He is Molly's comforter and adviser
at the time of her father's re-marriage. 'He was but a very
young man, and he was honestly flattered' that she had
accepted his counsel; 'perhaps this led him on to offer

more advice' (p. 153). This touch of youthful self-confidence redeems him here. Elsewhere, his inherent kindliness is simply, perhaps too simply, expressed—in his concern for Molly and for his brother. It is also a rather obvious device to have him rise in the reader's estimation by his parents' thinking him less promising than his brother, whereas the reader is quickly told otherwise. Mrs Gaskell wisely exiles him from the novel, but he is clearly necessary to provide the happy ending. Perhaps too suddenly we find him noticing the 'admiring deference which most men experience, when conversing with a very pretty girl' (p. 717). Molly seems to have grown up very quickly. At the end, of course, he must distinguish his feeling for her from his 'boyish love for Cynthia' (p. 746). Roger Hamley is the only young man in love in Mrs Gaskell's major novels, who may be said to come from the social group that she knew best of all. In these last years of her life, with eligible daughters, she must have seen a number of young men of Roger's class, and we know that she was interested in some of them, such as Charles Bosanquet. It is difficult to believe that she did not notice their behaviour in love. She seems, however, to have been deficient in the ability to represent this condition convincingly. On the whole, however, she had the wisdom of Jane Austen not to try to venture too far outside her range. We may be thankful for this self-imposed restriction, even as we regret the occasions on which she chose to ignore it or did not realize the necessity of doing so.

Lest we should end on too critical a note, it may be salutary to remember that *Wives and Mothers* has been called 'incomparably her richest and most satisfying' novel.[1] It is undoubtedly a work of a fine magnitude, if

[1] Rosamond Lehmann, op. cit., p. 5.

for no other reason than the characterization of Mrs Gibson and Cynthia. These two show Mrs Gaskell operating in a new, subtler and completely unsuspected dimension. Seen as a whole, *Wives and Daughters* is, like most of Mrs Gaskell's work, a moral view of life, but it is so much more refined, more delicate in its treatment than the others. It is this quality which reminds us of Jane Austen and of Henry James. We may leave the novel with the latter's commendation of it in a review in *The Nation*:

So delicately, so elaborately, so artistically, so truthfully, and heartily is the story wrought out, that the hours given to its perusal seem like hours actually spent, in the flesh as well as in the spirit, among the scenes and people described, in the atmosphere of their motives, feelings, traditions, associations. The gentle skill with which the reader is slowly involved in the tissue of the story . . . the admirable, inaudible, invisible exercise of creative power, in short, with which a new arbitrary world is reared over his heedless head . . . these marvellous results, we say, are such as to compel the reader's very warmest admiration, and to make him feel, in his gratitude for this seeming accession of social and moral knowledge, as if he made but a poor return to the author in testifying, no matter how strongly, to the fact of her genius (Vol. II, pp. 246–7, 22 February 1866).

CHAPTER XI

ESTIMATE

FROM *Mary Barton* to *Wives and Daughters* was a long literary journey and few, if any, in 1848 could have predicted the end it reached. The first book is the work of a gifted amateur, the last of a consummate artist. Mrs Gaskell profited from experience. She learned more and more about her craft as she went along. Hers was a career of progress. She had her limitations, but she also had tremendous receptivity and adaptability. It is time now to strike a balance, to summarize her achievement in the novelist's craft and to assess her place amongst the exponents of the novel.

Considering the ways in which a novel should be written, she herself placed plot first among the elements of the form. It will therefore be proper first to judge of that. Three qualities in particular are apparently considered most important, namely, growth or evolution to a climax, vividness or immediacy, and economy. Basically, most of Mrs Gaskell's novels have very simple plots. An error or crime, a deed that is done, a lie that is told, must bring its inevitable consequence. The difference between the various plots resides in such features as the nature and disposition of events leading up to the original error or crime, the portrayal of character between the error and its ultimate consequence, and the economy of means employed. *Ruth* is a comparative failure because the initial situation is inadequate. Her seduction is the conventional misfortune, and her previous history is too sketchy and too simplified. *Mary Barton* leads up powerfully to the murder and we await the retribution with interest, particularly as Mrs Gaskell introduces the complications of false accusation and divided loyalties, but the book as a whole lacks economy. It is marred by superfluous digressions. By contrast, *Sylvia's Lovers* is so powerful because it is so economical, at any rate up to Kinraid's return and Philip's departure. After that, it is spoiled by protracted anti-climax, the properties of which are all the more obvious by contrast with what has gone before. *North and South* lacks the power of *Sylvia's Lovers*, but its plot is at once more cleverly conceived and more harmoniously held together, and the prolonged tension of its later chapters is in marked opposition to the comparable sections of the other novel.

Because Mrs Gaskell relies so much upon so little, she is not often driven to unacceptable contrivance and coincidence. At times, however, resort of this kind stands out most awkwardly. Two examples may be cited, namely, the meeting of Philip and Kinraid on the battlefield at Acre, and the presence of Mrs Mason's sister in the same town as Ruth. Both, it should be noted, are required for moralizing purposes—the first, to show Philip in a reconciling, rescuing and redemptive capacity towards the man he has so gravely wronged, the second, to ensure that Ruth is not allowed to escape her doom, whatever means must be espoused to encompass it. This insistence upon moralizing results in that auctorial intrusion Mrs Gaskell so rightly deplored, but herself here failed to avoid. Her work, especially in the early novels, has an obvious and pervasive moral purpose. She is usually, however, more capable than in these two examples of that *ars celare artem*, of being subtle enough by manipulation of events and characters, to point to her moral without putting her finger right through the middle of it. Moralizing is sometimes one of her faults; lapse into melodrama is another and more serious shortcoming. This arises from the method she adopts for the basic construction of her novels. Simple plots demand crucial episodes. The critical nature of such episodes can often be conveyed by their suggested magnitude. Lord David Cecil has enumerated the murder in *Mary Barton*, the riot in *North and South* and the press-gang scenes in *Sylvia's Lovers* as 'melodrama; and bad melodrama at that'.[1] I cannot fully agree with his choice, least of all with the last, but Mrs Gaskell did rely on melodrama too much, particularly in *Mary Barton*. The melodrama often occurred when she trusted her imagination too much and her observation too little.

Her handling of character is, in general, more skilful than her handling of plot. Lord David Cecil has indicated her limitations. Her work, he says, is entirely feminine and completely Victorian. So it is. At times, indeed, one might say that her work is that of a Victorian Dissenting minister's wife, notably in *Ruth* with its kindly condescension to the heroine, the all but ideal piety of the Benson household, and the caricature of Bradshaw, the arrogant, autocratic, influential, repulsive member of the congregation. Again, in *Mary Barton* we find not only the energetic social concern of the minister's wife, but also a view of social relations, and especially an attitude towards the moral behaviour of the working classes, which betrays the position of the author. Elsewhere, however, it is not so easy to define Mrs Gaskell's position so narrowly. She does rely upon her own memories and experiences; in *Wives and Daughters*, in *Cranford* and in some of the

[1] *Early Victorian Novelists*, p. 234.

shorter works we can trace passages which are, in fact, a re-creation of Knutsford as she knew it in her own youth. It was a feminine world in which she there lived. It was a world also towards which her responses were always more natural and spontaneous than to that of workaday Manchester. The type of person she knew best in life she created best in her novels. There are some exceptions to this, as to most generalizations, but it remains true that her imaginative sympathy throve best alongside her actual experience. Thus, to distinguish between successful characters, those such as Molly Gibson, Cynthia Kirkpatrick, Margaret Hale and Miss Matty, who seem to come from worlds she knew well, represent one order of creation; others such as John Barton, Sylvia Robson and Philip Hepburn, powerfully conceived though they are, belong to another. The difference shows even among minor characters. Her servants generally are excellent. In particular, she understands their loyalty. Martha in *Cranford*, Sally in *Ruth*, Dixon in *North and South*, Betty in *Cousin Phillis*, even a man, Kester in *Sylvia's Lovers*, illustrate this achievement. With the upper classes she had less to do. We see more of them in *Wives and Daughters* than in all her other works, but even here none is portrayed at full length; the thinking and feeling of no single one of the Cumnor Towers group is intensively investigated. Instead, they are shown in their public activities and in their public personae. Lady Harriet, for example, is terrifyingly candid, Lord Hollingford is reticent and withdrawn. That is how they appear to Hollingford folk; that is all we know about them. The only other aristocratic character of much importance is Bellingham in *Ruth*; he is also a limited character, but in a more critical sense than the aristocrats of *Wives and Daughters*.

Mrs Gaskell might, and did, avoid some of the difficulties of sex and age. Her young men are worst. They are alternately melodramatically wicked like Bellingham, conventionally good like Jem Wilson and Roger Hamley or suitably dashing like Charley Kinraid. The exceptions are Thornton and Philip Hepburn—Thornton because Mrs Gaskell holds him dexterously in a middle state as a not too minor and, what is more important, not too major character, whilst endowing him with sufficient manly qualities for his situation which is more than that merely of a lover; Hepburn, because his is a serious, religious nature of a kind Mrs Gaskell seems to have understood well. By her portrayal of this nature she suggests the intensity of his character, the pathetic yearning of his love and the tragic poignancy of his whole situation. She had no qualities of like intensity with which to endow Roger Hamley, and the simple goodness of Jem Wilson is often too simple to be convincing. Her older men are better, partly because they are not involved in a love-situation and partly because life has done much more to them. Mrs Gaskell is recording what they are, rather than what they would be. Even someone so crudely conceived as Bradshaw in *Ruth* has a certain power. Like Jane Austen, Mrs Gaskell does not try to make much of the life of men with each other. She records rather what a woman would see, the sardonic frustration of a Gibson, or the amiability and subsequent puzzled despair of a Squire Hamley, the garrulous idleness of a Daniel Robson and the oppression and desperation of a John Barton. We know why these characters have become what they are. It is only when she refuses us necessary information as, say, with Mr Hale that a character hovers in a mist of vagueness.

The merely partial success she achieves with Mr Hale may be connected with her distrust of introspection; his inner struggles needed to be conveyed. In the letter quoted in the introductory chapter of this study Mrs Gaskell commends Defoe for 'the healthy way in which he set *objects* not *feelings* before you' (420). She does not seem to have been very deeply interested in questions of motivation. In general, her questions do not revolve upon whether or why something may or may not be done, but rather upon the consequences of hasty and ill-considered action. Perhaps if she had lived to write further novels after *Wives and Daughters*, we might have seen a change in this respect. That book certainly seems to indicate a major change of direction—but then who can be sure? Who could have prophesied that *Wives and Daughters* would follow *Sylvia's Lovers*? We need to keep in mind the versatility of Mrs Gaskell's genius.

In one set of feelings she manifests subtle understanding, namely, in young women's response to love. From the fairly elementary situation of Mary Barton she progresses through the trying and tender story of Margaret Hale and the tempestuous chronicle of Sylvia Robson to the parallel but so different experiences of Molly Gibson and Cynthia Kirkpatrick. After *Mary Barton*, so much depends upon what the girl is in herself, on her own character. The mere listing of these four girls' names is a reminder of the variety of Mrs Gaskell's young women. Together they illustrate her comprehension of both the depth and complexity of the female soul. Alongside these young women must be placed one older woman among the triumphs of Mrs Gaskell's characterization—Mrs Gibson, a personification of affectation and hypocrisy so intensely conceived as to arouse the exasperation of the reader almost as if she were an actual person. Of lesser achievements we may note Mrs Gaskell's success with rather querulous middle-aged women (Mrs Wilson in *Mary Barton*, Mrs Hale in *North and South* and Mrs Robson in *Sylvia's Lovers*) and slightly eccentric spinsters (in both *Cranford* and *Wives and Daughters*). The portrayal of these represents '*objects* not *feelings*', Mrs Gaskell preferring the world she sees rather than searching among its troublesome undercurrents.

Her preference for the world she sees helps to give her novels their vivid sense of actuality. The unusual group of characters in *Cranford* forms a very special world, but it is a world which convinces the reader of its complete authenticity. This quality arises from Mrs Gaskell's observation of detail in manner, action, speech and appearance. Her men and women have characteristic modes of speech. Sometimes they are easy to recognize, as, for instance, by their dialect, which, incidentally, she used well (witness John Barton or Kester). At other times recognition may be less easy, a matter of tone rather than accent, but the mode is always consistent. Once we have heard, say, Miss Matty, Mr Hale or Mrs Gibson, we are not likely to miss their manner. Mrs Gaskell knew also that speech has other functions besides that of revealing character. Most speech in the novel is conversation, and, as she said in the letter to 'Herbert Grey', conversation must advance the plot. This was a truth she recognized more and more in later years. There are conversational passages in *Mary Barton*, *Ruth* and even *North and South* which seem to be looking in directions other than those of advancing the plot; such passages are much harder to find in the last two novels.

The sense of actuality is vividly realized in Mrs Gaskell's descriptions. It is a commonplace to remark upon her representation of interiors. In this she shows her woman's eye for detail. Whether it is a drawing-room of Cranford, a worker's hovel in Manchester or the cosy farmhouse of *Cousin Phillis*, she gives a full picture of a scene quickly observed, minutely remembered and deftly delineated. Such passages, however, are not mere impersonal description; they also indicate attitudes, sometimes of the author, sometimes of the characters. Atmosphere arouses responses both directly in the reader and indirectly through the characters. It is not accidental that in two of the works which contain the most loving description— *Cranford* and *Cousin Phillis*—the narrator is also a participant. Mrs Gaskell's description of interiors illustrates her vivid sense of place. It is not therefore surprising that Knutsford which she knew so well and loved so much should appear so often in her tales. We must remember, however, that there are also some impressive evocations of other places in her work—Manchester with its slum houses, dingy streets and smoking mills in *Mary Barton* and *North and South*, sombre Whitby (Monkshaven), the sea and the adjacent moors in *Sylvia's Lovers* and, not least, Charlotte Brontë's Haworth in the *Life*.

Mrs Gaskell is also able vividly to establish a sense of time. When she has to move back into an era earlier than her own, she notes the differences that contrast immediately with the present; often they are details of dress or of the appearance of buildings, but she also mentions different customs and public activities that mattered, such as the work of the press-gang in *Sylvia's Lovers* and the building of the railway in *Cousin Phillis*. It may here be worth noticing a subtler use of time as it appears in *Wives and Daughters*, where change of season indicates not only chronological progress but also emotional conditions.

Mrs Gaskell made some use of the differing appearance of the countryside at the different seasons in both *Sylvia's Lovers* and *Cousin Phillis*, and the rural scene had earlier been important in *Ruth*. The treatment of the subject in *Wives and Daughters*, however, is more elaborate. Molly stays at Hamley in the last happy summer before her father's re-marriage amidst the scent of flowers, the buzzing of bees and the making of hay (pp. 92–3). She thinks of this occasion on the last day of a later visit in winter:

Now the trees were leafless; there was no sweet odour in the keen frosty air. . . . The thicket was tangled with dead weeds and rime and hoar-frost. . . . Then she thought of the day her father had brought her the news of his second marriage (p. 239).

It is autumn when Roger Hamley proposes to Cynthia (p. 433) and the winter that follows is indeed a season of discontent for Molly (p. 476). It is autumn again when Cynthia's entanglement with Preston becomes important (p. 531), and winter when Molly's kindly meant intervention is misinterpreted to bring scandal on her good name. Inevitably, it is spring blossoming into summer, when Molly is recovering from her illness and Roger returns home as prelude to their final happiness together (pp. 675, 684).

Molly experiences much ill-treatment and endures much suffering. Her creator's attitude towards her demonstrates one of Mrs Gaskell's most appealing qualities—her sympathy. She understands the delicate sensitivity of the human heart, and especially the female heart. She has a ready response towards suffering, and much of the poignancy of her work derives from her descriptions of the helpless, crushed beneath the weight of circumstances or the callousness of their fellow-men. From this arose her very urge to write. *Mary Barton* was born out of her feelings for the workers in Manchester's mills. She is asking others to show a sympathy similar to that which has moved her to write. Her capacity for sympathy gives to many of her death-scenes a moving power hardly surpassed in English literature. Much of this power derives from Mrs Gaskell's awareness of the relationship of death to life, of what might have been and what has been, of death often ending a life of needless suffering and giving an edge, an added poignancy to that suffering. There is the pathos, too, of lives which, though apparently tranquil, might have been so much happier, lives of disappointed hopes, supremely those of Miss Matty and Hester Rose. The pathos and tenderness occasionally declines into sentimentality, as with Margaret Jennings in *Mary Barton*. On the whole, however, Mrs Gaskell is tender without being too tearful. With her pathos she has also an acute sense of the human comedy. Sometimes it is sharp, even acid, as in the relationship of Gibson and his wife in *Wives and Daughters*, more often it is gentle as in *Cranford*. Even in a tale as dark as *Sylvia's Lovers* there is room for the unconscious comedy of Daniel Robson and Kester, and in *North and South* the humour of the servant Dixon makes its impact amongst all else.

Mrs Gaskell's modulation of pathos and humour reminds us of her generally skilful control and variation of tone. She realized the value of variation increasingly in the progress of her career. In her early work the tone often seems insufficiently varied; this is a criticism which can be levelled at both *Mary Barton* and *Ruth*. In *Cranford* there is plenty of variety and some of its tonal quality is peculiar to itself. It is not, however, until we reach *North and South* that we find that sureness of touch which is the mark of the mature artist. Here Mrs Gaskell cannot rely on a special atmosphere as she does in *Cranford*. She is dealing with a more ordinary world; and in addition she is trying to portray a fuller range of attitudes than in her previous novels. In *Sylvia's Lovers* and in lesser works such as 'Lois the Witch' she gives the impression of intensity of atmosphere through concentration and emphasis upon a narrow area of feeling and tone. It was for her last work, however, in *Wives and Daughters* that she reserved the display of resources that produces the subtlety of tone not only unmatched, but even unsuspected, in anything that had gone before. Moreover, the tone both of single passages and of the whole is always so right, so inevitable, so much an integral part of the whole. There is never any sense of striving for effect.

Mrs Gaskell controls tone as she manages characters and events by this time, seeing the novel as a unit and a whole. The moral impact of her work becomes thus something that emerges from the experience of reading, rather than something that has been conveyed in the process of reading. She thought of herself as a teacher. We know why *Mary Barton* was written, and this book together with *Ruth* and *North and South* gives her claims to recognition as a didactic novelist. Such writers are not in fashion nowadays, and Lord David Cecil even thinks that she had no talent for this sort of thing, that 'she wasted her time writing about subjects that did not inspire her'.[1] I differ from him, at any rate as far as *Mary Barton* and *North and South* are concerned. Mrs Gaskell, however, is never a propagandist; or if she is, she is only a propagandist for sympathy, pleading that others shall feel

[1] Op. cit., p. 238.

about the workers' lot as she does. In *North and South* she subordinates socio-economic matters to the characters' personal histories, and her treatment of these matters is more dispassionate than in *Mary Barton*. If inspiration has anything to do with feeling so deeply as to write about a particular subject, then certainly in *Mary Barton* she was inspired by the conditions of life and work in Manchester. Imaginative realization, perhaps not complete but nevertheless very impressive, proceeds in that book from emotional concern. *North and South* is a more mature work, in which the social problem is neatly placed within the novel as a whole. The more satisfying achievement of the later novels derives not from the difference of subject, but from increasing mastery of her art. The explicit commentary of earlier work gives way to more controlled disposition of event, more independent reliance upon characters to make their own impression, and more liberal use of dialogue. By these means she there conveys her moral view of life implicitly by contrast with its explicit imposition in the novels of earlier days.

How finally are we to define Mrs Gaskell's view of life? Here was neither a sustained comic nor a sustained tragic vision. She was too well-balanced for it to be simply either. Life for her consisted of comedy and pathos, sometimes one, sometimes the other, more often both, with now and again an intrusion of tragedy. Above all, life demanded and brought forth from her an abundant kindliness. Her humour is never vicious, her pity is always both ready and generous. The deepening understanding which enriches both her humour and her pity in her later work comes from a richer awareness of the profound mysteries of life. None can miss the sympathy which is embodied in the protests of *Mary Barton*; none can miss the tenderness of both the comedy and the pathos of *Cranford*; but none can miss either the new dimensions of the last works, the awe that mingles with and exalts the sympathy in *Sylvia's Lovers* and the sense of subtlety, of life-rending complexities in the apparently ordinary courses of the characters in *Wives and Daughters*.

This is one way in which Mrs Gaskell's development may be measured. It is only one way. Broader experience, deepening understanding of life, found appropriate correspondences in the maturing of her craft. She was always an 'instinctive' rather than a professional novelist, and economy was not amongst her technical virtues. She seems, incidentally, to have practised it most in her least successful novel, so that her lack of it may not be as serious as one might at first assume. Nevertheless, her tendency to let her novels sprawl had its sad effects. They show strongly in *Mary Barton*; but they are less serious later. What she lacked in economy, she tended in later novels to make up for by her sense of order. Because the deficiency in economy shows worst in plot, we may be grateful that there is some compensation in characterization. The last two novels, and *Wives and Daughters* in particular, seem to show that she more and more realized where her strength lay and that she was moving towards the psychological novel. This final novel does not possess the sheer passionate strength of its immediate predecessor, *Sylvia's Lovers*, but it does have the same depth of apprehension, though disposed upon less tragic, more 'normal' material, and it has in addition a fine and previously unexampled technical mastery of her medium. In seventeen years Mrs Gaskell had travelled far from the often crude, strident but energetic *Mary Barton* to this ultimate work, delicate at once in feeling and in execution.

She deservedly stood high in the esteem of her contemporaries and amongst her fellow-novelists at her death. It is easy to look at these latter and by comparison to list her deficiencies. She did not have the vitality, the vivid phantasmagoric genius of Dickens, able at once to suggest symbolic complexities and to do it by the sharpest simplicities. She had neither Thackeray's panoramic scope nor his gift of pungent satire. Nor, again, did she possess the intense, fevered, lurid subjectivism of the Brontës. Lord David Cecil has compared her with Trollope,[1] and it is true that they both move within similar ranges of Victorian thought and feeling, but Trollope's is a fuller world and a more tarnished world than Mrs Gaskell's, and his view of it is more worldly-wise, more disillusioned. Mrs Gaskell is less satirical, more kindly, even more noble than he. There is much, in fact, in George Eliot which makes her a more appropriate figure for comparison. There are obvious differences but they are mainly differences of degree rather than of kind. George Eliot is a more massive writer, more massive in intellect, in moral grasp, in psychological understanding, in mastery of the feelings, but we have her own word for the extent to which *Scenes from Clerical Life* and *Adam Bede* were indebted to Mrs Gaskell's work. The younger writer, better endowed, went on to greater things, but their admiration for each other was essentially the tribute of kindred spirits. It is this which I would allege to destroy the wholly deluded image of Mrs Gaskell as 'lavender and lace', derived as it is from the reading merely of *Cranford* and from a superficial reading at that. Read Mrs Gaskell's last two books, and my claims for her moral grasp, psychological understanding and mastery of the feelings are

[1] Op. cit., p. 198.

surely comprehensible. Add to these what all her work displays, its generous humour, gentle criticism, tender sympathy and immense regard for high principle, and thus her achievement is summed together. In his epilogue to *Wives and Daughters* Greenwood called her 'a wise, good woman' (p. 761). As a writer she lacked the highest imaginative power, as a thinker and teacher the highest realms of moral vision were beyond her reach. In these respects she falls below George Eliot. She remains, however, a considerable artist of the moral imagination, whose works possess unique flavour and provide unique reward.

INDEX

All the Year Round, 22, 178

Aristocracy, portrayal of, 226, 251

Athenaeum, The, 2, 59, 89

Atmosphere, evocation of, 10, 75, 173, 186, 190, 255

Austen, Jane, 63, 225, 231, 246, 247

Avonbank school, 13

Bald, Marjorie, 6–7

Bamford, Samuel, 59

Bentley's Magazine, 106

Biography, problems, 144–6

Bosanquet, Charles, 17, 182, 246

Briery Close, 23

British Quarterly Review, The, 3

Brontë, Anne, 25, 152, 159

Brontë, Branwell, 145, 152, 154, 155, 161, 166–8

Brontë, Charlotte

— Chapter Coffee House, 156, 160, 166

— Currer Bell, 147, 154, 165–6

— death, 142, 152

— and Elizabeth Gaskell, 18, 24, 63–4, 102, 139

— and Héger, 149, 150, 160

— history of, 151–4, 157, 159

— letters, 154

— *Shirley*, 162

Brontë, Charlotte, *Life of*, 2, 3, 21–2, 26, 139–71

— commission, 143–4

— Cowan Bridge, 149, 153, 155

— as hagiography, 159

— Haworth described, 152, 255

— Héger, 149–50

— objectors, 27, 164–71

— Mr Nicholls, 142, 148

— Patrick Brontë, 163–4

— writing of, 146, 149

Brontë, Emily, 25, 152, 156, 161–2

Brontë, Patrick, 26, 143, 153, 157, 163, 168

Browning, Elizabeth, 65

Carlyle, Thomas, 18, 34, 35, 41, 59, 128

Cazamian, Louis, 5

Cecil, Lord David, 7, 243, 250, 258

Chapman and Hall, 20, 23

Characterization, 4, 6, 10, 65–6, 193, 195, 213–15, 225, 260

— *Mary Barton*, 54, 56

— of men, 7, 57

— and narrative, 118, 128–9, 184–5

— *North and South*, 109, 124

— *Ruth*, 88, 91, 93–4, 103–4

— of women, 7, 184, 190, 253–4

Characters, complexity, 183–4

— and environment, 65, 193, 203, 225–6

— and events, 129, 198–9

Chartists, 32–3, 34, 41

Children, portrayal, 100–1

Christmas Storms and Sunshine, 20, 172

Church, 99, 201

Class relations, 51–2, 82

Collins, H. P., 8, 9

Comedy, 81, 85, 257

INDEX

Corn Laws, 33

Cornhill Magazine, 1, 4, 22, 29, 177–8, 194

Cotton industry, 20, 21, 39, 124–5

Countryside, 191, 256

Cousin Phillis, 22, 29, 173, 178, 186
— atmosphere, 255
— characterization, 191–2, 251, 255
— criticisms, 6, 7
— environment, 187, 191

Crabbe, George, 19–20, 64–6

Cranford, 2, 30, 62–85
— analogues, 63–4
— atmosphere, 75, 82–3, 255
— characterization, 66–8, 74–6, 78–80, 84, 250–1
— comedy, 81, 85, 257
— criticisms, 3, 4, 6, 7, 9, 63–4
— E.G.'s sympathy, 73, 84–5, 260
— and Knutsford, 68, 82
— *Last Generation in England*, 172
— publication, 22–3, 177
— social scene, 254
— structure, 66
— unity of, 66, 68
— women in, 254

Crime, 112, 174, 253

Criticism of E.G., phases, 4–5, 8–9, 25
— and Victorian ethos, 194

Crompton, Charles, 17

Crooked Branch, The, 176

Cross Street Chapel, 13, 18–19

Dark Night's Work, A, 176, 178

Death, E.G.'s use of, 42, 70, 76, 102, 123, 257

Defoe, Daniel, 253

Dialect, 217, 254

Dialogue, 47–8, 188, 236

Dickens, Charles, 4, 21, 23
— and E.G. compared, 25, 116, 123, 261
— *Hard Times*, 35, 62, 99
— *Household Words*, 109, 177, 178
— on *Mary Barton*, 59

Disraeli: *Sybil*, 34–5

Doom of the Griffiths, The, 174

Drama, 7, 91, 111–12

Dreams, E.G.'s use, 94, 95, 205–6

Eastlake, Lady, 165–6

Eccentrics, 184

Eclectic Review, The, 59

Economy, narrative, 92, 248–9, 160

Edinburgh, 13

Edinburgh Review, The, 21, 59

Eliot, George, 4, 25, 91, 261

Emigration, 19, 59

Engels, F., 40

Environment, and character, 65, 153, 193, 203
— portrayal, 187

Fairbairn, Sir William, 28

Ffrench, Yvonne, 7

Forster, John, 20

Fortnightly Review, The, 4

Fox, Eliza, 16, 20, 23, 86, 187

Fraser's Magazine, 59

Froude, Mrs, 140

Galt, John, 64

Gaskell, Elizabeth, as biographer, 139, 166
— and Charlotte Brontë, 139, 161
— comparisons, 225, 261
— death of, 30
— development, 194, 195, 248
— economic thinking, 50, 125

— family, 14, 16–17, 29
— feminine viewpoint, 252
— history, 12–30
— kindliness, 35, 50–1, 73, 259
— and London, 25
— marriage, 14–16
— moral view of life, 8, 10, 85, 106, 193, 247, 262
— psychological grasp, 134, 261–2
— social work, 15, 35
— sympathy, 256, 260
— versatility, 253
Gaskell, William, 13–15
Germany, 174
Goldsmith, Oliver, 64
Goodness, depiction, 192, 231
Greenwood, John, 142–3, 147–8
Greg, William Rathbone, 21, 59, 108–9
Grey Woman, The, 174, 179
Guardian, The, 89

Half a Lifetime Ago, 174, 177, 180–2, 186
Hand and Heart, 172
Haworth, 141–2, 152–3, 255
Heart of John Middleton, The, 181
Holland family, 13, 17, 63
Holybourne, 29–30
Hopkins, Annette, 1, 78, 151, 154, 171
Household Words, 21, 62, 63, 67
Howitt, William and Mary, 20
Humour, 190

Illegitimacy, 87, 98–9
Illness, E.G.'s use of, 88
Introspection, 253
Irony, 64, 73, 77, 113, 208–9, 221

James, Henry, 225, 247
Jameson, Anna, 22

Kay-Shuttleworth, Sir James and Lady, 23–4, 123, 139, 150, 159, 161
Kettle, Arnold, 7
Kingsley, Charles, 35, 59, 119
Knutsford in novels, 13, 62, 68–9, 173–4, 191, 226, 251, 255

Laissez-faire economy, 34, 128
Lake District, 174
Last Generation in England, The, 62, 172
Lea Hurst, 24
Lehmann, Rosamund, 1, 233
Lewes, G. H., 106, 165
Libbie Marsh's Three Eras, 20, 172
Lie, E.G.'s use, 89, 113, 197
Literary Gazette, The, 86
Lizzie Leigh, 21, 87, 172–3, 175, 180, 184
Lois the Witch, 174, 177, 180, 186, 193, 258
London, E.G. in, 12, 13, 14, 25
— in novels, 13, 111, 131–2, 241
Love, E.G.'s treatment, 135–6
Love, Benjamin, 40
Lumb, Aunt, 12, 63

Macmillan's Magazine, 2, 3
Madge, Travers, 35, 126
Manchester, conditions in, 35, 36–9
— in novels, 111–12, 131–2, 172, 174, 255, 257
Manchester Guardian, 39–40
Manchester Marriage, A, 184
Martineau, Harriet, 25, 60, 164–5
Mary Barton, 32–61
— background, 14, 32, 128–9
— characters, 54–5, 57, 250
— comparisons, 4, 25, 60–2
— cotton industry, 21, 40

Mary Barton (contd.)
— criticisms, 3, 7–8, 21, 39–40, 59, 62
— as didactic novel, 53–4, 258
— Esther, 44–6, 57–8, 87, 101
— John Barton, 20, 41, 53–4, 60, 129
— and *North and South* compared, 108–9, 118, 123, 137, 138
— plot, 42, 250
— social change in, 136
— and *Sylvia's Lovers* compared, 213
— sympathy, 257
— technical weakness, 92, 249, 260
— tone variation, 257
— women in, 254
Maurice, F. D., 59
Melodrama, 42, 250
Melville, Lewis, 5, 6
Memory at Cranford, 67
Men, E.G.'s portrayal, 80–1, 243–6, 252
Methodists, 181
Middle classes, portrayal, 46–7
Mr Harrison's Confessions, 173, 178, 187–90
Mitford, Miss, 64
Mohl, Madame, 24–5
Moorland Cottage, The, 173, 177–8, 180, 187–8
More, P. E., 9
Morton Hall, 176
Motivation, 253
My Diary, 16
My Lady Ludlow, 173, 174, 178, 187, 190
Mystery, 174, 176

Nation, The, 2, 5
New England, 174
Newby, T. C., 165

Newcastle, 13
Nicholls, Rev., 26, 28, 142, 162, 163, 169
Nightingale, Florence, 24
Nineteenth Century, The, 5–6
North British Magazine, The, 86
North and South, 10–11, 108–38
— characters, 109, 111, 124–8, 130–2, 134
— comedy in, 257
— comparisons, 116, 119, 123, 138
— contrasts in, 118
— criticisms, 7, 108, 214
— 'Death and Variations', 123
— didactic novel, 138, 258
— Dorset labourers, 108
— London in, 111, 117, 131
— Manchester in, 111, 119–20, 131–2
— Margaret, 109–10, 121–2, 137
— and *Mary Barton* compared, 108–9, 111, 118, 123, 137–8
— plot, 109, 111–12, 250
— publication, 22–3, 110–11, 177
— Thornton, 117, 124, 127, 136
— tone variation, 258
— unions, 125, 127
— women in, 120, 129, 132, 251
Northup, C. S., 6
Norton, Charles Eliot, 17, 31, 171
Novel, autobiographical view, 110, 186, 190, 255
— didactic, 53–4, 87, 95, 102, 106, 258
— E.G. on, 9–10, 19, 109
— serialization, 109
Nussey, Ellen, 143, 147, 151, 163, 164, 170

Old Nurse's Story, The, 174–5
Old People, 73
Oxford, 24

Parkinson, Canon, 39
Past, evocation of, 71–2, 121–2, 174
Pathos, 70–1, 77, 197, 257
Payne, G. A., 93
Periodicals, 175
Peterloo massacre, 32
Place, E.G.'s sense of, 44, 68, 193, 204, 254
Plot, 10
— and characterization, 184
— coincidence in, 178, 208
— contrivance, 88, 249
— development, 256
— improvement, 109, 248
— simplicity, 250
— weakness, 173, 178, 193
Poor Clare, The, 174, 179, 180–1
Poverty, Victorian views, 59, 60, 118
Press-gang, 201–2
Preston family, 182
Prostitution, 38
Psychology, 134
Puritans, 182

Research, 203–4
Right at Last, 176
Robberds, Mrs, 13
Robson, Nancy, 16, 23, 25, 86, 92
Rubenius, Aina, 7
Ruskin, John, 23–4, 62, 68
Ruth, 86–107
— Benson and Bradshaw, 87–9, 92, 97–100, 104–5
— characterization, 88, 91, 96–8, 100, 250
— comparisons, 90, 92, 101, 106, 227, 257–8
— criticisms, 2, 3, 4, 6, 7, 86, 91, 102
— didactic purpose, 87, 92, 105, 106, 258

— narrative, 89, 92, 102–3, 248, 249
— publication, 23
— purification and death in, 102
— scenic description, 92, 256
— suffering, portrayal, 95–7
— tone, 257
— women in, 254

Sampson Low, 28
Sanders, G. de Witt, 6
Sartain's Union Magazine, 62
Scenic description, E.G.'s use, 92–4, 152–3, 254–5
Scott, Lady, 27, 145–9, 165–8
Sentimentalism, 236, 257
Serialization, 109, 175
Servants, portrayal, 120, 122, 251
Sex, E.G. and, 80
Sexton's Hero, The, 20, 172
Shaen, Emily, 27
Sharpe's Magazine, 143
Short stories, 172–93
— as art form, 175
Shorter, Clement, 5
Six Weeks at Heppenheim, 174, 176, 184–6
Sketches Among the Poor No. 1, 19
Smith, Elder, 23, 26, 195
Smith, George, 1, 4, 22, 26, 28–9
— letters to, 27, 28, 143, 147–9, 151, 153, 165, 167, 224
Social picture, portrayal, 6, 64, 122, 243, 246
— change, 136
Squire's Story, The, 174
Stevenson family, 9, 12, 115
Stowe, Harriet Beecher, 18
Strikes, 125
Suffering, description, 256
Surprise, E.G.'s use, 176–7
Swift, Jonathan, 9

INDEX

Sylvia's Lovers, 4, 10, 16, 89, 194–223
— atmosphere, 205–7
— characterization, 6, 209, 213–216
— comedy, 257
— comparisons, 194, 213
— countryside, 256
— criticisms, 2–3, 6, 7, 194
— epic quality, 222–3
— Hepburn's lie, 89, 197, 220–1
— 'Philip's Idol', 212, 216
— plot, 249–50
— press-gang, 201–4, 255
— as psychological novel, 253, 260
— publication, 28, 77–8
— suffering in, 195
— themes, 196, 198, 211–12, 218–219
— tone variation, 257–8
— 'Too Late', 219
— women in, 254
Symbolism, 53–4

Taylor, Mary, 151, 162, 170
Technique, E.G.'s development, 248
Thackeray, W. M., 4, 261
Tillotson, Kathleen, 8, 50
Time, E.G.'s sense of, 255
Tone, 8, 257–8
Trade unions, 48–9, 125
Trollope, A., 261
Trollope, Mrs, 34, 106
Turner, Anne, 13

Unitarian church, 12, 13, 15, 17–18, 115

Victorian ethos, 145–6, 194
Violence, E.G. and, 125, 174
Vulgarity, 84

Wales, 14, 93, 174
Ward, A. W., 5, 89
Weavers, 37
Westminster Review, The, 86, 101
Whitby, 29, 174, 200, 255
Whitfield, A. Stanton, 6
Williams, Raymond, 8
Wilson, Rev. William Carus, 27, 166, 169–70
Winkworth, 111
Winkworth, Susanna, 30–1
Wives and Daughters, 1, 4, 10, 22, 173, 224–47
— 'An Everyday Story', 225
— characterization, 188, 225–6, 228–30, 233–7, 250–1
— comedy, 257
— comparisons, 225, 226, 231, 232
— criticisms, 2–3, 4, 5, 6, 7, 194
— Cynthia, 231–3, 238–42
— dialogue, 236
— as psychological novel, 6, 253, 260
— publication, 28, 29
— social scene, 226, 229, 241, 242–3
— structure, 226
— time, use of, 255
— tone, 258
— 'Two Mothers', 224
— women in, 233–7, 254
Women, portrayal, 7, 184, 190, 253–4
Wordsworths, 24, 154